HISTORY OF INDIA

150 A.D. TO 350 A.D.

BY

K. P. JAYASWAL

M.A. (OXON.); BARRISTER-AT-LAW, ESQUIRE, OF LINCOLN'S INN; DAVIS CHINESE SCHOLAR (OXFORD UNIVERSITY); VIDYĀ-MAHODADHI; AUTHOR OF TAGORE LAW LECTURES ON MANU AND YĀJÑAVALKYA, 'HINDU POLITY'; EDITOR, JOURNAL OF THE BIHAR AND ORISSA RESEARCH SOCIETY, ETC.; ADVOCATE, PATNA HIGH COURT

Low Price Publications

2015

Kashi Prasad Jayaswal (1871-1937)

First Published 1933
Reprinted in **LPP** 1990, 2015

ISBN 10: 81-85418-04-7
ISBN 13: 978-81-85418-04-9

Published by
Low Price Publications
A-6, 2nd Floor, Nimri Commercial Centre,
Ashok Vihar Phase 4, Delhi 110052 (INDIA)
tel.: +91-11-27302453 fax.: +91-11-47061936
url: www.LPPindia.com e-mail: info@LPPindia.com

Printed at
IIP Printers
Delhi

PRINTED IN INDIA

TABLE OF SUBJECTS OF THE HISTORY OF INDIA, *c.* 150 A.D. TO 350 A.D.

PART I.

India under the Nāga Dynasty [c. 150 A.D.—284 A.D.]

CHAPTER I.

INTRODUCTORY.

CHAPTER II.

CHAPTER III.

CHAPTER IV.

CHAPTER VII.

CHAPTER VIII.

CHAPTER IX.

CHAPTER X.

CHAPTER XIII.

CHAPTER XIV.

PART IV.

CHAPTER XV.

CHAPTER XVI.

PART V.

Conclusion.

CHAPTER XVIII.

APPENDIX A.

APPENDIX B.

APPENDIX C.

APPENDIX D.

APPENDIX E.

APPENDIX F.

APPENDIX G.

LIST OF PLATES.

CORRECTIONS AND ADDITIONS.

Read at p. 34, l. 4, Nāgabhaṭṭa *instead of* Nāgadatta.

Add to f.n. 1 at p. 51: See plate in Banerji's *History of Orissa*, i. 113, of coins of Kanishka and Huvishka, which were found, 112 in number, in a hoard along with 170 Puri Kushan coins, in Mayurbhanj, Orissa.

Statement about 'Meghas' at p. 87, l. 25, has been corrected in App. D; and that at p. 113, §111, and f.n. 3, about the 'first Gupta King' has been modified in App. F.

Read at p. 142, l. 11, with the family of Nāgabhaṭṭa *instead of* with the Nāgadatta.

,, p. 206, l. 31, Ayodhyā *instead of* Ajodhyā.

,, p. 210, l. 20, Guptas ,, Gupta.

HISTORY OF INDIA

c. 150 A.D. to 350 A.D.

[NĀGA—VĀKĀṬAKA IMPERIAL PERIOD.]

By K. P. Jayaswal.

FOREWORD

This work is divided in five parts: (i) INDIA UNDER THE NĀGA DYNASTY (150 A.D.—284 A.D.), (ii) THE VĀKĀṬAKA EMPIRE (284 A.D.—348 A.D.) with an APPENDIX on the LATER VĀKĀṬAKA KINGDOM (348 A.D.—520 A.D.), (iii) HISTORY OF MAGADHA (31 B.C.—340 A.D.) and SAMUDRA GUPTA'S INDIA, (iv) SOUTHERN INDIA [240 A.D.—350 A.D.] and THE UNIFICATION OF THE NORTH AND SOUTH; and (v) THE EFFECTS OF GUPTA IMPERIALISM. This reconstruction is based primarily on the Purāṇas, and has been executed in consequence of a suggestion of the Editor-in-Chief of the *Indian Antiquary* [1932, p. 100]. The author acknowledges his thanks to Mr. K. K. Roy, M.A., for his ungrudging help in preparing this volume and for several useful suggestions.

The reader will forgive a few repetitions due to the plan of the work having overlapping periods.

July 23rd, 1932.

* * *

The period 180 A.D. to 320 A.D. is called the DARK PERIOD. I undertake the work with the prayer

'*Lead me from darkness to light.*'

K. P. J.

PART I.

India under the Nāga Dynasty [c. 150 A.D.—284 A.D.]

'Daśâśvamedhâvabhṛitha-snānānāṁ BHĀRA-ŚIVĀNĀṀ'

'Of the BHĀRA ŚIVAS who had performed Ten Aśvamedhas followed by baths of completion'—[Vākāṭaka Royal Copper-plate Deeds]

I. INTRODUCTORY.

RE-FOUNDERS OF THE IMPERIAL HINDU THRONE.

Period regarded as blank.

1. Dr. Vincent Smith in the last edition (1924), as well as in the earlier editions, of his Early History of India declared:

A. 'So much, however, is clear, that Vāsudeva was the last Kushān king who continued to hold extensive territories in India. After his death there is no indication of the existence of a paramount power in Northern India' (page 290);

B. 'Probably numerous Rājas asserted their independence and formed a number of short-lived states......... but historical materials for the third century is so completely lacking that it is impossible to say what or how many those states were' (page 290);

C. 'The period between the extinction of the Kushān and Āndhra dynasties, about A.D. 220 or 230, and the rise of the imperial Gupta dynasty, nearly a century later, is one of the darkest in the whole range of Indian history' (page 292).

In other words, the period is a 'blank' in the history of India as he put it at page 291. This hopelessness has been tacitly acquiesced in up to this time. After working at the materials available I find that none of the three statements cited above can be accepted and need be repeated in future. The materials are copious, as we shall see below, and for two sections of the period, scientifically arranged for us by Hindu historians.

Revival of Imperial Power.

2. The statement that there was no paramount power before the Imperial Guptas is thoroughly incorrect and cannot be maintained for a moment. The history of the Imperial Hindu revival is not to be dated in the fourth century with Samudra Gupta, not even with the Vākāṭakas nearly a century earlier, but with the Bhāra-Śivas half a century earlier still. There is not a line about the Vākāṭakas in the history of Dr. Vincent Smith, nor a line about the Bhāra-Śivas in any text-book. About the latter I have not seen even a paper written upon in any of the historical or archæological journals, although the main history of both these dynasties is contained in well-attested documents on copper or stone, and as we shall see, fully set out in the Purāṇas, which is supported by coins. The miss and neglect is due to the fact that the editors of those records, Fleet and others, did not read the facts contained in the inscriptions though they read the inscriptions. And as Vincent Smith who surveyed the history of India missed the period, following the lead of Fleet and Kielhorn, the period was declared to be blank. But as a matter of fact it is unusually full as compared with many periods of Indian history. Dr. Fleet while translating the Vākāṭaka inscriptions even missed the prominent expression *Samrāṭ*, 'EMPEROR OF ALL-INDIA,'[1] the title of Pravarasena I, who assumed it after performing as many as four sacrifices of imperial sovereignty, that is, four *aśvamedhas*.

Vākāṭaka Emperor and the preceding Power.

3. The Emperor Pravarasena I, of the dynasty of the Vākāṭakas, who was crowned, as we shall presently see, a generation before the Emperor Samudra Gupta, was the Emperor of Āryāvarta and also a large portion of the South, if not of the whole of the South, im-

[1] See Matsya Purāṇa, ch. 113, verse 15, on the definition of *Samrāṭ*; in vs. 9–14 the limits of India [as distinguished from Further India, § 149A] are given, and *Samrāṭ* is the emperor of 'all' (*kṛitsnaṁ*) India.

mediately before Samudra Gupta. And it was the position of that Brahmin Emperor, Pravarasena the Vākāṭaka, which Samudra Gupta took over from his grandson Rudrasena I, described as Rudra Deva,[1] the leading sovereign of Āryāvarta in the list given in the political biography of Samudra Gupta published on the Allahabad pillar.

4. It was a continuation by Samudra Gupta of that imperial rule and paramount sovereignty which had been in the hands and the keeping of the Vākāṭakas for 60 years before Samudra Gupta, as is evident from the Vākāṭaka inscriptions and the Purāṇas. I say advisedly 'in the hands and the keeping of the Vākāṭakas', for they had inherited that paramountcy from the Bhāra Śivas whose dynasty had performed no less than Ten *aśvamedhas* on the Ganges—a repeated assertion of their imperial position in Āryāvarta. It is needless to state that the *aśvamedhas* were at the cost of the Kushan[2] Empire. That history written in the orthodox Hindu fashion of these imperial functions sums up the breaking-up of the Kushan Empire and the driving of the Kushans further and further north-west towards the confines of the Salt Range.

The Bhāra Śivas.

5. The Emperor Pravarasena got his son Gautamîputra married to the daughter of the Bhāra Śiva King, Mahārāja Bhava Nāga. This event was so important in the history of the Vākāṭaka dynasty that it was incorporated in their dynastic history and repeated in all the official deeds of the Vākāṭakas. There it is recorded that before this political marriage, the rājavaṁśa (dynasty) of the Bhāra Śivas had performed Ten Horse-Sacrifices on the Ganges which they had acquired by valour; that with the holy water of the Ganges they had been crowned kings. The Bhāra Śivas adopted Śiva as the presiding deity of their empire. The site of the *daśâśvamedha* of the Bhāra Śivas performed on the bank of the Ganges, seems to me to be the sacred site come down to us as Daśâśvamedha at Benares,

[1] See § 64, below.

[2] I have preferred the foreign form *Kushan* and have left it unpunctuated.

the earthly home of Lord Śiva. The Bhāra Śivas issuing from Baghelkhand must have reached the Ganges through what we now call the Ancient Deccan Road terminating at the town of the Goddess Vindhyavāsinī [Mirzapur, U.P.]. The district of Benares was at one end of the Kushan Empire. It was far removed from its western seat. If a new power arising from the Vindhya hills were to reach the plains and if it went, not through Baghelkhand but through any part of Bundelkhand, it would reach the Jumna and not the Ganges. The site of the home of the Vākāṭakas also gives an indication: the ancient town of *Vāgāṭ* (= *Vākāṭa*) from which the *Vākāṭaka* family derived its name, I have discovered in the northern part of the Orchha State in Bundelkhand; and the Vākāṭakas were evidently the neighbours of the Bhāra Śivas[1]. There are other indications which I shall discuss in their proper places, in the shape of monuments, place-names, and coins which fix the seat of the Bhāra Śivas between Kauśāmbī and Benares.

Beginnings of the Bhāra Śivas.

6. To perform ten *aśvamedhas* before or up to the time of Pravarasena I and his *aśvamedhas*, the dynasty of the Bhāra Śivas must have been in existence for about at least a century. To put it roughly here, their rise is to be dated about 150 A.D.

Contribution of the Bhāra Śivas.

7. The real contribution of the Bhāra Śivas is the foundation of a new tradition—or rather the revival of an old tradition—the tradition of Hindu freedom and sovereignty. The national law-book, the Mānava Dharma Śāstra, had laid down that Āryāvarta was the God-given land of the Āryas and that the Mlechchhas must live beyond that and outside. This was their political and international birth-right[2] prescribed by the sacred law of the land. It had to be vindicated. The tradition initiated by the Bhāra Śivas was kept up by the Vākāṭakas and was taken over by the Guptas and fully maintained by the

[1] There is a pillar at Durehā (Jāso State, Baghelkhand) which bears the inscription *Vākāṭakānām* and below it their royal wheel-mark. See appendix at the end of the book.

[2] For this ruling idea see the references cited under § 38.

subsequent emperors from Chandra Gupta Vikramāditya to Bālāditya. If there had been no Bhāra Śivas there would not have come into existence a Gupta Empire and the Gupta Vikramādityas.

Miniatured Bhāra Śiva history.

8. The history of those Bhāra Śivas is set in lapidary by the Vākāṭaka historiographer. Never so shortly, yet so pregnantly, was a history in miniature set in, as in these three lines of the copper-plate[1]:

aṁsabhâra-sannivêśita-Śiva-liṅgôdvahana-Śiva-suparitushṭa-samutpâdita-râjavaṁśânâṁ parâkram=âdhigata-Bhâgîrathy=amala-jala-mûrddhâbhishiktânâṁ daśâśvamêdh=âvabhṛitha-snânânâṁ Bhāraśivânâṁ

'Of [the Dynasty of] the Bhāra Śivas whose royal line owed its origin to the great satisfaction of Śiva on account of their carrying the load of the symbol of Śiva on their shoulders—the Bhāra Śivas who were anointed to sovereignty with the holy water of the Bhāgīrathī which had been obtained by their valour—the Bhāra Śivas who performed their sacred bath on the completion of their Ten Aśvamedhas'

End of Kushan Power.

9. The last Kushan emperor was Vāsudeva who was ruling up to the year 98 of the Kushan era as evident from a Mathurā inscription.[2] Either in the last years of Vāsudeva (*c.* 165 A.D.) or on his death (176 A.D.) the imperial rule of the Kushans came to an end. The end of the Kushan rule synchronizes with the rise of the Aśvamedhin Bhāra Śivas. When they rise, the power they had to face and break was the imperial Kushan.

II. Identification of the Bhāra Śivas.

The Bhāra Śivas and Purāṇic Chronicles.

10. After a century of Kushan domination, a Hindu king in the person of the Bhāra Śiva king was consecrated to Hindu sovereignty with the holy waters of the Ganges. The significance of this statement is that after an interregnum of hundred years he became the first legal king. In this connection we may recall the Purāṇic statement about the foreign kings in India in those days, namely that they were not consecrated kings: *naiva mūrdhâbhishiktās te.*

[1] Fleet, *Gupta Inscriptions*, pp. 245, 236.

[2] Lüders, *List*, No. 76 (*Epigraphia Indica*, vol. X, supplement).

Now, is it possible that the Purāṇas will fail to record these *Mūrdhâbhishikta* kings, consecrated to the throne with Vedic hymns and Vedic rites, a line of lawful kings, who performed not one or two but ten *aśvamedhas* in the sacred land of the Āryas—an achievement which was not to the credit of any of the ancient dynasties of the Kali Age whom the Purāṇas have described? The Śuṅgas performed two, and the Śuṅgas are in the Purāṇic list of the Emperors. The Sātavāhanas performed two, and the Sātavāhanas have been recorded. The Bhāra Śivas, who performed ten, could not have been left out. And in fact, they have not been left out.

Bhāra Śivas were Nāgas.

11. We have in the Vākāṭaka inscriptions one of the Bhāra Śivas named, and we have in that name that he was a Nāga king—'of the Bhāra Śivas—[i.e. of the dynasty of the Bhāra Śivas]—Mahārāja Śrî Bhava Nāga'. The Purāṇas describe, after mentioning the fall of the Āndhras and their contemporaries the Tukhāra-Muruṇḍa dynasty [i.e. the dynasty we now call the Imperial Kushan], the rise of Vindhyaśakti on the Kilakilā, that is, the Vākāṭaka dynasty in Bundelkhand, 'Kilakilā' being a river near Panna.[1] The Purāṇas in explaining the importance of the rule of the son of Vindhyaśakti begin to describe the Nāga Dynasty. The Nāga Dynasty arose at Vidiśā, the well-known seat of a viceroyalty under the Śuṅgas.

The Nāgas of Vidiśā.

12. The Purāṇas divide the Nāga dynasty of Vidiśā into two parts:

[1] To Rai Bahadur Hira Lal I am indebted for the information that the *Kilakilā* is a small river near Pannā. I have since ascertained, through the kind offices of Mr. Śaradā-Prasad of Satnā (Rewah) that one crosses it on the road Satnā-to-Pannā, about 4 miles E. of Pannā, and the river enters the town of Pannā. It still bears its original name. It finally falls into the Ken under the name *Mahāur*. Probably the entire table-land of Pannā was termed *Kilakilā* at the time. It agrees with the contemporary designations of other territorial units like *Kosalā* and *Mekalā*. [Since the above information I have personally seen the river and found it called 'Kilkila' on two tablets on its bridges in Pannā, erected in 1870 A.D., marked 'Kilkila Bridge'.]

(A) Those kings who flourished before the end of the Śuṅgas, and

(B) those kings who flourished after their end.

We must recall here that the Matsya and the Bhāgavata chronicle[1]:

'Suśarmāṇam prasahya (*or*, pragṛhya) taṁ
'Śuṅgānāṁ ch=aiva yach=chheshaṁ kshapitvā tu balaṁ tadā.'

'[The Āndhra king] having taken Suśarman (the Kāṇva king) a prisoner and having destroyed whatever had been left of the Śuṅga power at that time.'

This statement would refer to the Śuṅga power which had been left in Vidiśā, their ancestral home. And as the Purāṇas here are dealing with the Vaidiśa kings, the statement about the Vaidiśa Nāgas coming into power before and after the Śuṅgas, must refer to the Āndhra or Sātavāhana period when the Sātavāhanas become the emperors of Āryāvarta in addition to their being the emperors of Dakshiṇāpatha, i.e. about 31 B.C.[2]

13. The kings before 31 B.C. in the Nāga dynasty, according to the Purāṇic chronicles, were:

(1) *Śesha*, 'king of the Nāgas', 'conqueror of his enemy's capital' (Surapura[3]—according to the Brahmāṇḍa).

(2) *Bhogin*—son of King Śesha.

(3) *Rāmachandra*, chandrāṁśu,[4] as the second descendant, i.e. a grandson of Śesha.

(4) *Nakhavān* (or, *Nakhapāna*), i.e. *Nahapāna*.

It is noteworthy that the Vishṇu Purāṇa omits this name from the list, evidently for the reason that it was not to be read in the line of the Nāgas.

[1] Pargiter, *Purāṇa Text*, p. 38.

[2] J.B.O.R.S., I, 116:

Pushyamitra: acc. 188 B.C.
Śuṅgas: 112 years } 157
Kāṇvas: 45 years } 31 B.C.

[3] *Surapura* may be *Indrapura*, now *Indor Kheṛā* in the Buland-Shahr district, where a large number of the so-called Mathurā coins have been found. See A.S.R., XII, p. 36 ff.

[4] I do not read Chandrāṁśu separately, as the Vishṇu Purāṇa does not read it so.

(5) *Dhana-*, or *Dharma-varman* (Dharma, according to the Vishṇu).

(6) Vaṅgara.[1] The Vāyu and the Brahmāṇḍa without naming him call him the fourth descendant, i.e. he was the fourth descendant from Śesha; probably Dharma (5) was the third descendant of Śesha.

The Purāṇas, after this, make the definite division from the next king, the Bhāgavata omitting the previous names altogether and the Vāyu and the Brahmāṇḍa stating that the next kings flourished '*after the end of the Śuṅga Dynasty*',[2] that is, after the conquest by the Sātavāhanas of Nahapāna, and their arrival in Central India and their conquest of the Kāṇvas and the Śuṅgas. These post-Śuṅgan Nāgas were:

(7) *Bhūta Nandi* or *Bhūti Nandi*.

(8) *Śiśu Nandi*.

(9) *Yaśo Nandi* [younger brother of Śiśu Nandi]; other kings are left unnamed.

The Vṛisha or Nandi Nāgas.

14. Before proceeding further we should notice here that the Vāyu calls these Vaidiśa Nāgas '*Vṛisha*'[3]—Śiva's bull, i.e. 'Nandi', with which the names of the kings coming after the close of the Śuṅga dynasty end. It seems that the title *Bhāra Śiva*, which was taken up later, is connected conceptually with the '*Vṛisha*' of the Vāyu and the '*Nandi*' of the names.

A Nāga inscription.

15. There is a positive confirmation of the existence of these post-Śuṅgan Nāgas in the first century A.D. At Padampawāyā, which is the site of Padmāvatī, a statue of Yaksha Maṇibhadra was dedicated by some members of a public body in the fourth year of the reign of '*King Svāmin Śiva Nandi*'.[4]

[1] This name, as a name, is traceable in a village-name *Vaṅgara* [near Nāgaudh] in the Khoh copper-plate of Mahārāja Hastin. G.I., page 105.

[2] भूति[भूत]नन्दिस्ततश्चापि वैदिशे तु भविष्यति शुङ्गानां तु कुलस्यान्ते । [Pargiter's PT., p. 49, *n.* 15.]

[3] वृषान् वैदिशकांश्चापि भविष्यांस्तु निबोधत । (II. 37–360.)

[4] *Archæological Survey of India Report*, 1915-1916, p. 106, plate LVI.

The script of the inscription is earlier than that of the early Kushans. The 'i'-vowel-marks do not curve and are straight; seriph is not developed. The style of the Yaksha image is also early. The script will place the record in the first century A.D. Śiva Nandi would be one of the unnamed kings coming after Yaśaḥ Nandi. As the Purāṇas generally omit the names when a dynasty comes under an overlordship, Śiva Nandi was probably the king superseded by Kanishka. It is stated in the Purāṇas that Padmāvatī passed under a ruler named Vinvasphāṇi who is to be identified with the viceroy of Kanishka, Mahākshatrapa Vanaspara (§ 33). Śiva Nandi up to his fourth year was an independent king, for the inscription is dated in his regnal years and not in the Kushan Era. Under the Kushans the dating was universally in their imperial era. The royal style '*svāmî*' is exactly after the fashion of the earlier Sātavāhanas.[1] It was a term denoting '*sovereign*' which was borrowed from Hindu politics, and which was adopted by the early Śaka rulers of Mathurā, for instance, in the Āmohinī inscriptions of Samvat 42 of the reign of '*Svāmî*' Mahākshatrapa Śoḍāsa—a style which went out of use at Mathurā since the rule of Kanishka.

16. It seems that from the time of Bhūta Nandi when the dynasty was re-established as treated by the Bhāgavata, they made Padmāvatī their capital. A famous Śivaliṅgam called Svarṇabindu was established there, and seven centuries later in the time of Bhavabhūti it was popularly alleged (*ākhyāyate*) that it had no human origin. The platform of the Svarṇabindu Śiva has been discovered by Mr. Garde at Pavāyā.[2] An image of

Padmāvatī.

[1] See Lūders, List No. 1100 for Puḷumāvi. *Cf.* No. 1174 for Nahapāna. See below § 26 A.

[2] A.S.R., 1915-1916, p. 100 ff. On the description of Padmāvatī, see Khajuraho inscription, E.I., Vol. I, page 149. The description (1000-1 A.D.) is worth quoting. It runs:—'There was on the surface of the earth a matchless (town), decorated with lofty palaces, which is recorded to have been founded here between the golden and silver ages by some ruler of the earth, a lord of the people, who was of the Padma dynasty, (a town which is) read of in histories (and) called *Padmāvatī* by people versed in the Purāṇas. This most excellent (town) named Padmāvatī built in an

Nandi with human body and bull's head has also been found there, and also a number of sculptures in the 'Gupta style'.

Nāga Coins.

17. Let us take a series of coins which, in my opinion, belongs to this early Nāga dynasty. Some of the coins are generally assigned to Mathurā. In the British Museum there are coins of *Śeshadāta*, *Rāmadāta*[1] and *Śiśu-chandra-dāta*. The script of the Śeshadāta coin is the oldest and belongs to the first century B.C. In the same series there are coins of Rāmadāta. These three kings, in my opinion, are identical with Śesha-Nāga, Rāma-chandra and Śiśu-Nandi of this dynasty. Amongst themselves they are connected by their coinage—a fact already recognised.[2] The coins of Śesha and Śiśu are intimately connected with those of Vīrasena, as already pointed by Prof. Rapson (J.R.A.S., 1900, page 115). Vīrasena's coin, reproduced by Prof. Rapson, has a serpent rising over the throne, on which is seated a female figure holding a jar in her up-raised right hand, the figure being evidently that of Gaṅgā. Another coin of Vīrasena, reproduced by General Cunningham, has a nāga standing by a male figure. The Nāga figures there, on the analogy of the coins of Nava Nāga (§20), complete the name as 'Vīrasena *Nāga*'. The *Vṛisha* or *Nandi*, serpent and *triśūla* are prominent on the Nāga coins.

18. The word '*dāta*' in *Śiśu chaṁ. dāta*[3] and *Śesha dāta*, *Rāma dāta*, etc. may not correspond to '*datta*', as hitherto held, but to '*dātṛi*' or '*dātva*', which is evident in *Śiśuchandra dāta*—meaning 'liberal,' 'sacrificer,' 'protector,' 'donor'. This is further evident from the legend '*Rāmasa*'—without *dāta*—on some coins of the series.[4]

unprecedented manner, was crowded with lofty rows of streets of palaces, in which tall horses were curvetting: with its shining white high-topped walls, which grazed the clouds, it irradiated the sky; (and) it was full of bright palacial dwellings that resembled the peaks of the Snowy Mountain.'

[1] Mr. Carlleye found at Indor Kheṛā a coin of 'Rāma' (*Rāmasa*) without the addition of *dāta*. A.S.R., Vol. XII, p. 43.

[2] Rapson, J.R.A.S., 1900, p. 109.

[3] J.R.A.S., 1900, pl. opposite p. 97, fig. No. 14.

[4] A.S.I., Vol. XII, p. 43.

19. There are also coins of *Uttama dāta* and *Purusha dāta*,[1] *Kāma dāta* and *Śiva dāta* (mentioned by Prof. Rapson as *Kāmadatta* and *Śivadatta* in J.A.R.S., 1900, p. 111), and also of *Bhava dāta* [illustrated in J.R.A.S., 1900, p. 97, pl., fig. No. 13, which, read by Prof. Rapson as of *Bhīmadāta*, really reads as of *Bhavadāta*][2]. Against these there are the unnamed kings of the line in the Purāṇas amongst whom figures *Śiva Nandi* of the Pavāyā inscription who can now be easily identified with *Śiva dāta* of the coins.

21. Thus we have the following names of the dynasty against which we have coins of this connected series:—

(1) Śesha, Nāgarāja .. (coins) Śesha dāta.
(2) Rāma chandra .. ,, Rāma dāta.
(3) Śiśu Nandi .. ,, Śiśu chandra dāta.
(4) Śiva Nandi (from inscription: one of the unnamed kings of the Purāṇas) ,, Śiva dāta.[3]
(5) Bhava [Nandi ?] [one of the unnamed kings] ,, Bhava dāta.

Indrapura and Mathurā.

22. Whether the early Nāga princes, Śiśu Nāga and others, ruled at Mathurā or not we cannot say. For, Mathurā was the mart where coins from adjoining territories, e.g. Padmāvatī, Vidiśā, Ahichhatra, etc., came. We have, however, the Purāṇic datum that they ruled at Vidiśā and that the first king, Śesha, was the conqueror of his enemy's capital. In view of the fact that the Brahmāṇḍa gives *Surapura* as the description of the town conquered, we would be authorised in assuming that he took *Indrapura*, now in the Buland-shahr district, a very important town in those days[4] where a number of coins of these early Nāgas have been found. We do find Śiva Nandi's rule extending up to Padmāvatī. In any case, the political connection of Mathurā with Vidiśā had been very old, and it was again

[1] V. Smith, C.I.M., pp. 190, 192.
[2] Cf. V. Smith, C.I.M., p. 193.
[3] Described by Prof. Rapson as *S'va-datta* in J.R.A.S., 1900, p. 111.
[4] A.S.R., Vol. XII, p. 36 ff.

firmly established in the later Nāga history. The presumption that the earlier Nāgas played a part in ousting the Mathurā satraps is not discounted by the fact that we have a line of kings at Mathurā with 'Mitra'-ending names in coins found there in the period succeeding the satraps, as these coins seem to be later.[1]

The Vidiśā Nāgas' Chronology.

§ 22A. Approximately the following table will represent the chronology of the Vidiśā Nāgas:

C. 110 B.C. to 31 B.C. 5 successions but four generations.	Śesha (110–90 B.C.)	(Coins)
	Bhogin (90–80 B.C.)	(No coins)
	Rāma-chandra (80–50 B.C.)	(Many coins)
	Dharma-varman (50–40 B.C.)	(No coins)
	Vaṅgara (40–31 B.C.)	(No coins)

The time of the kings after 31 B.C.—probably henceforward at Padmāvatī—would be as below:

Circa 20 B.C.–10 B.C. Bhūta Nandi (No coins).
10 B.C.–25 A.D. Śiśu Nandi (Many coins).
C. 25 A.D.–30 A.D. Yaśaḥ Nandi (No coins).

[The unnamed kings in the Purāṇas: under whom will come, *c.* 50 A.D., Śiva Nandi (from the inscription of his 4th year and from coins as '*Śiva dāta*'); *c.* 80 to 175 A.D., comes the Kushan rule with the withdrawal of the Nāga kings to Purikā and Nāgapura-Nandi-vardhana in the Central Provinces (§§ 31A, 44).]

Reconstructing the list of the early Nāgas, we get the following kings:—

1. Śesha Nāga.
2. Bhogin.
3. Rāma chandra.
4. Dharma-varmā.
5. Vaṅgara.
6. Bhūta Nandi.
7. Śiśu Nandi.
8. Yaśaḥ Nandi. [We know the relationships of the kings up to No. 8, § 13.]

[1] Vincent Smith, C.I.M., p. 190.

9 to 13:

Purusha dāta Uttama dāta Kāma dāta Bhava dāta Śiva Nandi or Śiva dāta	Five kings from inscription and coins. (Order of succession uncertain.)

They cover about 200 years, from about *c.* 110 B.C. to 78 A.D.

III. The Senior Nāga Dynasty and the Vākāṭakas.

Main Vidiśā Nāga line merged into a daughter's son.

23. The Senior Nāga dynasty merged into the Vākāṭakas by a marriage, according to the Purāṇas, which is confirmed, as we shall see, by the Vākāṭaka inscriptions. After Yaśaḥ Nandi, say the Purāṇas, 'there will be kings in the line of Yaśaḥ Nandi' or in the Vidiśā line:

tasy=ānvaye bhavishyanti rājānas tatra yas tu vai
dauhitraḥ Śiśuko nāma Purikāyāṁ nṛipo 'bhavat[1]

In his line there will be kings, and therein he who was a daughter's son, popularly called the Infant, became king at Purikā.[2] In place of *rājānas tatra yas tu (dauhitraḥ)*, some manuscripts read *rājānas taṁ* [or, *te*] *trayas tu vai*, which is a clear misreading, because the article '*te*' before 'trayaḥ' would not be needed, and *taṁ* would give no meaning. If the reading 'trayaḥ' (three) be there, which I doubt, it will have to be interpreted as three lines of kings arising from Yaśaḥ Nandi and not three kings, in view of what the Vishṇu says later, that the *Nava Nāgas*[3] ruled from three capitals, Padmāvatī, Mathurā, and Kāntipurī. The

1 P.T., p. 49, *n.* 23.

2 On Purikā, see Pargiter, *Ancient Indian Historical Tradition*, p. 262, J.R.A.S., 1910, 445. The location agrees with Hoshangabad.

3 '*Nava-Nāgāḥ Padmāvatyāṁ Kāntipuryāṁ Mathurāyāṁ; anu-Gaṅgā-Prayāgaṁ Māgadhā Guptāś cha bhokshyanti.*' As the Guptas are qualified by 'Māgadhāḥ', so the Nāgas are qualified by the word 'Nava'. In both cases the Purāṇa does not give any number. It cannot mean here '*nine*'. It may mean either the 'New', 'Later', Nāgas or the Nāgas of Nava's Dynasty. See § 26.

dynasty of Y a s a ḥ N a n d ī, or at least one line of it, lapsed and got merged into 'the d a u g h t e r ' s s o n ', popularly known as the 'Infant'. The Nāgas had, under the evident pressure of the Kushans, left Padmāvatī. We have the definite statement in the Purāṇas that Vinvasphāṇi ruled at Padmāvatī and ruled up to Magadha (§§ 33-34). Therefore, we may take it that about 80–100 A.D. the Nāga dynasty takes shelter, away from the trunk road between Mathurā and Vidiśā, into the inaccessible jungles of the Central Provinces (§ 31 A).

Nāga *dauhitra* and Pravîra-Pravarasena at Purikā and Chanakā.

24. The Purāṇas, when they reach 'the Infant' in the Nāga line, again take up the line of V i n d h y a - ś a k t i in the person of Vindhyaśakti's son, about whom they say that he was popularly known[1] as P r a v ī r a , 'the Great Hero'. The Vishṇu expressly states that the two, the Infant and the Great Hero, ruled together: '*Śiśuka-Pravīrau.*' The Vāyu applies to them a plural verb, '*bhokshyanti*'—a Prakritism for the dual.[2] The Bhāgavata omits the Infant altogether and only gives Pravīra. It is thus evident that the Purāṇic historians are signifying here that the Infant succeeded to the territories of the Nāga king, his maternal grandfather, and that in the name of the grandson (the Infant), Pravīra son of Vindhyaśakti ruled. The joint rule is emphasised by the word '*ch=āpi*' ('*Vindhyaśakti-sutaś chāpi*') of the Vāyu and the Brahmāṇḍa. The Vishṇu expressly places the Infant first while the Vāyu and the Brahmāṇḍa imply it. The Vāyu and the Brahmāṇḍa give a rule of 60 years to Pravīra, at '*Purī Kāñchanakā*' or at 'P u r i k ā *and* C h a n a k ā'[3], the latter reading being, more likely, correct, owing to the presence of the 'a n d' [*cha*]. All this is fully confirmed by, and fully tallies with, the known details of the Bhāra Śiva and Vākāṭaka history as contained in inscriptions (§ 25).

[1] प्रवीरो नाम वीर्यवान्. [2] Pargiter, PT., p. 50, *n*. 31.

[3] '*bhokshyanti cha samā shashṭiṁ puriṁ Kāñchanakāñ cha vai*' where, it is possible to read, following the Prakrit forms *Pulakā* and *Chalakā* of Pargiter's *e* Vāyu, '*Purikāṁ Chanakāñ cha vai*'. *Chanakā* may be the same as *Nachnā*. Such transpositions of syllables are a common phonetic

Purāṇas corroborated by Inscriptions.

25. According to the Vākāṭaka inscriptions[1] Gautamīputra, son of the Emperor Pravarasena and father of Rudrasena I, did not succeed, but Rudrasena I both as the grandson of the Emperor Pravarasena and as the grandson of the Bhāraśiva Mahārāja Bhava Nāga, succeeded; and with this marked distinction that he comes in as the maternal grandson of the Bhāraśiva first and then as a Vākāṭaka—quite unlike Samudra Gupta who comes in the inscriptions as a Gupta king first and as a Lichchhavi grandson next. In one of the Vākāṭaka copper-plates (Bālāghāṭ—E.I., vol. IX, 270) Rudrasena I is expressly described as a 'Bhāra Śiva' Mahārāja [Bhāraśivānāṁ Mahārāja-Śrī-Rudrasenasya]. The Vishṇu Purāṇa is here thus fully supported by the Vākāṭaka dynastic inscriptions. Then, the Vākāṭaka inscriptions mark off the period at the death of Rudrasena I and separate it from the next Vākāṭaka period commencing with Pṛithivīsheṇa I, his son and successor. This is, as we shall see later, because of the extinction of the imperial position of the Vākāṭakas with the defeat and death of Rudrasena at the hands of Samudra Gupta [§ 52 ff], who calls him 'Rudradeva', just as in the Nepal inscriptions *Vasantasena* is called *Vasantadeva*.[2] At the accession of Pṛithivīsheṇa I the dynasty had completed 100 years with which the inscriptions mark off the previous period which is the period of independence: '*varshaśataṁ=abhivardhamāna-kośa-daṇḍa-sādhana-*'.[3] There is '96 years'

phenomenon. Nachnā is an ancient capital in the Ajayagarh State where Vākāṭaka inscriptions and monuments have been found. [A.S.R., XXI, 95.] The name *Chanakapura* is known to the Jaina literature as the older name of Rājagṛiha [*Abhidhāna-Rājendra.*]. *Chanakā* will mean 'celebrated'. Very likely *Kāñchanakā* and *Chanakā* were alternative names. The Kalki-Purāṇa III, 14, 2-21; Veṅkaṭeśvara ed., p. 298) gives the name of the capital of the Nāgas as *Kāñchanī purī*, which was a secluded (*guptā*) hill-fortress (*giridurgāvṛitā*). See also § 60 on Nachnā.

[1] Fleet, G.I., pp. 237, 245: भारशिवानां महाराज-श्रीभवनाग-दौहित्रस्य गौतमीपुत्रस्य-पुत्रस्य वाकाटकानां महाराज-श्रीरुद्रसेनस्य

[2] Fleet, G.I., *Introduction*, pages 186 to 191.

[3] '[Who belonged to an uninterrupted succession of sons and sons' sons], whose treasure and means of government had been accumulating for a hundred years' [Fleet].

given to the dynasty of Vindhyaśakti in the Vāyu and the Brahmāṇḍa.[1] The '100 years' of the inscription stands for what we will say to-day—'well-nigh a century'. The result is that the identity of the Bhāraśivas with the family of Bhūta-Naṇdi Nāga is established.

IV. The Kings and Chronology of the Bhāra Śivas.

26. Classified under a tentative name [*De*]*va* we have a coin of the Kauśāmbī mint which is reproduced by Vincent Smith in the Catalogue of Indian Museum, page 206, plates XXIII, 15 and 16. The coin is 'common in the United Provinces of Agra and Oudh'. The first letter of it has not been read with any confidence uptill now. I have compared this letter with the letters occurring in the scripts from the first century A.D. to the third and I read it as '*Na*'. The *n* is of the early Kushan type.[2] The coin is '*Navasa*' and above 'Navasa' there is a figure of a nāga (serpent) with raised hood. It stands for the dynastic name *Nāga* which is expressly given on other coins of the dynastic series (§ 26B). I read it as the coin of N a v a N ā g a. The palm symbol occurring here occurs on the coins of the series and on Bhāraśiva monuments (§ 46A).

Nava Nāga.

This coin has been a great puzzle to numismatists.[3] Its large area point to the king having been an important figure in history. But his personality could not be discovered, his name and dynasty remained concealed. These things are certain about him:

1 समाः षण्णवतिं भूत्वा [ज्ञात्वा], पृथिवी तु गमिष्यति. P.T., p. 48, *ns.* 86, 88—'On completion of 96 years, the Empire (see Part III, § 125, below) will pass away.'

2 See the *N*'s in E. I., vol. i, pl. opposite p. 388, no. 2A. of the year 15, no. 7 B of the year 35; cf. also in vol. ii, p. 205, no. 29 of the year 79.

3 Cf. V. Smith, C.I.M., p. 199: 'The D e v a s a class (separately numbered) is puzzling. The coins are common in the United Provinces of Agra and Oudh, and a good specimen which I formerly possessed came from Kōsam in the Allahabad District. The upper characters look like numerals in the old notation. The reading d e v a s a is due to Prof. Rapson. The first character, being peculiar in form, has been read

(1) He was a king who ruled in the United Provinces.

(2) His coins were issued from Kauśāmbī where they are often found and the coins have symbols and fabric of the Hindu mint of Kauśāmbī.

(3) His coins are of the same series which Dr. Smith has published on Plate XXIII of the C.I.M., and called them 'unassigned' (see below, § 26 B).

(4) His coinage bears affinity with the Vidiśa-Mathurā Nāga coins.

(5) He had a reign of at least 27 years, as his coins are dated in the years 6, 20 and 27.[1]

(6) By his coinage he is connected with Padmāvatī and Vidiśā on the one hand and with Vīrasena and the kings of the Kauśāmbī coins on the other.

As we shall see in § 26 B below 'the Kauśāmbī coins' are really Bhāraśiva coins. Several of them bear names ending in '-*Nāga*'. This N a v a N ā g a of our coins seems to me to be no other than the king after whose name the Purāṇas designate the N a v a N ā g a or N a v a N ā k a D y n a s t y. He was the founder of the Nava Nāga dynasty whose official title was *Bhāra-śivas*. The letters on his coins being in form identical with those of the Huvishka-Vāsudeva records, we should take him as a contemporary of Vāsudeva and assign him approximately to 140–170 A.D.

§ 26 A. About 175 or 180 A.D., we find a Nāga king re-establishing Hindu sovereignty at Mathurā. It was V ī r a s e n a. The rise of Vīrasena is a turning point not only in the Nāga history but also in the history of Āryāvarta. His coins have been largely found in Northern India, almost all over the United Provinces, and also in the Punjab.[2] They are most common at Mathurā where Cunning-

Bhāraśiva Power at Mathurā, established c. 175–180 A.D. under Vīrasena.

generally as N e, but D e appears to be the correct reading. There is nothing to indicate who Deva was.'

[1] V. Smith, C.I.M., p. 206.

[2] In the words of Mr. Vincent Smith, they 'are tolerably common in the North-Western Provinces and the Punjab'. J.R.A.S., 1897, p. 876.

ham obtained about a hundred. Carlleyle obtained thirteen at Indor Kherā, Bulandshahr district. They have been also collected in the Etah district, as well as at Kanauj and at other places in the Farukhabad district.[1] It is thus evident that he occupied Mathurā and ruled all over the Āryāvarta Doab. 'The commonest variety' of his coinage is the small rectangular piece 'with a palm tree on obverse'[2] and a figure seated on a throne[3] (V. Smith, C.I.M., p. 191). The palm tree, as already pointed out above, is a Nāga symbol. It recurs, as we shall see later, in the architectural monuments of the Bhāraśivas (§ 46A). Another variety of his coinage is the one illustrated by General Cunningham in his *Coins of Ancient India*, pl. VIII, fig. 18, where a human figure[4] probably seated, holds a standing nāga. A third issue is illustrated by Prof. Rapson in J.R.A.S., 1900, fig. 15, in the plate facing page 97, where a female figure is seated on a canopied throne and a nāga rises from the bottom of the throne up to the chhatra (canopy) as if upholding the canopy and protecting the throne. It is the figure of Gaṅgā as the right-hand holds a jar.[5] There is a palm tree on the reverse flanked by a symbolic design of the same type on each side of the tree. The coin is artistically connected with those of Nava; the Nāga figure is made to complete the title. It is dated like Nava's. The *nāga* represents the dynasty and the palm tree, the royal emblem. In the issue where the nāga rises up to the chhatra of the throne, probably a double significance is artistically intended to denote *Ahi-chhatra*, i.e. it is the issue of the Ahi-chhatra mint. There is also an issue of the Padmāvatī mint of this king,[6] with the legend *Mahārāja V(i)*

See also 'Catalogue of Coins in Lahore Museum', Pt. III, 128; Rodgers, C.I.M., Pt. III, pp. 32-33.

[1] V. Smith, C.I.M., 191. [2] *Ibid.*, p. 191.

[3] The *chhatra* or canopy part of the throne has been often mistaken for a crown. [Cf. C.I.M., p. 197.]

[4] See Plate I herein. The reproduction of Cunningham is a hand-copy, not a photograph.

[5] See Plate I herein. [The standing figure in the cast coin of the period in C.I.M., pl. XXIII, fig. 1 seems to be of Gaṅgā.]

[6] Cunningham, *Coins of Mediæval India*, pl. II, figs. 13 and 14.

Bhāraśiva Coins.

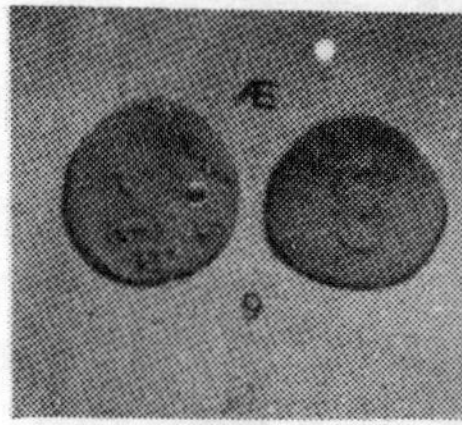

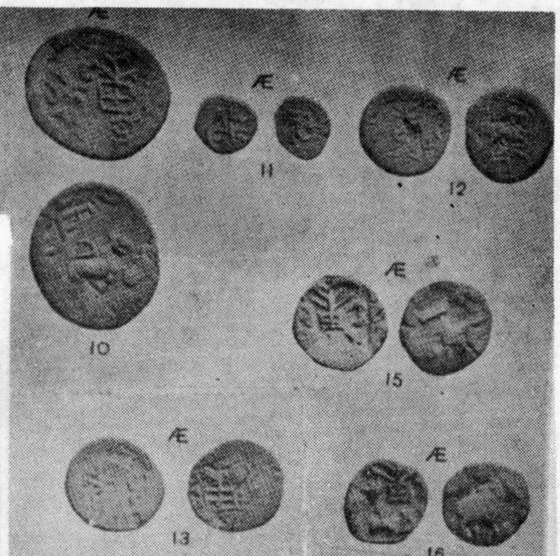

[C. I. M. Plate XXIII.]

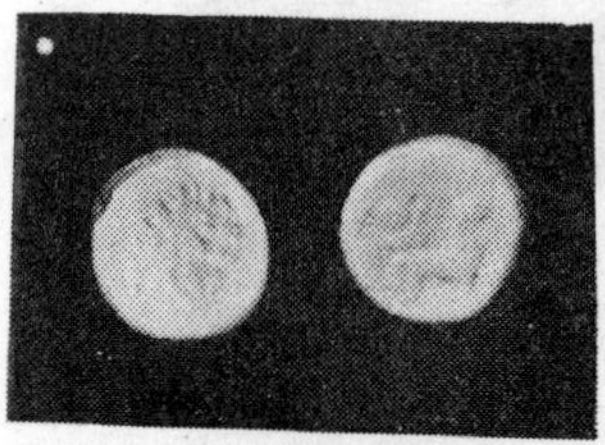

Traya Nāga
(Indian Museum)

C. A. I Plate VIII.

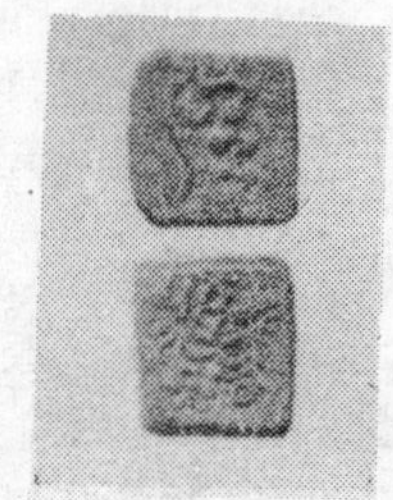

J. R. A. S., 1900, P. 97.
Virasena.

Bhāra Siva Sculptures, cir. 200 A.D., at Jānkhat.

Probably a Makara   Gangā on Makara   Lion-Capital   Two-handed   Indistinct

and a figure of the peacock which is the 'vāhana' of the god Vīrasena or Mahāsena. It is the earliest coin of the series of the Padmāvatī Nāgas [§ 27]. All these coins go back to the Hindu system, both in weight and shape and in the matter of symbolic language. In other words, Vīrasena discarded the Kushan coinage. We have also an inscription of this king discovered by Sir Richard Burn thirty-six years[1] back, at a village called Jānkhaṭ in the Tirwa tahsil of the district of Farukhabad. It is now published in the *Epigraphia Indica*, Vol. XI, p. 85, edited by Mr. Pargiter. There are a number of broken sculptures and carved pieces, and this inscription is on the head and mouth of a sculptured animal.[2] It bears the same royal symbols as the coin reproduced by Prof. Rapson. There is a rough representation of a tree, which on the analogy of the coins is to be taken as a palm tree. The side decorations are the conventional marks denoting the same thing as on the coin, but the significance of which is yet undisclosed. I regard the record as one of a royal foundation on account of the royal symbols. The inscription is dated in the thirteenth year of the reign of '*Svāmin Vīrasena*' (*Svāmisa Virasenasa saṁvatsare* 10, 3). The other portion of it is too fragmentary to give the object of the record. It is dated in the fourth fortnight of the summer season on the eighth day......... The letters are identical with the letters on the Ahi-chhatra coin. Further, they agree in all their characteristics with the inscriptions of Huvishka and Vāsudeva, found at Mathurā, published in vols. I and II of the *Epigraphia Indica* by Dr. Bühler. For instance, compare the inscription of the 90th year of the Kushan era given in the plate opposite page 205 in vol. II, where the heads of the perpendicular lines in '*s*' and '*k*' and '*n*' are thicker. The '*y*' in the Jānkhaṭ inscription is older in shape, but very near

Vīrasena's inscription.

[1] J.R.A.S., 1900, 553.

[2] These pieces are undoubtedly examples of the Bhāraśiva art. Fortunately I could obtain a photograph of these. It was taken in 1909 by the Archæological Survey of India. See Plate II herein. For the photograph I have to thank Rai Bahadur Daya Ram Sahani, Director-General of Archæology. The pillar is a *Makara-toraṇa* (bracket). The female figure is the royal Gaṅgā.

the shape in the record of the 90th year. Compare also the slanting vowel-marks in this inscription with the same forms in the Mathurā inscription no. 11 of the 4th year of the Kushan era in line 3, words '*saha*' and '*dāsena*' and in '*dānaṁ*', line 3 of the inscription no. 13 dated in the 18th Kushan year, also those in '*gaṇāto*' and the other '*to*'s in line 2, and in the inscription of the 98th year (*kshuṇe gaṇāto*). Most of the characteristics of the Jānkhaṭ writing being earlier than the inscriptions of the time of Vāsudeva and a few being contemporary, we have to assign the record to a period not later than the time of Vāsudeva Kushan.[1]

[1] Mr. Pargiter (E.I. XI. 85) has misread a passage on the date of Vīrasena's coins in Dr. Vincent Smith's *Catalogue of Coins*. Mr. Pargiter thought that Dr. Smith accepted the date about 300 A.D. for Vīrasena. But he missed Vincent Smith's distinction which he made between the Vīrasena of the coins of Cunningham and Rapson and the so-called Vīrasena of a later series. [The later 'Vīrasena' is really Pravarasena (§ 30)]. The result of this unfortunate mistake in regarding the two series of coins as one by Mr. Pargiter has been a sad one. Although he notes that the forms '*Y*' and '*V*' are found in inscriptions varying in date from the *first century B.C. to the second century A.D.*, and that of '*sh*' 'not until the second century A.D.', yet to bring the age of the inscription in agreement 'with Mr. V. Smith's conjecture regarding Vīrasena's age' [which Dr. Vincent Smith never made about the Vīrasena we are concerned with] Mr. Pargiter would place the inscription in the third century A.D., and 'very possibly' in 'the latter part of it'. Mr. Pargiter never realised that Dr. Smith postulated two Vīrasenas. Mr. Pargiter put forward two reasons for assigning a late date, both of which are absolutely untenable. One is that the bar denoting the long 'ā'-value shows a slight curve upwards, which he regards to be a Gupta tendency and not Kushan. His second reason is that the heads of the letters in this inscription are slightly wedge-shaped. Mr. Pargiter is entirely wrong both on principle and on fact. His principle for determining a later age of an inscription is to find out as to when 'later or new forms found in this inscription came into use'. I am not the first to question this principle. Dr. Fleet himself has questioned it by a footnote (E.I. XI 86: '*any particular record may easily give the first available instances of types found in it, and so may carry them back to earlier times than had been previously established for them*'). The two grounds of Mr. Pargiter, assuming them to be correct on fact, cannot make a record whose letters admittedly range from the first century B.C. to second century A.D. and not later, a record of the end of the third century A.D. But the facts of Mr. Pargiter are also wrong. The slight

Vīrasena, like Nava, assumed full sovereignty from the first year of his reign. The Jānkhaṭ record is dated in his own regnal years,[1] while the universal practice under the Kushan régime was to date records in the Kushan era. As in Śiva Nandi's inscription, the title of '*Svāmin*' is employed, which in the Hindu law and politics (Manu, IX, 294; VII, 167) means the '*sovereign-in-the-state*'. Vīrasena thus reverts here also to the orthodox system, as in his coinage. He adopts the ancient technical title and ignores the pompous royal style of the Kushans.

The distribution of the coins and the different issues prove that Vīrasena ousted the Kushans from Mathurā and from the whole of the Doab of the Gaṅgā and Yamunā which constitute the present territory of the United Provinces. From the evidence of the Kushan inscriptions and the age of the coins and the inscriptions of Vīrasena it is certain that soon after the 98th year of the Kushan era, the new king Vīrasena occupied Mathurā, which we may date about the year 180 A.D. The date, therefore, of the Jānkhaṭ inscription would be about 180–185 A.D. Vīrasena had a fairly long reign. His coin reproduced by General Cunningham bears a date, which I read as year 34. Giving him a reign of about 40 years, we place him from 170–210 A.D. as the sovereign replacing the Kushans.

His predecessor Nava Nāga must have been an independent ruler in the eastern part of the United Provinces in the reign of Vāsudeva, and Vīrasena's 10th or 13th year would have coincided with the last years of Vāsudeva. He would have thus come to the throne about 170 A.D.

thickening of the heads of the letters are as early as the records of the year 4 of the Kushan era. (Inscription no. 11 in the plate facing page 203 of vol. II of the *Epigraphia Indica* and even earlier as in the Śuṅga inscription of Ayodhyā edited by me in J.B.O.R.S., vol. X, p. 202, and in the Pabhosā inscriptions in E.I., vol. II, p. 242, which everybody has accepted to belong to the B.C. centuries). His view about the slightly upward tendency of the 'ā'-vowel-marks, which one would find throughout in line 1 of the Pabhosā inscription given in E.I., vol. II, plate facing page 243, and in numerous other examples, is one which cannot be entertained for a moment.

[1] Dr. Vincent Smith was wrong in supposing it to be dated in the year 113 of the Kushan era [C.I.M., p. 192] and Sir Richard Burn was right when he read it as 13.

The intimate connection between his coins and the coins of the undoubted Bhāraśiva kings (§ 26 B), the Nāga emblem on his coins as if to complete his name, the period of his rise and his establishing himself at Mathurā, mark V ī r a s e n a out as one of the earliest B h ā r a ś i v a N ā g a s of the inscriptions and the N a v a N ā g a s of the Purāṇas.

Other Bhāraśiva kings.

§ 26 B. We have discussed Vīrasena. The other kings may be taken up now. We know from the inscriptions that B h a v a N ā g a was a Bhāraśiva and the last Bhāraśiva king. Coins reveal a series of kings of his line, preceding him. They also prove that the family ruled in the United Provinces of Agra and Oudh—the area of these coins, and that there was a definite mint at Kauśāmbī of these kings. These coins hitherto have not been assigned by numismatists or historians to any dynasty. Nor has their connection *inter se* been realised. I discuss them in full below.

This series of coins belongs to the Indian Museum, Calcutta. They are grouped in section X, as the '*Unassigned Miscellaneous Ancient Coins of Northern India*'. Its subdivision IV (C.I.M., pp. 205, 206) has the following coins[1]:

Serial No. 7, A.S.B., Plate No. XXIII, fig. no. 9. Dr. Smith describes it: 'Peculiar object springing from railing. Br. *na* r. [Reverse]—Aśokan *ja* (?)'

Serial No. 8, A.S.B., Plate No. XXIII, fig. no. 10. A tree in railings with five branches or leaves, with Brāhmī legends in characters of the second century A.D., read by Dr. Smith as *Chīja*. On obverse: lion, railing above, Brāhmī writing, unread before.

Serial No. 9, A.S.B., Plate No. XXIII, fig. no. 11. A smaller coin, with Brāhmī writing, read by Dr. Smith as *Charāja* or *Charāju* (large letters).

[1] For the sake of convenience, I reproduce these coins on Plate I. The coins have been slightly reduced in size. I have had the advantage of obtaining their casts from the Indian Museum, thanks to Mr. K. N. Dikshit.

On reverse: one Brāhmī letter in field, read by Dr. Smith as '*la*'.

Serial No. 10, A.S.B. It is not reproduced by Dr. V. Smith. 'Tree in railings. Obverse: lion standing, a disc above, marginal legend read by Dr. Smith as '*traya nāgasa*; before traya—'*yana* (?)'. Its symbols and shape are noted to be similar to the next coin, serial no. 11, plate XXIII, fig. no. 12. [I am reproducing the coin here.]

Serial No. 11, A.S.B., Plate No. XXIII, fig. No. 12. (Tree in railing, Brāhmī legend, read by Dr. Smith as '*ratha yaṇa gicha m(i)ta(sa)* ?' On reverse, 'lion standing'. Over its back Brāhmī letters which Dr. Smith read, with doubt, as '*ba*', and a letter below which he read as '*ya*'.

Serial No. 12, I.M., Æ., Plate XXIII, 13. Dr. Smith described it: 'Tree in railing', 'thunderbolt, traces of marginal legend'. [This is really reverse, not obverse.] ['Reverse—Tree in railing, and obscure symbols; marginal Br. legend' (?) *ga bhemanapa* (or,-*ha*).]

[Just below the group of the above coins, under sub-heading (2), Dr. Smith has catalogued 8 coins which he, with doubt, read as coins of '*Deva*' (pp. 206, 207, 199). They, as pointed out above, really belong to *Nava* (Nāga). These coins have the same tree in railings which is to be found on the coins above-noticed and which he and other numismatists call the 'Kosam' symbol (Plate XXIII, figs. 15 and 16). The reverse bears sometimes the bull and sometimes the elephant. The obverse has a small hooded *nāga* above the name of the king.]

The following peculiarities of these coins are to be noted:

The 'five-branched' tree in railings is identical on figures 10, 12, 15 and 16, and serial no. 13. The shape and form of 12, 15 and 16 are identical. The size of 10 is larger but the shape is the same. The size of 11 is very small but the shape is the same. A look at these coins will convince one that they belong to the same series. Further, all these coins are dated.

Serial No. 10, not reproduced by Dr. Smith, has been studied by me. I have examined casts of the coin. The reading *traya nāgasa*, about which Dr. Smith was certain, is clear and correct.[1] I reproduce this coin from a cast. In photographing, it has become slightly reduced. Its real size is just the same as of the serial no. 12, plate XXIII, fig. 13 of Dr. Smith. It has the same tree-symbol as the others. *Tra* begins near the bottom of the railing. There are no letters before it. There might have been a figure-symbol there, but I am not certain about it. What Dr. Smith read as *sa* in *Nāgasa* is probably *sya*. Over the lion, on reverse, sun and moon [not 'disc'] are in relief. Its great value lies in the fact that it establishes the Nāga coinage of these issues of the United Provinces. About the findspot of the '*Deva*' [cor. *Nava*] series, Dr. Vincent Smith has given his opinion that they evidently belong to the Kosam mint, as a coin of that series he received from Kauśāmbī, and the particular tree-symbol is known to be connected with the Kauśāmbī mintage. I now give my reading of the published coins of the series.

Serial nos. 8 and 9 [Pl.-figs. 10 and 11] bear the same name. They read *Charaja*. The letters on no. 8 read *Charaja*; the '*ra*' being between '*cha*' and '*ja*' was missed by Dr. Smith on account its being finer than the other letters. The second line on the obverse of this coin (Plate XXIII, fig. 10) reads *nāgaśa*; and above the lion (reverse) there are the figure-symbols for 20, 8 (28)[2]. It is thus the coin of Charja Nāga dated in his 28th year. *Chara* is a name of Maṅgala, i.e. Mars.

Serial no. 11 (Plate-figure no. 12) reads '[*Śri*] *Haya-Nāgaśa*, 20, 10'. What Dr. Smith read as '*ra*', taking it to be a perpendicular stroke, is probably part of *Ś*[*ri*]. What he read as '*tha*' is really a '*ha*' and his '*nāgi*' is '*nāga*'. What he read as '*cha*' I read as the figure for 20. His '*ma*' stands for the figure '10'. There is no '*ta*' and '*sa*' about which

[1] I have to thank Mr. N. Majumdar of the Indian Museum for the casts of this coin and of Serial no. 12 of C.I.M., p. 206. The letter *Tra* is clear on the cast, though not in my photograph.

[2] There is a fragmentary letter before 20, probably *sa*=year.

he himself was doubtful; a part of the foundation of the railings was supposed by Dr. Smith to be writing. On the top of the reverse side, what Dr. Smith read doubtfully as '*ba*' and *ya* on its top is the taurine symbol. There is no letter below the animal. Dr. Smith's has the reverse upside down. The whole legend is: [*Śri*] *Haya-Nāgaśa*; 30.

Here we should take the coin of the smaller denomination, Serial no. 7, plate XXIII, fig. no. 9. Dr. Smith read only one letter—*na* on the obverse, and one letter on the reverse as Aśokan *ja*. The so-called Aśokan *ja* is the figure-symbol for 6, and it is the date. The obverse reads *sa ya ha*. The legend reads in the reverse way—a feature not unknown on coins and seals. It has to be read from the right beginning with *ha*. It is *Hayasa* [=*Haya-Nāga's*]. It should be compared with the smaller coin of Charaja for its small size, with which it agrees.

The small coin of '*Charaja*' has on its reverse a date. Dr. Smith read it as '*la*'. I read it as the symbol-figure 30. The coin is of a smaller denomination and was struck after his bigger coin.

Serial no. 12, [plate XXIII, fig. no. 13]: I read on the obverse [misdescribed by Smith as reverse]: [*Śri*] *Ba*[*r*]*hinasa*; the left-side leaves of the tree are combined with the tail of a peacock, i.e. looked at from the bottom they are branches, turning the coin upside down the branches become the tail of the peacock. The peacock represents the name of the king [*Barhina*]. The reverse bears the same tree and a legend which is partially worn out; I read from a cast: [*Nā*]*ga*[*sa*]. What Dr. Smith took as *vajra* has probably the symbol for 7 at the bottom of a taurine symbol.

We have thus four kings after Nava Nāga and Vīrasena, namely, H a y a N ā g a who ruled for 30 years or more, C h a r j a N ā g a who also ruled for 30 years or more, B a r h i n a N ā g a (7 years), and T r a y a N ā g a whose years we do not yet know. The script of the coin of H a y a N ā g a is the earliest and is referable to the period of V ī r a s e n a. He should be placed immediately after Vīrasena, i.e. *c*. 210 A.D. It should be noted that the coins of all these kings bear dates and the palm tree, which, according to Prof. Rapson, is also on the coin of Vīrasena and which I have identified with the tree-symbol in his inscription. The tree is essentially the same as on these Bhāraśiva coins. Giving the latter four kings 80 years after 210 A.D. (Vīrasena) we get approximately their date as 210–290 A.D. Some of these kings evidently had long reigns; probably some younger sons succeeded as in the case of the imperial Guptas. The date for **Bhava Nāga**, *c.* 300 A.D., I have assigned on the considerations of the Vākāṭaka and Gupta chronology [§ 67, 68]. Bhava Nāga was a contemporary of Pravarasena I, who was an elder contemporary of Samudra Gupta. Thus the dates for these kings as allotted here receive an indirect corroboration from the date of **Bhava Nāga**.

The **Nava Nāgas** of the main line or the **Bhāraśivas** may be listed as follows on the consideration of the lettering on their coins and their artistic connection *inter se*:

[c. 140–170 A.D.]	(1) Nava [Nāga] ..	[coins] ..	ruled for 27 years or more.
[c. 170–210 A.D.]	(2) Vīrasena [Nāga]..	[coins and .. inscription]	ruled for 34 years or more.
[c. 210–245 A.D.]	(3) Haya Nāga ..	[coins] ..	ruled for 30 years or more.
[c. 245–250 A.D.]	(4) Traya Nāga ..	[coins] ..	..
[c. 250–260 A.D.]	(5) Barhina Nāga ..	[coins] ..	ruled for 7 years or more.
[c. 260–290 A.D.]	(6) Charaja Nāga ..	[coins] ..	ruled for 30 years or more.
[c. 290–315 A.D.]	(7) Bhava Nāga ..	[inscriptions]	..

This agrees fully with the Purāṇas which give 7 successions to the Nava Nāgas.[1] We shall now take up the subsidiary dynasties of the Nava Nāgas at Padmāvatī and other centres and the question of the seat of the senior, the Bhāraśiva, line.

The Bhāraśivas, and Kāntipurī and other Nāga capitals.

27. The period of the Kushan imperial rule is of about a century. This is to be gathered from the Kushan inscriptions at Mathurā running up to the 98th year of their era which falls under the reign of Vāsudeva and

[1] Nāgā bhokshyanti sapta vai—V., Br.; PT., 53.

after which we get no date for Vāsudeva.[1] The Bhāraśivas re-issuing from the jungles of Hoshangabad and Jubalpur, seem to have reached the Ganges through Baghelkhand. The place where the road from Baghelkhand brings one to the Ganges is the old fort of Kantit[2] between the towns of Mirzapur and the Goddess Vindhyavāsinī or modern Vindhyāchal. This *Kantit* seems to represent the *Kānti-purī* of the Vishṇu. I found in the fort on a stone pillar-slab the name *Kānti* in modern Devanāgarī. It is a large mud fort, about a mile long, on the Ganges, marked with several pieces of Gupta sculpture[3] and a big stepped well. It is now in the zemindari of the Rajas of Kantit who are the direct descendants of the Gāhaḍwāla kings of Kanauj and Benares. The fort was destroyed in Muhammadan times and the Raja's seat was removed into the neighbouring hills at Bijayapur and Māṇḍā where the family, now in two branches, reside. The local tradition at Kantit is that long before the 'Gaharwārs' the fort belonged originally to the Bhar kings. The 'Bhar' kings here are evidently a corruption of the 'Bhāraśiva' kings, and not the Bhar tribe of whose rule in Mirzapur-Vindhyachal there is no evidence. The same tradition is repeated about the '*Bhar Deul*,'[4] once a magnificent Śiva's temple covered all over with the figures of Nāga [Serpent-] kings, built near Maughāṭ in the Vindhya hills, 25 miles to W.S.-W. of Allahabad. It is in the region of *Bhārahut*[5] (=*Bhāra-bhukti*), 'Bhāra Province'. We have no historical fact proving the existence of a rule of the aboriginal Bhars in historical times in the district of Mirzapur.

[1] J.B.O.R.S., XVI, 311, Lüders, *List*, nos. 76-77, E.I., X, App., p. 8. The *Rāja-Taraṅgiṇī* (C.I., 169–172) also gives only three generations to the Turushka rule in Kashmir: Hushka (Huvishka) Jushka (Vāsishka) and Kanishka, put in an order from the last, backwards.

[2] See A.S.I., XXI, 108 ff. on Kantit in Muhammadan times.

[3] There is a characteristic Gupta statue of Sūrya, about 7 ft. in height, there. It is worshipped at present as Bhairava guarding the fort gate.

[4] A.S.R., Vol. XXI, plates 3 and 4, description at pages 4–7.

[5] I heard the name pronounced as *Bhārahut* and *Bharahut*. Its original will be *Bhāra-bhukti*, 'the Bhāra Province'.

Allahabad and the neighbourhood. The tradition stands explained if it is taken to refer to the Bhāraśiva dynasty. The name *Bhar deul* which is prominently associated with Nāgas in sculpture and in popular tradition recorded by Kittoe in whose time it was called the 'Temple of Karkoṭ Nāg,' evidently supports the view that the 'Bhar' here stands for Bhāra Śiva. The place names *Nāgaudh*[1] and *Nāgadeya* mark the occupation by the Nāga kings of Baghelkhand, and so does *Bhārahut* and also probably *Bhar deul*.[2]

The situation of K a n t i t[3] admirably suits the Bhāraśiva history for their descent on the Ganges from Baghelkhand. The Vishṇu Purāṇa has :—

'Nava-nāgā Padmāvatyāṁ Kāntipuryāṁ Mathurāyaṁ'

It is significant that the other Purāṇas omit K ā n t i p u r ī. The reason for this may be the absorption of the line of Bhava Nāga into the Vākāṭaka line. In place of the '*Bhāraśivas*' the Purāṇic designation is the 'Nava Nāgas'. The first, the V i d i ś ā N ā g a s, i.e. Śesha to Vaṅgara, are the earlier Nāgas; from Bhūta Nandi, when the style of the name changes to Nandi ('Vṛisha'), then or certainly at their re-rise about 150-170 A.D., they are the Bhāraśivas. The coins of King Nava and his successors are marked off from the earlier coins of the Nāgas by dropping '*dāta*' and adopting 'Nāga'. The B h ā g a v a t a does not mention the Nava Nāgas but concerns itself with the princes from Bhūta Nandi to Pravīraka. The Nava Nāgas, to the author of the Bhāgavata, are therefore covered by the line of Bhūta Nandi and the rule of Pravīraka. Pravīra-Pravarasena was guardian to Rudrasena 'the Infant', and according to the

[1] I have passed this town three times. It is called *Nāgaudh* and *Nāgod.* The form *Nāgaudh* would mean the '*boundary*' (*avadhi*) '*of the Nāgas*'. *Cf.* the use of *avadhi* in this sense in the Matsya, 113. 10.

[2] The roof of this temple was flat, with sloping stones over the verandah. The cusped bracket, which is a restoration on the plate by Cunningham, is found generally in mediæval architecture, but no one can be definite as to how ancient its origin is. The large bricks found there and other features are decidedly early.

[3] Yule identified *Kindia* of Ptolemy with Mirzapur. See McCrindle, *Ptolemy*, p. 134.

other Purāṇas they two ruled together. The Vishṇu Purāṇa which had some materials not used by others, gives the order of the Capitals as Padmāvatī-Kāntīpurī-Mathurā. It probably implies that the original seat of the Nāgas was Padmāvatī and the next seat was Kāntīpurī and the third was Mathurā. This is verified by the known facts. Bhūta Nandi's line, up to Śiva Nandi and about half a century later, was at Padmāvatī. Padmāvatī then passes to the Kushan viceroys [§§33-34]. The Bhāraśivas in the latter days of the imperial Kushans, about 150 A.D., reach Kāntipurī on the Ganges. They performed their *aśvamedhas*[1] and coronations at or near Benares where the place Nagwā, the present site of the Hindu University, seems to be associated with their name. From Kāntipurī they move westwards and under Vīrasena, who strikes coins extensively and whose coins are found from the east of Ahichhatra up to Mathurā, regains Padmāvatī and Mathurā. The early coins with the letters '*Vi*'[2] and '*V*(·)' amongst the Padmāvatī coins are the first of the Padmāvatī series, and belong to Vīrasena. The peacock on the reverse of these two coins is the well-known symbol of Vīrasena who seems to be the same as Mahāsena, meaning the general of the Gods. As Bhīma Nāga and Skanda Nāga both follow the peacock design,[3] these two princes seem to have followed Vīrasena. For though with Skanda the peacock is connected, with Bhīma it is unconnected. Vīrasena having reached Mathurā and even beyond, Indor Kheṛā, where his coins have been largely dug out[4], would have naturally recovered the old Nāga territories in western

Vīrasena's Padmāvatī coins.

1 '*Haya*'-*Nāga* was probably a name given to a child born after one of the '*Aśva*'*medhas*.

2 It is read as '*kh*(*a*)' by Cunningham but I read it as '*Vi*', as the hook turns upwards disclosing it to be an *i*-mark, and identify it with the series having *Mahārāja V*(.), as the reverse of both and their letterings are identical (Cunningham, *Coins of Mediæval India*, Plate II Nos. 13 and 14).

3 Cunningham, *Coins of Mediæval India*, Plate II, Nos. 15 and 16, p. 23.

4 Cunningham, A.S.I., Vol. XII, pp. 41-42.

Bundelkhand which had passed under the Kushan rule a century back.

28. The Purāṇas advisedly use the term Nava Nāgas. For if they used the term Bhāraśiva or their own term Vaidiśaka or Vṛisha Nāgas, the idea of their revival as practically a new dynasty would have been lost and the practical break by the intervention of the Kushan rule would have been lost and confused. After describing the empire of the Vindhyakas, i.e. the Vākāṭakas, the Purāṇas total up and close the Nava Nāgas immediately before beginning the imperial line of the Guptas and their empire. The reason for doing this was the peculiar situation of Rudrasena the Śiśuka, who, though a grandson of Pravarasena Vākāṭaka, had succeeded as a Bhāraśiva *dauhitra*, so much so that the Vākāṭaka plates of Bālāghāṭ describe him only as a Bhāraśiva Mahārāja and not also as a Vākāṭaka.[1] And as we shall see below [Part II, § 64], it was Rudrasena, described as *Rudra Deva* ('His Majesty', or 'King' Rudra) who was killed in battle by Samudra Gupta. The Nāga line thus continued up to the time of Samudra Gupta in the Vākāṭaka period. The position of the Nava Nāgas, both chronological and territorial, is accurately given by the Purāṇas. They are placed between Vi(n)vasphāṇi (the Kushan viceroy) who ruled in Magadha and at Padmāvatī and the Guptas of Magadha who are said in the Vishṇu to have risen while the Nava Nāgas were ruling. And this insertion is made in the general history of Magadha which starts as a new section after the Vākāṭaka imperial history. The Nava Nāgas were not only rulers of the United Provinces but also of both eastern and western Bihar, for the Vāyu and the Brahmāṇḍa in all their copies describe their capitals both as Mathurā and Champā[2] ('Champāvatī'—Bhagalpur). That the Guptas established a government of

'Nava Nāgas.'

1 Legally the Bhāraśiva dynasty superseded the Vākāṭakas in the person of Rudrasena I (a *putrikāputra*), and the Vākāṭaka imperial dynasty and rule ended with Pravarasena I from that point of view.

2 There were only two Champās—one in Aṅga, now Champānagar at a distance of about 5 miles from Bhagalpur, and an old town with Jaina temples to Vāsupūjya who was born and died at Champā; and the other was in the hills now called Chambā.

their own at Champā (as we shall see in Part III, below) is especially noticed by the Purāṇas when dealing with the Gupta imperial system.[1] The Gupta emperor there was substituting himself in the Bhāraśiva-Vākāṭaka system.

Nāga Government.

29. The system of the Nāga Government was a federation consisting of (1) three main monarchical Nāga families, one of which the Bhāraśivas, was the imperial leader, with a number of gubernatorial families under them, and (2) a number of republics. Two branches—at Padmāvatī and Mathurā—were set up by the Bhāraśivas, with distinguishing dynastic titles of their own. The Padmāvatī dynasty had the official designation—the Ṭāka-vaṁśa, which is given in the *Bhāvaśataka*, a book dedicated to Gaṇapati Nāga (§ 31). The Mathurā family had the official title—the Yadu-vaṁśa, which is given in the drama *Kaumudīmahotsava* written about the same time as the Bhāvaśataka. The two titles incidently furnish ethnological data regarding the Nava Nāgas. They were Yādavas and had migrated from the Ṭakka-deśa [in the Punjab].[2] The Mathurā family never minted any coin. But the

1 The Purāṇas are specially full on the Vākāṭaka and Gupta Empires. The chronicles of those periods seem to have been composed in the Vākāṭaka country where, in the Vākāṭaka secretariat, the details of both could be easily available. The imperial system of the Āndhras is also attempted in the Purāṇas by recording their feudatories [see Part IV, below], though not in such detail. As in the case of the Vākāṭakas they go back to the early Nāga history from the imperial land-mark of the merging of the Nāgas into the Vākāṭakas, so also in the Āndhra history they go back to the origin, from the point of imperial succession to the Magadha throne. The Purāṇas have thus followed a system of going back to the beginning of a dynasty from a critical point and giving the earlier history of the imperial families. This they have done in the case of the Āndhras, the Vindhyakas and the Nāgas, and they would have done so regarding the Guptas if they could give their full history. Yet the earlier history of the Guptas is attempted in the Vishṇu (see Part iii, § 122).

2 See Cunningham, A.S.R., Vol. II, p. 6 ff. on the Ṭakkas and Ṭakkadeśa, and p. 14 ff. on the Yādavas in the same area. Hemachandra in his *Abhidhāna-Chintāmaṇi* (IV. 25) equates *Vāhika* with *Ṭakka*.

Padmāvatī family did so from the beginning to the end. They were thus a sovereign family, and their subordination to the Bhāraśivas was evidently of an imperial type. The Mathurā family and the family to which Nāgadatta (father of Mahārāja Maheśvara Nāga of the Lahore seal) belonged and who ruled somewhere in the Ambālā district, probably at the old capital Srughna, seem to have been under the direct control of the Bhāraśivas. There was a ruling family at or near Indrapura (Indor Kheṛā) in the district of Bulandshahr. At Bulandshahr the seal of Mattila with a Nāga symbol (Śaṅkha-pāla) [1] and without the title '*rājan*' was found. This Mattila has been identified by Growse and Fleet with the Matila of Samudra Gupta's inscription [2]. This area is described as the governorship of Antarvēdī (western part of the land between the Gaṅgā and the Yamunā) in the Indor plates issued by a Nāga ruler of the name of Śarva Nāga, governor of Skanda Gupta.[3] Nāga-datta, Nāga-sena or Matila or their ancestors did not strike any coin, nor did any governor of Ahichhatra in the time of the Bhāraśivas. At Ahichhatra the ruler called Achyuta on his coins and Achyuta Nandi in Samudra Gupta's inscription, strikes his coins for the first time, but that was under the Vākāṭakas, which indicates that the Vākāṭakas set up a feudatory family next-door to the Province of Kośala [Oudh], probably as a counter-poise against the Lichchhavis and the Guptas. As far as the Bhāraśiva government is concerned, we find only two sovereign centres—Kāntipurī and Padmāvatī. The seat at Champāvatī (Bhagalpur), given by the Vāyu and the Brahmāṇḍa[4], was evidently a subordinate seat, as we find no coins of Champāvatī. As we shall see in due course [§§ 132, 140], in Samudra Gupta's inscription the Āryāvarta rulers are divided into two groups—one beginning with Gaṇapati Nāga, which is the group of the kings killed in the first

1 See Part III on Gupta history (§ 140). I.A., XVIII, p. 289, pl., where a conch and a serpent are sculptured. Light radiates from the serpent's body.

2 I.A., XVIII, 289.

3 G.I., p. 68.

4 Nava-Nākās [Nāgās] tu bhokshyanti purīṁ Champāvatīṁ nṛipāḥ. P.T., p. 53.

Āryāvarta War of Samudra Gupta, and the other being the group of those rulers who were attacked in or after the second campaign and who are enumerated in territorial order beginning with Rudra Deva, i.e. Rudrasena the Vākāṭaka. The first group is headed by G a ṇ a p a t i N ā g a; he was the chief sovereign among the Nāga rulers in the Vākāṭaka times, which is confirmed by the Bhāvaśataka (§ 31). The republics in Malwā and Rajputana and probably also the Kuṇindas in the Punjab, who strike their respective coins in the Bhāraśiva times, were also sovereign members of the Bhāraśiva Federation (§ 43).

§ 29 A. The Purāṇas give to the Padmāvatī and the Mathurā Nāgas—or, in view of the Vishṇu, to the Padmāvatī-Kāntipurī-Mathurā Nāgas—seven successions (p. 28 above). This is fully borne out by the names gathered from the coins and inscriptions as tabulated below.

Nāga Lines.

BHĀRAŚIVAS: Rise at Kāntipurī, c. 140 A.D.

NAVA NĀGA, (Year 27 on his coin) [C. 140–170 A.D.] .. Founder of the Nava Nāga Dynasty [Bhāraśiva].

VĪRASENA (year 34 on coin) [170–210 A.D.] .. .. Founder of Mathurā and Padmāvatī Branches.

Padmāvatī (*Ṭāka* Dynasty)	Kāntipurī (*Bhāraśiva* Dynasty)	Mathurā (*Yadu* Dynasty.)
c. 210–230 A.D. BHĪMA NĀGA.	*c.* 210–245 HAYA NĀGA (year 30 on coin)	Name unknown.
c. 230–250 A.D. SKANDA NĀGA.	*c.* 245–250 TRAYA NĀGA	Name unknown.
c. 250–270 A.D. BṚIHASPATI NĀGA.	*c.* 250–260 BARHINA NĀGA (year 7 on coin)	Name unknown.
[*Vākāṭaka Suzerainty begins c.* 284 *A.D.*]		
c. 270–290 A.D. VYĀGHRA NĀGA.[1]	*c.* 260–290 CHARAJA NĀGA (year 30 on coin).	....
c. 290–310 A.D. DEVA NĀGA.	*c.* 290–315 A.D. BHAVA NĀGA.	*c.* 315–340 A.D. KĪRTI-SHEṆA.
c. 310–344 A.D. GAṆAPATI NĀGA.	[*c.* 315–344 Rudrasena at Purikā.]	*c.* 340–344 A.D. NĀGA-SENA.

[1] Cunningham read only '*Vyāghra* . .' but the plate [C.M.I., Pl. II, fig. 22] shows '*Vyāghra-Nāga*'.

Gubernatorial Nāga families.

Ahichhatra family.	*Antarvedī* family with capital, probably at *Indrapura* (Indor Kheṛā).	*Srughna*(?) family.	*Champāvatī* family.
c. 324–344 A.D. ACHYUTA NANDI.	c. 328–348 A.D. MATILA.	c. 328–348 NĀGA-DATTA. [c. 348–368 Mahārāja MAHEŚVARA NĀGA.]	Names unknown.

My reasons for assigning the above order in the succession of the Padmāvatī kings are these: Gaṇapati Nāga is the last king; about his date we are certain from the date of Samudra Gupta. As he has left several thousands of coins—in fact, he has left the largest number of coins out of all the kings of Hindu times—we have to assign to him a long reign. The issues of his coins are also many (I have counted about 8). I have, therefore, given him a reign of 35 years. Bhīma Nāga's coins immediately follow Vīrasena's; and Skanda Nāga's coinage follows his. Deva Nāga seems to have immediately preceded Gaṇapati Nāga, for they both add at times '*Indra*' (A.S.R., 1915-16, p. 105) behind their names—*Devendra, Gaṇendra.* Between Bṛihaspati Nāga and Vyāghra Nāga, the latter preceded immediately Deva Nāga, as both have the [Vākāṭaka] imperial wheel-mark [§§ 61*A*, 102 [1]] on their coins.

In the Mathurā dynasty, the last name, Nāgasena, is taken from the record of the conquest of Samudra Gupta. His seat, on the basis of Samudra Gupta's inscription, which is discussed in Part III below, seems to be, almost certainly, at Mathurā. Kīrtisheṇa is described in the *Kaumudī-mahotsava* as a friend of Sundara-varman and as the father-in-law of Kalyāṇa-varman, son of Sundara-varman, who dispossessed Chandra Gupta I from Pāṭaliputra. His date is discussed in Part III in the Gupta history [§ 133]. On the basis of that date Nāga-sena is given only 4 years and Kīrtisheṇa, c. 315–340 A.D. To complete seven successions

1 See also Appendix at the end, on the Durehā Pillar.

there should have been three more kings after Vīrasena at Mathurā. The Nāgasena of the *Harsha-charita* was a prince at Padmāvatī and not at Mathurā, and he probably flourished under the Guptas as he has left no coin at Padmāvatī.

The Ahichhatra family is located from the coins of Achyuta and the occurrence of his name in Samudra Gupta's inscription, which I discuss in Part III. His coins bear the same imperial wheel-mark (C.I.M., Pl. XXII, 9) as the coin of Devasena of Padmāvatī (C.M.I., Pl. II, 24). I restore the territorial unit, the province of Antarvedī, from the Indor plates of Skanda Gupta's reign, issued by **Śarva Nāga**, governor (*vishayapati*) of the Province (G.I., p. 70). I regard Indrapura [Indor Kheṛā] as its capital on account of its probable mention in the Brahmāṇḍa as *Surapura* and on account of the antiquity of the place, where also the Indor plates were found. **Śarva Nāga** was very likely a descendant of Matila whom I discuss in Part III (§ 140). The location of Nāga-datta of Samudra Gupta's inscription is discussed in Part III (§ 140). His headquarters must have been at or near Srughna, in the Ambala district. His son's seal was found at Lahore (G.I., p. 282) who, in his time, must have ruled as a Gupta feudatory or servant. The seat of Champāvatī is mentioned in the Vāyu and the Brahmānda, but names of the rulers have not yet been found.

Pravarasena's coin alleged to be that of Vīrasena.

30. As we have been dealing here with the Bhāraśiva coins, I may discuss a coin which has been taken as a coin of Vīrasena but which I take to be a Vākāṭaka coin, of Pravarasena I. It belongs to the same series as the coins we have been noticing. It is of the old orthodox Hindu type post-Kushan in script and pre-Guptan in style. The coin is illustrated in the Catalogue of the Coins of the Indian Museum by Dr. Vincent Smith on plate No. XXII, fig. no. 15[1] It is read by him as '*V(i)rasenasa*'. He reads the 'i' doubtfully, and although he takes the coin on the whole as a coin of Vīrasena, yet he says that this is subsequent to the coins of the earlier Vīrasena.[2] His estimate of the difference between the

[1] See Plate III herein. [2] C.I.M., p. 192, p. 197, *n.* 2.

two in point of time and the decision to take it as belonging to another and a later king is correct, but he is incorrect in reading the name as 'Vīrasena'. I read the legend on the coin as *Pravarasenas[y]a*, reading '*Pra*' as the first letter in the left-hand bottom-corner, beginning the legend with it. And I also read as 76 [70, 6], below the name. On the obverse there is seated a female figure with a jar in her right hand, which denotes that it is the figure of the River Goddess Ganges [*cf.* § 17].[1] In the right-hand bottom corner there is the Vākāṭaka wheel which we meet at Nachnā and Jāso (see last App.).

The Bhāva-śataka and the original Nāga home.

§ 31. The family history of Gaṇapati Nāgā has been yielded by a manuscript in Mithilā of a poetic work written in the reign of Gaṇapati Nāga and dedicated to him. The author says that both '*Vāk*' (Sarasvatī) and '*Padmālayā*' (=Padmāvatī) adore the Nāga king (Nāgarāja)[2] whose name he gives in verse as '*Gajavaktra Śrī* (the "Elephant-faced Majesty") *Nāga*'.[3] In one of the verses he says that by looking at '*Gaṇapati*,' the other Nāgas feel afraid.[4] The king is called the overlord of Dhārā (Western Malwa).[5] His family is described as *Ṭāka vaṁśa* and his gotra is called Karpaṭi. Neither his father, Jālapa, nor his grandfather, Vidyādhara, was king; he evidently succeeded from a collateral line. The name of the book is 'Bhāva-śataka' which consists of a little over a hundred verses, 95 verses of which are mostly on sentiments. Every verse is complete in itself with one poetic idea, as in Amaru. Many verses, however, are in praise of Śiva who was the *ishṭa devatā* of the author's patron. The author's patron is described as of a severe and austere character,

[1] There is no 'rayed crown' on the head of the figure (C.I.M., p. 197), but it is the canopy (*chhatra*) part of the throne. See also § 61 below on Vākāṭaka coins.

[2-3] Jayaswal, *Cat. of Mithilā MSS.*, Vol. II, 105.

नागराज-समं [श्रतं] ग्रन्थं नागराजेन तन्वता ।

चकारि गजवक्त्र-श्रीर्नागराजो गिरां गुरुः ॥ १ ॥

[4-5] पद्मगपतयः सर्वे वीचन्ते गणपतिं भीताः (80). धाराधीश! (62).

who did not take interest in beautiful women and who is noted to be of a warlike temperament and a veteran warrior. The book is printed in the Kāvyamālā series, Part IV, 1899, pages 37 to 52.[1] But in the second śloka of the Kāvyamālā text the name of the king is wrongly given as *Gatavaktra-Śrīr Nāgarājaḥ*,[2] while in the Mithilā manuscript it is *Gajavaktra-Śrīr Nāgarājaḥ*, i.e. Śrī Gaṇapati Nāgarāja, which led me to identify the king with Gaṇapati Nāga. The Ṭāk Nāgas living near Jammu and elsewhere in the Punjab are well known.[3] Their royal race is mentioned by the chronicles of Rajputana, Chandbardai and Muhammadan historians. Their gotra Karpaṭi is to be traced in the Mahā-Bhārata where we have the Five Karpaṭas placed in the company of the Mālavas in the Punjab-Rajputana region, evidently as republican communities.[4] The Nāga family seems to have been akin to their next-door neighbours the Mālavas who were worshippers of Karkoṭa Nāga and had migrated from the Punjab to Rajputana (see Pt. III of this book, §§ 145–6).

The Refuge of the Nāgas from A.D. 80 to 140 A.D.

31 A. The Nandi-Nāgas, when they leave Padmāvatī and Vidiśā in the Kushan period about 80 A.D., migrate to the Central Provinces where they live and rule in the security of mountain fastnesses for over half a century. There is a definite piece of evidence of their occupation of the district Nāgpur (C.P.). The Deoli plates of the Rāshṭrakūṭa king Kṛishṇarāja II (E.I., Vol. V, p. 188) which was found within a few miles of Nagpur, the modern capital of the Central Provinces, and is dated in the Śaka year 852 (940-41 A.D.) describes the gifted estate to be in the district of 'Nāgapura-Nandivardhana'. Now, both these names are connected with the Nandi-Nāgas. We find *Nandivardhana* much earlier than this

1-2 On character see verses 76, 66, 62, etc. See Kāvyamālā text, verses 1, 98–100, where the family is described.

3 Cunningham, A.S.R., Vol. II, p. 10. For *Ṭakkārikā* a Bhaṭṭa village in Madhyadeśa in the Middle Ages, see I.A., XVII, 245.

4 See my *Hindu Polity*, Part I, page 156; *M.Bh.*, *Sabhā*, C. XXXII, verses 7–9.

inscription, going back right to the time of the Vākāṭakas who were the immediate successors of the Bhāraśiva Nāgas. In the Poona plates of Prabhāvatī Guptā, edited in E.I., vol. XV, p. 39, the town of *Nandivardhana* figures. This Nandivardhana has been identified by Rai Bahadur Hira Lal, as pointed out by Mr. Pathak and Mr. Dikshit in E.I., XV, p. 41, with *Nagardhan*, which is 20 miles from Nagpur.[1] The name *Nandivardhana* could not have come into existence under the Vākāṭakas or the Bhāraśivas when the title *Nandi* had dropped, and would go back to a period before the Bhāraśiva rise. When the Nāga kings left Padmāvatī and Vidiśā they at the time bore the dynastic style *Nandi*. It seems that the Nandi-Nāgas for about half a century made the country on the other side of the Vindhyas in the Central Provinces their place of refuge and haven of freedom where the Kushans could not reach. This migration of an Āryāvarta dynasty into the heart of the Central Provinces had a tremendous effect upon the subsequent history which united Āryāvarta with a part of Dakshiṇāpatha in the reign of the Bhāraśivas and their successors the Vākāṭakas. From 100 A.D. up to 550 A.D. the Central Provinces became absolutely interwoven and one with the Vindhyan Āryāvarta, i.e. Bundelkhand—a unity which has obtained and come down to our own days. A part of Bundelkhand and the Nagpur part of the ancient Dakshiṇāpatha have remained a Hindusthānī province, wholly become Northern in race, language and culture; and Āryāvarta has been *de facto* extended up to the confines of the Nirmal range. This is a legacy of the history of those sixty years of the Nāga exile. From Nagpur up to Purikā (Hoshangabad) on one side and through Seoni and Jabalpur on the other, they maintained touch respectively with Eastern Malwā (from which they had been dispossessed) and with Baghelkhand (Rewah) through which ultimately they reached the Ganges. This new home became the second and subsequent home of the Vākāṭakas in the Gupta time and led to the enrichment of Ajaṇṭā, which had been throughout its main history under the influence and direct possession of the

[1] Hira Lal, *Inscriptions in C.P. and Berar*, p. 10. *Nāga-vardhana*= *Nagardhana*

Bhāraśivas and the Vākāṭakas. The art of Ajaṇṭā in the main is the Nāgara (Bhāraśiva) and Vākāṭaka art; Ajaṇṭā passed hands from the Sātavāhanas to the Bhāraśiva-Vākāṭakas about 250–275 A.D.

Later history of the Nāgas.

§ 32. Up to the reign of Skanda Gupta there were some Nāga feudatories, as Skanda Gupta is described to have dealt severely with a Nāga rebellion.[1] Chandra Gupta II married a Nāga princess, Kubera-Nāgā, who was *mahādevī* and the mother of Prabhāvatī Guptā, and, if not identical with Dhruva-Devī, was probably the second wife of Chandra Gupta. A Nāga family of feudatories in Koṭā, Rajputana, is found in the Middle Ages.[2] The Nāgavaṁśī families of the Bastar inscriptions, published by Rai Bahadur Hira Lal, descend very likely from the Nāgas of the Central Provinces who have left a memorial to their name in the place-namee *Nāgpur*[3] and *Nagar(var)-dhana*, and are the probable remnants of the Bhāraśiva occupation.

V. The Kushan Rule at Padmāvatī and in Magadha (c. 80 A.D. to 180 A.D.).

Vanashpara.

33. The Purāṇas, to complete the history of Padmāvatī and Magadha before the rise of the Nava Nāgas and the Guptas, insert the history of Vanashpara, spelt in the Purāṇas as *Viśvasphaṭi(ka)*, *Viśvasphāṇi* and *Viṁvasphāṭi*,[4] where Kharoshṭhī *n* has been misread and misreproduced as *ś*,[5] as in the case of *Kunāla* misspelt

[1] G.I., p. 59 (Junagarh, *l*. 3). [2] I.A., XIV, 45.

[3] *Nāgapura* (present Nāgpur) is found in an inscription of the 10th century. See Hira Lal's *Inscriptions in the Central Provinces and Berar* (2nd ed.), p. 10; E.I., Vol. V, 188. For the Nāgavaṁśis of the 11th and later centuries see his *I.C.P.B.*, pp. 209-210 and references in that book (p. 196). *Nagar-dhana*, as pointed out above (§ 31A), is the ancient site of *Nandi-vardhana*, the town mentioned in the Poona plates of Prabhāvatī Guptā, and in the Rashṭrakūta inscription (Deoli plates). It is now called *Nagar-dhana*, i.e. "*the Nāgas' Vardhana*," where *Nagar* stands for *Nāgar*.

[4] Pargiter, *Purāṇa Text*, p. 52, *n*. 45 and others on that page.

[5] *Ibid*., p. 85.

as *Kuśāla*. *Viṁvasphāṭi* and *Vi(n)vasphāṇi* stand for the name found in inscriptions at Sarnath, spelt as *Vanashpara* and *Vanaspara*. We know from two Sarnath inscriptions (E.I., Vol. VIII, p. 173) that Vanaspara ruled as governor of the province wherein Benares was situated, under the reign of Kanishka in his year 3. Vanashpara (Vanaspara) was at that time only a governor (Kshatrapa), while his chief Kharapallāṇa was a Mahākshatrapa (Viceroy). Vanashpara would have become a Mahākshatrapa later. We may, therefore, place him at about 90 A.D. to 120 A.D., for he seems to have had a long rule. This is the period when the Vidiśā-Nāgas must seek security in obscurity.

His policy.

34. This Vanaspara was so important that his descendants, the Banāphars of Bundelkhand, retained military reputation down to the Chandel times. They were considered low in origin and found it difficult to marry into Rajput families and their position is low still to-day. A dialect—Banāpharī—in Bundelkhand goes by their name. Viṁvasphāṭi established himself at Padmāvatī (according to the Bhāgavata) and up to Magadha (according to all the Purāṇas). The Purāṇas record that he was very brave, that he conquered capitals, i.e. from Padmāvatī to Bihar; that in war he was powerful like Vishṇu; that he looked like a eunuch. The Purāṇas here anticipated the description which Gibbon, the great historian, gave to the Huns:—'*as they were almost destitute of beards, they never enjoyed the manly graces of youth or the venerable aspect of age*'. Vanaspara evidently had a Hun-like, Mongolian appearance. His policy is specially noted. He made the population practically Brahmin-less (*prajāś ch-ā-brahma-bhūyishṭhāḥ*). He depressed the high-class Hindus and raised low-caste men and foreigners to high positions. He abolished the Kshatriyas and created a new ruling caste. He made his subjects un-Brahmanical. The same policy was followed by the later Kushans as we shall see hereafter (§ 146 B)—a policy of social tyranny, and religious fanaticism—both actuated by political motives. Vanaspara created a new ruling or official class out of the Kaivartas (a low caste of aboriginal agriculturists, now called *Kewaṭ*) and out of the

Pañchakas, i.e. castes lower than the Śūdras—the untouchables. He imported [into Bundelkhand-to-Bihar] the *Madrakas* who had their home in the Punjab, and the *Chakas* and *Pulindas* or *Chaka-Pulindas* or *Pulinda-Yavus*[1]. The detail about the first class of men imported for administrative purposes from the north to the east is useful as showing the policy of importing mercenaries from one part of India into another. The *Chaka-Pulindas* are really *Śaka-Pulindas*, *Śaka* often being rendered as *Chaka* in India, e.g. in the Garga-saṁhitā.[2] They are qualified as *yapu-* or *yavu-Pulindas* and are called *Pulinda-yavu* and *Pulinda-abrāhmanāṇām.*[3] In other words, they were non-Brahmanical Scythic Pulindas, as opposed to the Indian Pulindas. They seem to be the *Pāladas* or *Pāladu-'Shākas* who appear prominently in the fourth century and the beginning of the fifth century on account of their coinage and their acceptance of the coinage of Samudra Gupta and Chandra Gupta.[4]

35. This description of the rule of the Kushan viceroy gives us a great insight into the character of the Kushan rule in India. This is further confirmed by what we read in the history of Kashmir [the *Rājataraṅgiṇī*] about the Kushan rule [i, 1,174–185]. In Kashmir they stopped the prevalent worship of the Nāgas and imposed Buddhism. Buddhism was the only religion whereby the foreigner Śakas could claim equality with an old, orthodox, proud society organised on exclusive, ethnic lines. These Mlechchha rulers felt the ignominy which the Brahmanic system of society automatically imposed upon them, and they

[1] Pargiter, P.T., p. 52, *n.* 48:
Vishṇu: Kaivarta-yad(v)u-Pulinda-abrāhmaṇānāṁ (°nyān) rājye sthāpayishyati utsādyākhila-kshatra-jātim.
Bhāgavata: karishyaty aparān varṇān, Pulinda-yavu-Madrakān | prajāś ch-ābrahma-bhūyishṭhāḥ, sthāpayishyati durmatiḥ |
Vāyu: utsādya pārthivān sarvān, so 'nyān varṇān karishyati | Kaivartān Pañchakāṁś chaiva Pulindān(a)brāhmanāṁs tathā ||
Other readings: 'Kaivartyānāṁ Cakāṁś chaiva Pulindakān', and 'Kaivartān yapumāṁś chaiva' (etc.).

[2] J.B.O.R.S., Vol. XIV, p. 408.

[3] Pargiter, P.T., p. 52, note 35 and others.

[4] J.B.O.R.S., XVIII, 209. [There were Northern Pulindas, in Afghanistān, probably, now called *Povindāh*. See Matsya Pu., 113-41.]

tried various means to destroy that social system which excluded them. The consequent agitation in Kashmir was great, and it is recorded that Gonarda III restored the Nāga-worship which the Turushka [i.e. the Kushan] rule of Hushka, Jushka and Kanishka had abolished. In Hindustan we have a similar tale, without understanding which we cannot understand the national movement under the Bhāraśivas.

Pre-Kushan orthodox monuments and Kushan social policy.

36. Of Buddhism and Jainism alone we have monumental evidence in the period of the Kushan rule. Of the orthodox worship of the Hindu system we have no trace in monuments. And we have[1] no trace of earlier orthodox monuments, although we know that orthodox motifs and orthodox architecture and orthodox iconography had already been established facts before the earliest Buddhist monuments were erected. That Hindu temples of various styles and Hindu Gods and Goddesses of various forms existed before 300 A.D. is proved by their elaborate and scientific treatment in the Matsya Purāṇa, and orthodox books are full of reference to them.[2] In the face of that evidence there can be no manner of doubt that before the Gupta period the national art and architecture of the orthodox Hindus had reached a point which was not repeated in all its details in the revivalist period of the Bhāraśivas, the Vākāṭakas and the Guptas. This is established by the internal evidence of Buddhist and Jaina monuments themselves. To take one example: There was no scope for the rise of the *Apsaras* in sculpture on Buddhist and Jaina sepulchral memorials. But we do find the Apsarā with her lover, the Gandharva, in loving attitude at the Bodh-Gayā railing gate, at the Mathurā Jaina stūpas, at the Nāgārjuni Koṇḍā stūpas, etc. The origin of the Apsarā motive is not to be found in Buddhism and Jainism but in the Hindu texts (e.g. in the Matsya Purāṇa), which at least go back to the third century. Their treatment with citations of 18 previous authorities

[1] One exception is the five-faced liṅgam at Bhīṭā (A.S.R., 1909-10) which bears an inscription of the second century B.C.

[2] These have been ably collected by Mr. Brindaban Bhattacharya in his book 'The Hindu Images'.

shows that they must go back centuries earlier.[1] The Hindu texts lay down that the doorways must be decorated with *Gandharva-mithunas*, the Gandharva couples[2], and that Apsarases, Siddhas, Yakshas and others must be sculptured on the temples. The toilet scenes at Mathurā are of Apsarases in their characteristic, toilet-bathing poses which give them the name '*water-nymphs*'. Now, where did the Buddhists or Jainas get the Apsaras from; from where did the Buddhists and Jainas get their Gaja-Lakshmī; wherefrom did the Buddhists get the Vaishṇavī carrying the Garuḍadhvaja? My answer is, they got them from the orthodox Hindu buildings. There they had become too stereotyped for the architect and the mason to ignore; without these motives and decorative icons no building could be regarded as a sacred building when the Buddhists started erecting their sacred monuments which had to be in the style current in the country. On Hindu temples they all have a meaning, mystic (yogic) and traditional, dating back to the Vedic age and Vedic conceptions and are intimately connected with the previous history of Hindu mythology, which faithfully descended down to the last days of Hindu sacred architecture and iconography. But they have no meaning with Buddhist and Jaina structures where they are mere architectural, conventional decorations, i.e. borrowed and repeated from orthodox Hindu buildings. The orthodox buildings themselves of the pre-Kushan period are completely wiped out. And, who destroyed them? My answer is, the Kushan rule destroyed them. It is recorded[3] that one of the early Kushans destroyed temples of the Sacred Fire and raised in their places Buddhist temples. We see from the recorded policy of the Kushan viceroy that he suppressed Brahmins and orthodox castes and made the popu-

1 The subject is treated in the Matsya Purāṇa in chapters 251—269, and the text is avowedly based on 18 named authorities (Ch. 251, 2-4). From chapter 270, chapters dealing with history (Chs. 270–274) begin, which end about 240 A.D. The eighteen authorities will take back the science to about 600 B.C. at least, for its initial stage.

2 Matsya, 257, 13-14 (re. Vishṇu's Temple):

toraṇān choparishṭāt tu Vidyādhara-samanvitam |
devadundubhi-saṁyuktaṁ Gandharva-mithunānvitam |

3 J.B.O.R.S., XVIII, 15.

lation practically Brahmin-less. Alberūnī took note of the character of the Śaka rule referring to the period of **78 A.D.**

'The here-mentioned Śaka tyrannised over the country between the river Sindhu and the Ocean after he had made Āryāvarta in the midst of his realm his dwelling place. He interdicted the Hindus from considering and representing themselves as anything but Śakas.' [ii. 6].

The Garga Saṁhitā has a similar history to repeat:

'The king of the Śakas [was] greedy, very powerful, sinful.......... The terrible and the numerous Śakas [made] the population lose their character and degraded in their acts.' (J.B.O R.S., Vol. XIV, pp. 404 and 408.)

Guṇāḍhya in the first century A.D. gives a similar description of their doings, the doings of the Mlechchhas, the foreigners, defeated by Vikramāditya Śālivāhana (J.B.O.R.S., XVI, 296):

'(These) Mlechchhas slay Brahmins, interfere with sacrifices and other sacred ceremonies. They carry off daughters of hermits. Indeed, what crime do not the villains commit?' (Kathāsarit., Bk. XVIII.)

Mahā-Bhārata on social conditions, c. 150 A.D.–200 A.D.

36 A. How the Hindu nation looked at the Buddhist India of the Kushans is summed up in the Mahā-Bhārata, Vana-parvan, chapters 188 and 190[1]:—

'Then will rule over the land many Mlechchha kings. These sinful kings, addicted to falsehood, will govern on principles that are false, and they will be given to false controversialism. The Āndhras, the Śakas, the Pulindas, the Yavanas (i.e. Yaunas), the Kāmbhojas, the Vālhikas, and the Śūra-Ābhiras will then be rulers (188. 34–36). Then,

[1] Ch. 190 is mostly repetition of Ch. 188. It seems that Ch. 188 was the original text which was revised in the shape of Ch. 190 and the name of Kalki introduced at the end which is not to be found in Ch. 188, and which was expressly borrowed from 'the Purāṇa by Vāyu' (Ch. 191.16). It is not to be found in the present Vāyu P., though it is in the *Vāyu-prokta*-Brahmāṇḍa Purāṇa. The period (c. 150 A.D.–200 A.D.) is fixed by the rulers mentioned in Ch. 188.

the utterings of the Vedas become futile, the Śūdras address (Brāhmaṇas) with 'Bho' (term of equality), while Brāhmaṇas address them with 'Noble Sir' (39). Citizens will lose character on account of the terror of the burden of taxation (46). They become addicted to materialism ('*this-worldism*'—*aihalaukikam*) which ministers to their flesh and blood (49). The whole world will be Mlechchhanized; all rites and sacrifices will cease (190. 29). The Brāhmaṇas, Kshatriyas, and Vaiśyas will disappear; at this time all men will become one caste, the whole world will be Mlechchhanized, men will no more gratify the Celestials with *śrāddha* or manes with libations (46). Prohibiting the worship of the Celestials, they will worship bones. In the settlement of the Brāhmaṇas, in the Āśramas of the Great Ṛishis, in places sacred to gods, in sacred spots and in temples which had been dedicated to the Nāgas—the land will be marked with tombs ('Eḍūkas'=Buddhist stūpas) containing bones. They will have no temples dedicated to the Celestials.'[1] (65, 66, 67.)

This in places textually corresponds with the description of India under the Śaka rule given in the Garga Saṁhitā. The description seems to be a description by an eye-witness. The times to which the description applies is fixed by the mention of the rulers—the Āndhras, Śakas, Pulindas, Bactrians (i.e. the Kushans), Ābhiras—that is, the latter part of the Kushan times. I have said before that the Kushans destroyed the Hindu temples. This is borne out by this Mahā-Bhārata passage. The whole Hindu world was turned into Mlechchhas; all castes were abolished and practically one caste was created. Śrāddha and other rites were suspended; people worshipped bone-relics instead of Hindu gods. The *Varṇāśrama* system had been superseded. Oppression resulted in loss of character. Moral decay is set out at length in the same chapters.

[1] Eḍūkān pūjayishyanti, varjayishyanti devatāḥ. Śūdraś cha prabhavishyanti na dvijāḥ yugasaṁkshaye. Āśrameshu Maharshīṇām Brāhmaṇāvasatheshu cha, Devasthāneshu chaityeshu Nāgānāmālayeshu cha, Eḍūka-chinhā pṛithivī na devagriha-bhūshitā. (Kumbakonam Text, p. 314.)

The Śakan rule aimed at denationalising the Hindus and at the basic destruction of their national system. The social revolution which the Śakas strove for with a calculated policy, was a scheme to depress the high and the aristocrat, the custodian of national culture and the trustee of national liberty—the Brahmin and the Kshatriya. The Śakas were more afraid of the Hindu social system than the arms of the Hindu rulers whom they had already conquered. They aimed at sapping character from the common people by systematic terrorisation and proselytisation. The Garga Saṁhitā says that they carried away one-fourth of the total population from the Siprā to their own capital, i.e. Bactria. Their massacres are noted both by the Garga Saṁhitā and in their summing up by the Purāṇas.[1] They must have carried away as well great wealth from the country to Bactria. Their infamous greed was notorious. They systematically imposed a non-Brahmanical religious system on the Hindus. Hindu life, in short, was suspended. No book written between 78 A.D. to 180 A.D. is to be traced in the orthodox literature of Northern India. It became, therefore, imperatively necessary for the Hindus to undertake to deliver their country from such a political and social scourge.

VI. The Achievements of the Bhāraśivas, and their Empire.

The motive-cult of the Bhāraśiva time.

37. The undertaking to deliver the country from such a national calamity (§ 36) was shouldered by the Bhāraśivas on the Ganges. Now, here we have to take note of the contemporary motive factor which rules national undertakings in every human community and in every age and clime. That factor is the spiritual sentiment and the faith for the time-being. If the historian misses to read that, and merely attempts to record the catalogue of facts, he misses the bird and counts the feathers. It is more than doubtful whether he can read his facts correctly without reading the curves of national thought and sentiment.

1 See below, Pt. III, §§ 146B—147.

38. Then, what was the National Cult and Faith with which the Bhāraśivas entered on their mission? We find in that period everywhere—Śiva. Śiva rules over the actions of the Bhāraśivas and continues to preside over the Vākāṭaka India. In their period even books on poetic sentiments, which ought to be devoted to love, were devoted to Lord Śiva. National service of Hindu state-makers was always a solemn dedication to the Supreme Force which presides over human destiny. The dedication was made to a particular aspect of Him to a particular temperament of His, according to the national temperament of the time. The presiding God to whom political service was this time dedicated, was the God of Destruction. The Bhāraśivas called in Śiva who stood up in Yoga for a partial Tāṇḍava through his people of the Gangetic valley. We find Śiva everywhere in this period. The air is surcharged with the belief that the Destroyer Himself has founded the Bhāraśiva State, that He is the guarantor of the king and the people of the Bhāraśiva kingdom. He has stood up to see His people free—free to follow their *dharma*, free to be their own masters, free to be in Āryāvarta, the land of the Āryas, their God-given home. This politico-geographical idea of 'legitimacy' of the Hindu sovereign in Āryāvarta, which we may call *Āryāvartism*, is laid down in the Mānava Dharmaśāstra (II, 22-23), and is traceable from the time of Patañjali (180 B.C.)[1] down to Medhātithi [*ākramyākramya na chiraṁ tatra Mlechchhāḥ sthātāro bhavanti*],[2] and to Vīsala-deva [1164 A.D.] as a living belief [*Āryāvartaṁ yathārthaṁ punarapi kṛitavān Mlechchha-vichchhedanābhiḥ*].[3] This sacred principle had been violated, and He must set the wrong right. He must do it by His own method, by His own process, the dance of destruction. The Nāga kings became *Bhāraśiva*. They undertook to execute and they successfully executed that national dance of destruction in the valley of the Ganges. The names assumed by the Bhāraśiva Nāgas—'Vīrasena,' 'Skanda Nāga,' 'Bhīma Nāga,'

[1] J.B.O.R.S., IV, p. 202.

[2] Tagore Lectures, *Manu and Yājñavalkya*, pp. 31-32.

[3] Delhi Pillar, I.A., XIX, p. 212.

'Deva Nāga,' 'Bhava Nāga'—all prove that sense of Śaiva responsibility and necessity which the time required. Their repeated *aśvamedhas*, like the revival of the names of divine heroes, are records in themselves. A series of acts of valour continued, and repeated exertions resulted in progressive destruction of the Kushaṅ power in Āryāvarta. Soon after the rise of Vīrasena we find the Kushans pushed back as far as the neighbourhood of Sirhind from the Gangetic valley. About 226–241 A.D., the Kushan king (*Junāh*=Yauvan)[1] had diplomatic dealings with Ardashir, the first Sassanian emperor, from Sirhind.[2] By that time North-Eastern India up to the confines of the Punjab had been freed. This is amply borne out by the coins of Vīrasena which are found all over the United Provinces, and parts of the Punjab. The Kushans were so pressed by the Bhāraśivas that they ultimately sought the protection of the Sassanian Emperor Shapur (between 238 and 269 A.D.) whose effigy they had to stamp on their coins. Before Samudra Gupta, the greater portion of the Punjab as well had been liberated. The Mādrakas were striking their own coins once more and negotiated peace with and accepted the suzerainty of Samudra Gupta. The hills up to Kāngrā once more were under Hindu rulers when Samudra Gupta appeared on the scene. Most of this achievement is to be credited to the Bhāraśiva Nāgas, performers of ten aśvamedhas; and the maintenance of that free inheritance for 50 years, with further progress, to the Vākāṭakas, who carried on the Bhāraśiva policy.

Bhāraśiva Nāgas' success against the Kushans.

39. To appraise the success of the Bhāraśivas we have to imagine and visualize the immense prestige of the Bactrian Tukharas whom we call to-day the Kushans. Here was a power whose reserve forces were centred in their homeland in Central Asia and which was constantly fed from that centre—a power which had become firmly established from the banks of the Oxus up to the Bay of

Prestige and strength of the Kushans, and the Bhāraśiva boldness.

[1] J.B.O.R.S., XVIII, 201.

[2] V. Smith, E.H.I., 4th, p. 289, *n*.

Bengal,[1] from the Jumna down to the Narbada,[2] and in the west, from Kashmir and the Punjab to Sindh and Kathiawāḍ and to the sea beating against the coast of Gujarat, Sindh and Beluchistan—a power which for nearly one hundred years had insisted on its divine right as the Son of Heaven (*Daiva-putra*[3]) to rule over the Hindu humanity—a power which had the established fact of an iron rule in its favour. That power now to be challenged by a leader risen from obscurity, was a bigger fact than the challenge by the subject Greeks against the mammoth Persian Empire. The Greeks had not been under the direct administration of Persia, while the area now called the United Provinces of Agra and Oudh and Bihar had been under the direct imperial administration of the Kushans. It was not the question of merely throwing off a suzerainty, it was not the case of merely tearing off the veil of prestige hanging from a distance, but attacking directly a mighty power bodily installed in the country. The Bhāraśivas did it and did it successfully. While the Sātavāhanas in the West were still struggling against the Śaka power—the Sātavāhanas who had been emperors of the South for three centuries—the Bhāraśivas attained the result where the Emperors of Dakshiṇāpatha failed.

Simplicity of the Bhāraśiva Rule.

40. The Bhāraśiva rule was marked with Śiva's asceticism. They have no grandeur except the grandeur of their severe and austere undertaking. They ignore the imperial coinage of Kushans and revert to the old Hindu coinage. They assume no grandeur, unlike the Guptas. Like Śiva, they have a self-imposed non-richness. Like Śiva, they bestow and not partake. They give freedom to the Hindu Republics; they give them freedom to mint their own money and to live their own full life. Like Śiva's domestic polity, they have a *gaṇa*, of

[1] Coins of Vāsudeva were found in Pāṭaliputra excavations. A.R.A.S., E.C., 1913-14, p. 74. The Kushan and Pūrī Kushan coins would indicate their influence up to the Bay of Bengal, though beyond Bihar they seem to be limited generally by the Rajmahal Hills. The Orissa tradition about a *yavana* invasion probably refers to the Kushan *yaunas*.

[2] At Bheṛāghāṭ a Kushan inscription has been found.

[3] *Cf.* Alberūnī, II, 10, on the pretensions of the *Barha-takin*, ancestor of Kanishka (J.B.O.R.S., XVIII, 225).

Hindu States, around them. They are the true Śiva-made Nandi, the lord of the *Gaṇas*. They merely preside over a confederacy of states and foster freedom everywhere. They perform aśvamedhas, but do not become *eka-rāṭ* Emperors. They remain political Śaivas and international ascetics amongst their countrymen.

41. A worshipper of Śiva is a worshipper of a symbol, a *bindu*. The Śaiva worshipper would have looked down upon the Buddhist idol-worshippers as followers of a low cult.[1] Whether the Bhāraśiva did so or did not, we can be certain of one fact that Buddhism could not but have declined in the Nāga country, if for nothing else, at least for its political alliance with the enemy of the national civilization. It had become the foster-child of a tyrant and with the uprooting of the tyranny it must fall. This is the explanation of the decay of Buddhism which was so marked by the time of the early Guptas. The decay was in an advanced stage by the end of the Bhāraśiva period. Buddhism had become a denationalized system and assumed a non-Hindu character by its contact with the Kushans, in whose hands it had lost its spiritual independence and become a political instrument. The Buddhist Bhikshus in the Kushan period in Kashmir were felt, on the evidence of the *Rāja-taranginī*, as a social nuisance and a load of oppression. They must have been so felt also in Āryāvarta. Śaiva asceticism became a necessary antidote for a readjustment of society. The Sakas had weakened the character of the Hindu population; Śaiva asceticism was a necessary factor of correction. The greedy imperialism of the Kushans was destroyed; the Hindu people were purged of deteriorated morals. And when the task was done, the Bhāraśivas retired. Śiva's mission was complete, and in Lord Śiva the Bhāraśivas re-entered in spiritual triumph. Unconquered till the last, untainted by any material selfishness, the true servants of their Lord and His people exit from the stage of history—a rare, honourable and noble finis which the Bhāraśiva fully deserved. The Bhāraśivas

1 During the Nāga-Vākāṭaka period, the Ceylonese Buddhists transferred the tooth-relic from Andhra to Ceylon (§ 175). It indicates that Buddhist worship at the time stood discredited in India [*cf.* § 126].

re-established Hindu sovereignty in Āryāvarta. They restored the Hindu imperial throne and the national civilization and gave a new life to their country. They revived aśvamedha after a lapse of some four centuries. They restored the sanctity of the Mother Ganges, the river of Lord Śiva, throughout its length by freeing her from sin and crime, and made her worthy to be sculptured at the doors of the temples of the Vākāṭakas and the Guptas as a symbol of purity.[1] They did all this, and left no memorial to themselves. They left their deeds and obliterated themselves.

Nāgas and Mālavas.

42. The Nāga performers of the ten *aśvamedhas*, to put it in modern phraseology, the Nāga emperors, fostered the republics which covered the whole of [Eastern and Western] Malwā, and probably also Gujarat (Ābhīras), the whole of Rajputana (Yaudheyas and Mālavas), and probably also a portion of the Eastern Punjab (Madras)—all connected territory, to the west of the valley of the Ganges. These were certainly free in the next, the Vākāṭaka period, when Samudra Gupta emerges on the stage. The Malwā republics seem to have been formed by peoples and clans akin to the Nāgas. Those around Vidiśā were worshippers of Nāgas from early times, as the republican coins of Eran prove. Eran, the Airikiṇa town, is itself after the name Airaka, a Nāga, and the Eran coins bear a Nāga (serpent) figure. The Mālavas, near Jaipur, had founded their capital, Karkoṭa Nāgara, naming it after the Nāga Karkoṭa, which now lies within the territory of the Raja of Uniyāra—a feudatory of

[1] The oldest form of Gaṅgā in stone is at Jānkhat (see Plate II herein). The next one, together with that of the sister-river Yamunā we find at Bhūmarā; then those at Deogarh, described by Cunningham in A.S.R., vol. X, p. 104, Temple No. 5, where the figures are '*canopied by a five-hooded Nāga*'. They are on the lower faces of the jambs, just as at Samudra Gupta's Vishṇu temple at Eran. The Nāga-canopy at Deogarh is unique, nowhere repeated. Nāga is unconnected with the mythology of Gaṅgā and Yamunā. The river motifs themselves are referable to the Bhāraśiva period (see § 30) and its association with Nāga lends strong support to that view. The *Nāga-Gaṅgā* and the *Nāga-Yamunā* signify the two sacred rivers of the Nāga territory freed by them. *Cf.* § 86 on the conscious, political significance of the river motifs.

the Mahārāja of Jaipur, about 25 miles E.-S. from Ṭonk. The word *Nāgara* itself in the capital *Karkoṭa Nāgara* is connected with the word *Nāga*. It is important to recognise this fact that the Nāga monarchs and the republican Mālavas were, by their civilization and also probably ethnically, connected. Rāja-śekhara says that the Ṭakkas and the people of Maru used *apabhraṁśa* idioms. As we have already seen, the family of Gaṇapati Nāga of Padmāvatī was a *Ṭāka-vaṁśa*, which means that the family came from the Ṭakka-deśa. Thus we see that the Mālavas and the Nāgas spoke the same dialect. It seems that with the original migration of the republican Mālavas from the Punjab, the Ṭakka Nāgas had also migrated, and that the Nāgas themselves originally belonged to a republican community [the Five Karpaṭas] [§ 31], and that they were a Punjab people settled in Malwā.

Other Republics.

43. The Nāga emperors became the leaders of a movement for freedom from the Kushan rule. The Mālavas, the Yaudheyas, and the Kuṇindas (Madrakas) all re-strike their coins in the Nāga period. It may be possible to discern on a minute study their connection with the Nāga coinage disclosing the symbols of hegemony or suzerainty of the Nāgas.[1] The connection of the Mālava republican coins with those of Padmāvatī has been already realized and noticed. Dr. Vincent Smith says, 'they (Nāga coins) are closely related to some of the later Mālava coins'.[2] The Mālava coins re-appear, after a break, about the same time as the Nāga coins of Padmāvatī, about the second century A.D.[3] The Yaudheya coinage revives about the second century A.D.,[4] and the Kuṇinda coinage in the third century,[5] who are, evidently, the last to be liberated. In other words, the re-rise of the Yaudheyas and the Mālavas is contemporaneous with the Nāgas.

1 The peculiar tree symbol with the side designs of the Bhāraśiva coins (§§ 26A, 26B) is met with on several republican coins of the period.

2 C.I.M., p. 164.

3 Rapson, I.C., pp. 12-13; *Cf.* C.I.M., pp. 176-177.

4 C.I.M., p. 165.

5 Rapson, I.C., p. 12.

Nāga Empire: its character and extent.

44. The main blow to the Kushan power came from the Nāga emperors, but it is almost certain that on account of the confederate sovereignty enjoyed by these large republics the Nāgas must have been helped in their campaign by these republican communities. The Nāga empire was, what we may call, a Democratic Empire. In Magadha, the Kota dynasty seems to have arisen under them (Part III). The Gupta dynasty takes its root in the Nāga period, which the Purāṇas expressly mention (Part III, § 110). It should be noted here that the Guptas were also northern emigrants domiciled in the east (Part III, § 112). The Kotas of Magadha and the Guptas of Prayāga were evidently subordinate members of the Nāga Empire. In Bihar, Champāvatī is noted by the Vāyu and the Brahmāṇḍa, as a capital of the Nava Nāgas. The Nāgas extended their sway into the Central Provinces, a fact borne out by the subsequent Vākāṭaka history and the place-names like *Nāgavardhana*, *Nandi-vardhana*, and *Nāgapura*. At Purikā, they had a capital in the heart of the Vindhyan mountains, as a gateway to Mālwā. We may take it that, speaking roughly, the empire of the Bhāraśivas included Bihar, the United Provinces of Agra and Oudh, Bundelkhand, the Central Provinces, Malwa, Rajputana and the Madra republics in the E. Punjab. The Kushans accepted the suzerainty of Ardashir just in the middle of the Bhāraśiva period, 226–241 A.D., and they adopted Shapur's effigy on their coins between 238 and 269 A.D. This was the result of the Bhāraśiva pressure. Thus the ten aśvamedhas of the Bhāraśivas were not an empty rite.

Nāgara Architecture.

45. Apart from the *aśvamedhas* which are symbols both of a political revival and a revival of orthodox culture, there is independent evidence of a revival of orthodox culture which marks a new era. The word *Nagara* as in *Karkoṭa-Nāgara*, is undoubtedly connected with the word *Nāga* and is a vernacular form, denoting a derivative from that word, just as in *Nagar-dhana* [= *Nāgara-Vardhana*] (§ 32). The architectural term 'Nāgara style' could not be explained on the basis of assuming its connection with the word *nagara* (city). This style-name is un-

known to the Matsya Purāṇa which closes its historical data at about 243 A.D., i.e. before the close of the Nāga period. But it is known to the *Māna-sāra*, a Guptan or post-Guptan work. The style designated by the term N ā g a r a seems to be the style made popular by the N ā g a kings. In this connection, we should notice the same term applied to Brahmins called N ā g a r Brahmins of the Gangetic valley (Bulandshahar) [1] who became Muhammadan in Muhammadan times, and the term applied to the Jāṭs called *Nāgrā* Jāṭs near Ahi-chhatra.[2] The former were *Nāga* priests and '-*r* (*a*)' is added to show their connection with *Nāga*. The '*V e s a r a*' style, which again is a vernacular term taken, like the *Nāgara*, from the vocabulary of the mason, is distinguished by its being in the '*ornamental*' style: Sanskrit *veśa*, 'dress', 'make-up', Pkt. *Vesa*, *besa*, or '*ornamental*' [vide *Śilpa-Ratna*, ch. xvi. 50: '*vesaram veśya uchyate*'].[3] In both *Nāgara* and *Vesara*, *ra* has been added to the base-word forming a vernacular derivative, as *gaṭṭhar* ('bundle') from '*grantha*' ('tie'). The base in *Nāgara* is thus *Nāga*. *Vesara* was the type of religious buildings which was 'artificial', 'architectonic'. *Nāgara* was that in which we mostly find the Gupta square temples, and the Vākāṭaka temple of Pārvatī at Nachnā, and the Bhāraśiva temple of Bhūmarā (Bhūbharā, see App. A.). It was a *griha* ('dwelling-house') of one room (Matsya, 252. 51; 253. 2).

The Nāga antiquities have not been explored, yet we know that at Karkoṭa Nāgara, the capital of the Mālava Republic, the true type of also the *vesara* style existed. Carlleyle, in vol. VI, A.S.R., at page 186, describes the temple which he excavated and calls '*peculiarly-shaped*'

[1] F. S. Growse, J.B.A.S., 1879, p. 271: 'The principal residents of the town are Nāgar Brahmans by descent, though since the time of Aurangzeb, Muhammadan by religion, who believe that their ancestors were the priests employed by Janamejaya to conduct his sacrifice and that in return for their services they had a grant of the township and the surrounding villages.'

[2] Rose, *Glossary of the Tribes and Castes of the Punjab and the N.W.F. Province*, 1919. Vol. I, p. 48.

[3] Compare *Visika* in the Hathigumpha inscription (E.I., XX, p. 80, line 13) for 'architect'. *Vesar* (*Besar*) in Hindī is a nose ornament.

Chaunsath Joginī Temples at Khajurāho.

'This small temple is remarkable for having been composed almost entirely of an exteriorly circular (or circularly many-sided) building, which probably once terminated upwards in a *sikar* [śikhara], and which contained within it a square chamber built of massive, rough-hewn stones; for the temple did not appear to have possessed either a pillared portico, or a vestibule, or antechamber.

There is found in the period a śikhara style: on the square body [Nāgara plan] a four-sided *śikhara*.[1] Of this type, I have discovered a very small temple at Suraj Mau, which though dedicated to a lingam, now outside the temple, is called the *Nāg Bābā* Temple. The small temples of Karkoṭa Nāgara with Śikharas, were out of a class. The temple which I discovered at Suraj Mau has in its lower square portion the perfect 'Gupta'-body, while the śikhara part is a suggestion of so many storeys rising one on the other, tapering in imitation of a mountain peak. Such shrines at Khajurāho of Chauṅsaṭh Joginīs belong to that class. Cunningham rightly dates the latter before the grandfather of Dhaṅga, i.e. about 800 A.D. (A.S.R., XXI, 57). A glance at the two (the Suraj Mau Nāg Bābā)[2] and the Jogini shrines[3] will at once convince one that the Nāga Bābā is much older. Cunningham found at Tigowa foundations of 34 such small temples,[4] open on the east and closed on three sides, i.e. like the Suraj Mau Temple and of similar dimensions. He assigned them to the Gupta period, a date which he gave to the sculptures there. Smith after the publication of his *History of Art*, amended the date of the Tigowā remains by placing them in the Vākāṭaka period, contemporaneous with Samudra Gupta.[5] I found there numerous four-sided śikhara pieces. The small śikhara temples at Karkoṭa Nāgara would also go back, at the latest, to 350 A.D., after which date the Mālavas disappeared, and the deserted town yields no coins subsequent to that date. These small temples, remains of which were found at Karkoṭa

[1] *Cf.* Gopīnath Rao, *Iconography*, ii, 1, p. 99, on Nāgara plan: *Nāgaraṁ chaturasraṁ syāt.* See *Śilpa-Ratna*, XVI, 58.

[2] See *Modern Review*, August 1932. Suraj Mau is near Chhatarpur, C.I.

[3] I have not found them illustrated anywhere yet. [See plate II A.]

[4] A.S.R., IX, 41-44. [5] J.R.Å.S., 1914, p. 334. I agree; the details there are in line with Nachnā. The place-name is *Tigawāṅ*.

Nāgara and Tigowā, were Hindu *votive* temples after the fashion of the *votive* stūpas of the Kushan period. Architecturally thus they would follow immediately the Kushan period. A normal, as opposed to a 'votive', śikhara temple must have been large. Śikhara had been an old thing; '*excellent śikharas with carved interior*' are noted in the Hathigumphā inscription (*c.* 160 B.C.); their artists, one hundred in number, received land-grants from the Emperor Khāravela (E.I., XX, p. 80, Insc. line, 13). The Nāgara śikhara was a particular, probably a new, variety, which arose in the time of the Nāgas, i.e. the Bhāraśiva dynasty, and after their name received a permanent and wide name as 'Nāgara'. The Vākāṭaka period, which follows the Nāga period, affords an example of the Nāgara śikhara in the shape of its Chaturmukha Śiva Temple at Nachnā. Its Pārvatī Temple is an imitation of a mountain (*parvata*) with caves and wild animals; while the Śiva Temple has the śikhara (*Kailāsa*). Both are contemporary, and both styles existed contemporaneously. The age of both are fixed by what we call 'Gupta' sculptures, that is, the temples cannot be post-Guptan, yet they are not Guptan.[1] The figures and decorations on both were done by the same masons. The Chaturmukha Temple has a tall śikhara with slightly curved sides and having a height of about 40 feet. It stands on a raised platform. Pillars and halls it lacks [App. A].

The Bhūmarā Temple.

§ 46A. The Bhūmarā Temple, discovered by the late Mr. R. D. Banerji, near Uch-harā (the *Uchchakalpa* of the inscriptions of the Gupta-Vākāṭaka period), Nagod State, Western Baghelkhand, has been assigned by him to the fifth century A.D.[2] This temple is

[1] Scholars have gone into wild guesses over the Chaturmukha Temple. They hold that the śikhara temple of Chaturmukha is probably a later building. They, however, forget that the two temples make one scheme, and sculptures in both are by the same chisel. The buildings are in their original shape and material. They are parts of the same scheme, to make Pārvatī, the Goddess living in the *Parvata* which is imitated on the walls, while the Chaturmukha lingaṁ is installed under a śikhara, denoting Kailāsa. They escaped the hand of the iconoclast, being in an out-of-the-way place. [See App. at the end.]

[2] Archæological Memoir, No. 16, pp. 3, 7. The Memoir illustrates

surely a Bhāraśiva building. It is a Śaiva shrine. A large lingam, like the Chaturmukha at Nachnā, was established in the temple which is in the style followed in Samudra Gupta's time at Eran. What connects this temple with the Nāga traditions is the peculiar palm designs. Palm was the Nāga emblem, which has been also found at Padmāvatī, one of the Nāga capitals. At Bhumarā we have whole pillars (pilasters) carved in imitation of palm trees (Pl. IV), a feature nowhere else found. I shall designate it a Nāga (Bhāraśiva) motif. Scrolls of palm-leaf (fan) are used as decoration. Its human figures stand out classically. They express a fullness of life where nothing of the primitive the decadent is traceable. They are entirely of a different technique, conception and execution, to what we are accustomed at Mathurā. Here we have the real, old Hindu Art, practically come down direct from the art of Bhārahut which is within a few miles of Bhūmarā. To Bhūmarā, Bhārahuṭ is primitive, although in itself Bhārahut marks a decadent close of a preceding line of Hindu Art. Bhūmarā supplies a missing link connecting the Guptan Udaygiri-Deogarh with the past of the national orthodox art. The national orthodox art seems to have survived only in Baghelkhand and Bundelkhand where the Kushan rule could not be sufficiently destructive. As there is very little difference between the Bhāraśiva and the Vākāṭaka culture—the latter being a continuation of the former, we may, with some confidence, assume that the national plastic art did revive under the Bhāraśivas, which is attested by the Jānkhaṭ fragments for its early and independent existence. The śikhara before the Bhāraśivas was a four-cornered spire, as evidenced from the 'Bodh-Gaya' plaque found at Pāṭaliputra with a Kharosṭhi inscription of the first or the second century A.D., and the two sculptured replicas of śikhara temples found at Mathurā of about 150 A.D., to which Dr. Coomaraswamy has drawn attention.[1] The Bhāraśiva and Vākāṭaka śikhara, on the other hand, is a four-cornered spire over a four-cornered

the remains, some of which have now been removed to the Indian Museum, Calcutta. [See App. A. at the end here on the date.]

[1] *History of Indian and Indonesian Art*, Pl. XIX.

sanctum, with a bulge in the spire. This post-Kushan new type of śikhara is definitely datable in the Bhāraśiva period, and we may call this style the *Nāgara* śikhara.

47. The śikhara style goes out of fashion in the Gupta times in stone temples. But the Nāgara type asserts itself in the Gupta period itself more in brick.[1] In mediæval architecture, there is a combination of the pillar and the śikhara, of the square and the round plans, i.e. of the Nāgara and the Vesara types, the Nāgara type predominating.

Nāgara painting.

48. There was a Nāgara style of painting. That was also evidently connected with the Nāga period, but we are not in a position to distinguish it yet. I should not, however, be surprised if one day it is discovered in some distinctive style amongst our old frescoes of Ajaṇṭā. Ajaṇṭā became part of the Nāga Empire about 250 A.D.

Language.

49. It is certain that the Nāgas did not discourage Prakrit. On their coins they use Prakrit. Rājaśekhara, though later, noted the Ṭakkas for using apabhraṁśisms. The official language, as before the Kushans, remained Prakrit. They were democratic in politics, and they remained so in the matter of language.

Nāgara script.

49A. In the same way the script name *Nāgarī* is to be explained. I think, the origin of this name lies in the Nāga dynasty under whom originated the headed type of writing, evidence of the existence of which we get from the time of Pṛithivīsheṇa I in the inscriptions of Nachnā and Ganj.[2] In the Vākāṭaka inscriptions the letters are bound with a box-like heading which was reduced to a line in the Nāgarī script beginning from about

[1] *Cf.* Cunningham, on Gupta brick-temple at Konch, A.S.R. XVI, plate 17, p. 52.

[2] I emphatically disagree with the new view propounded in the Epigraphia Indica, Vol. XVII, p. 362, that the Nachnā and Ganj inscriptions belonged to Pṛithivīsheṇa II. I have carefully compared the scripts, and it is impossible to hold that they can be later than the fourth century A.D. The view of Fleet on the age of these inscriptions was perfectly right. Pṛithivīsheṇa II's plates clearly show that the Nachnā Pṛithivīsheṇa flourished long before. [See 61A for the Vākāṭaka inscriptions.]

800 A.D. The name *Nāgarī* seems to have been applied to what is called the box-headed script of the fourth and early fifth centuries. It is significant that the box-headed writing is found exactly where the Nāga government was most prominent, viz. in Bundelkhand and the Central Provinces. In the Central Provinces before the Nāga period, we have a Kushan inscription found at Bheṛāghāṭ which is in the ordinary Brāhmī script. The peculiar box-headed writing, therefore, came into existence after the Kushans and before the Vākāṭakas. We can confidently date it in the Nāga period.

Gaṅgā and Yamunā.

50. The Gaṅgā and Yamunā motifs and their connexion with the Nāga period have been noticed above. The motifs continue in the Vākāṭaka period (§ 86) and are carried down to the Gupta art and further down to the Chandel art.[1]

Sacredness of the Cow.

51. In the next big period, i.e. the Guptan, we find a sudden change in a social matter. Bull and cow are declared in Gupta inscriptions to be sacred and not to be killed. The beginning of this cult is probably to be dated in the Nāga period. The Kushans used to kill bulls and cows.[2] The Bhāraśivas had the bull as their sacred symbol, with which they identified themselves. With them the sacredness of the bull probably became universal in their empire, punctuating the difference of their age from the last political period when the bull was freely slaughtered for the kitchen of the Kushans. In the Gupta period, the kings take pride in being protectors of the bull and cow, emphasizing the character of their own rule as contrasted with that of the Kushans. The foundations of modern Hinduism were laid by the Nāga Emperors and that edifice was reared by the Vākāṭakas and elaborated by the Guptas.

[1] Cunningham, A.S.R. XXI, 59. The gate mentioned by Cunningham is now at the Museum gate, Khajurāho.

[2] See below on Kushan rule in the Gupta Section (§ 146 B).

PART II

The Vākāṭaka Kingdom (248 A.D.–284 A.D.): The Vākāṭaka Empire (284 A.D.–348 A.D.) with an Appendix on the Later Vākāṭaka Period (348 A.D.–550 A.D.)[1]

'*Vākāṭaka-lalāmasya kramaprāpta-Nṛipa-śriyaḥ.*'—[Vākāṭaka Seal.]

VII. THE VĀKĀṬAKAS.

The Vākāṭakas and their importance.

52. From the Vākāṭaka inscriptions the following facts are well-established. A dynasty, which took for its name *Vākāṭaka*, came into existence about a century before Samudra Gupta's conquests. The first king of the dynasty was Vindhyaśakti[2], a Brahmin. Their *gotra* was *Vishṇu-vṛiddha*—a subdivision of the Bhāradvājas. The second king of the dynasty was Pravarasena; the kings coming after him all assume their regnal names ending in °*sena*. Pravarasena, son of Vindhyaśakti, to be known hereafter as Pravarasena I, not only performed four *aśvamedha* sacrifices but also assumed the title of *Samrāṭ*, i.e. the Emperor of India. He had a long reign, so much so that his eldest son Gautamīputra could not succeed him, but his grandson Rudrasena I succeeded him. His son Gautamīputra was from a Brahmin lady, which is clear from his name. But Gautamīputra himself was married to the daughter of the Bhāraśiva king Bhava Nāga—a Kshatriya. The son of this union was Rudrasena, grandson of Pravarasena I and Bhava Nāga. We have to call him Rudrasena I, as names were repeated in consonance with the orthodox Hindu law—a practice also followed by the Guptas. Rudrasena's son was Pṛithivīsheṇa I, by whose time the family had existed for 100 years:

[1] The later history of the Vākāṭakas [348 A.D.—550 A.D.] is included owing to its cultural importance and for its not having been treated before.

[2] This seems to be an assumed name, an *abhisheka-nāma*, after the name of the country of his rise.

[1] 'Varsha-śatam-abhivardhamāna-kośa-daṇḍa-sādhana-' meaning:

> '—whose treasure and means of government had been accumulating for a hundred years'—(Fleet, G. I., p. 241).

This Pṛithivīsheṇa, whose political wisdom, heroism and good government are praised, subjugated the king of Kuntala, which was the name for a part of the Kārṇāṭaka country and the Kadamba kingdom, with which we shall deal later. Rudrasena II, son of Pṛithivīsheṇa I, was married to the daughter of Chandra Gupta II, Vikramāditya, whose name was Prabhāvatī Guptā, born of the Empress Kubera Nāgā, a princess of the Nāga dynasty. Prabhāvatī Guptā ruled as regent after the death of her husband Rudrasena II, as guardian to her minor son Yuvarāja Divākarasena who was in his thirteenth year when the Poona Plates were issued by the Queen-Mother, and subsequently to another son called Damodarasena-Pravarasena who succeeded Divākarasena and who issued a charter in his nineteenth year, which has come down to us.[2] The double name *Damodarasena-Pravarasena* proves the practice that these kings had two names, one the pre-coronation, and the other the coronation name which in the Champā (Cambodia) inscription is called the *Abhisheka-nāma*.[3] Similarly the Gupta Emperor Chandra Gupta II had two names, one *Deva Gupta* and the other *Chandra Gupta*.[4] Damodarasena-Pravarasena would have assumed kingship when 25 years of age, as that is the age laid down by the Śāstras for obtaining coronation.[5] Prabhāvati Guptā had thus a regency of about 20 years during the minority of her two sons. Neither Prabhāvatī Guptā nor her son when he came of age, ever used the Gupta Era. We may, therefore, conclude with certainty that the position of the Vākāṭakas was such as the Gupta Era was not required to be used in the Vākāṭaka dominions during the reigns of Chandra Gupta II and his successors. Although the Vākāṭakas after Samudra Gupta were in the Empire

[1] The Chamak, Dudia, and Bālāghāṭ plates (See § 61A.).

[2] Second Poona plates. I.A., 53, p. 48.

[3] *Champā*, by Dr. R. C. Majumdar, p. 157.

[4] J.B.O.R.S., XVIII, p. 38.

[5] *Hindu Polity*, II, p. 52.

of the Guptas, they were full sovereigns. From the Ajaṇṭā inscriptions and the Bālāghāṭ plates it is also clear that they had their own feudatories and they made war and peace on their own account. They subdued the kings of Trikūṭa, Kuntala, the Andhras, etc. and kept them as their feudatories. Their kingdom commenced in the western portion of Bundelkhand where Bundelkhand begins, in Ajaygarh and Pannā, and covered the whole of the Central Provinces and Berars, and with the Trikūṭa territory which was situated in northern Konkan, they were also masters of the northern part of the Maratha country, up to the sea. They were next-door to Kuntala, i.e. Karṇāṭaka, and the Andhra country. Their direct rule covered all the land on the table-land of the Vindhyas and the valley between the Vindhyas and the Satpura with the Maikal range. They controlled the passage through the Ajaṇṭā ghats to the South. Their feudatory empire included S. Kosala and Andhra, Western Malwā and Northern Hyderabad (§§ 73 ff.), apart from their Bhāraśiva inheritance. They had thus a very large kingdom under their direct control, which in the reign of Samudra Gupta had been reduced, but which in the next reign was fully restored and revived, and very likely it was so restored in the reign of Samudra Gupta himself, as Pṛithivīshēṇa I waged war against the newly constituted Kadamba kingdom and reduced its king to a subordinate position (§§ 82, 203).

53. Their history remains mostly uninterpreted without the aid of the Purāṇas and without reference to the history of India under the Bhāraśiva empire. With their aid we shall now relate the Vākāṭaka history. It is really the history of India for over half a century which we have to call the Vākāṭaka Period. Its importance is very great, both for the period and as explaining the rise and course of the next imperial period, i.e. of the Gupta Empire. The Guptas merely took over the empire already established by Pravarasena I, both territorially and culturally. If there had been no Vākāṭaka Empire, there would have been no Gupta Empire.

54. Pravarasena I was the first king who superseded the old orthodox imperial title of *Dviraśvamedha-Yājin*,

'Performer of Two Aśvamedhas,' which had been revived some five centuries before, after a lapse of several centuries, by Pushyamitra Śuṅga, Emperor of Āryāvarta, and by Śrī Sātakarṇi I, Emperor of Dakshiṇāpatha. The Emperor Pravarasena performed Four Aśvamedhas, and also *Bṛihaspati-sava*—a ritual open only to Brahmins. Along with them he performed Vājapeyas and several other Vedic sacrifices. Unlike the Bhāraśivas, he assumed the title of *Samrāṭ*, to which he was fully entitled as he seems to have brought the South also under his control (§§ 82, 176), and achieved a result which had been unachieved after the imperial Mauryas. A great portion of northern Dakshiṇāpatha, we find, becoming integral part of his dominions.

Position of Pravarasena I.

55. It is possible, though strange, that the empire of the Vākāṭakas should not receive up to this time even a line in modern text-books on Indian history, but it is not possible for the Purāṇas not to include the dynasty of Vindhyaśakti and Pravarasena in their chronicles. It was not a small thing to perform Four Aśvamedhas, and assume the title of Samrāṭ bringing oneself in line with Māndhātā and Vasu. The Purāṇas, which register even the foreign dynasties in India, could not have missed Pravarasena and his family. And, as a matter of fact, they have not missed them. After registering the fall of the Tukhāra, i.e. the Kushan dynasty they immediately give the dynasty of the *Vindhyakas*, of which they give the founder's name as *Vindhyaśakti*, whose son is called *Pravīra*. That name is described as a 'popular name' and it literally means 'the great hero'. His Vājapeya sacrifices are recorded by them and one edition of the Vāyu Purāṇa which is really the original Brahmāṇḍa,[1] instead of reading *Vājapeya* reads *Vājimedha*, i.e. 'Horse-Sacrifice', and the

The Purāṇas and Vākāṭakas.

[1] e Vāyu of Pargiter agrees fully with the Brahmāṇḍa of Dr. Hall. The present printed text of the Brahmāṇḍa is an amended edition. Brahmāṇḍa MSS. are so rare that neither Mr. Pargiter nor I could find any.

word is put in the plural [*Vājimedhaiś cha*] [1] which means, according to Sanskrit grammar, that he performed three or more Horse-Sacrifices. His reign is given as one of 60 years, which as being long, stands corroborated by the Vākāṭaka inscriptions and by the fact of his four aśvamedhas which must cover, on account of the protracted nature of the sacrifice and the intervals necessary, 40 to 50 years. Three facts completely establish the identity, viz. (1) the period of the rise of Vindhyaśakti and Pravīra which comes in the Purāṇas before the Guptas and after the Tukhāras, (2) the name of the founder of the dynasty being identical, (3) the vājimedhas (Horse-Sacrifices) and the long reign of Pravīra. Add to this, the inter-connection which the Purāṇas establish between the Nāga dynasty and Pravarasena through the grandson which I have already discussed above. In the light of this identification we gain the whole history of the Vākāṭakas from the Purāṇas which the inscriptions by themselves fail to impart.

The Original Home of the Vākāṭakas.

56. That the Vākāṭakas were Brahmins admits of no doubt. They did *Bṛihaspati-sava* sacrifices, which are intended for and open to Brahmins only. About the exclusive character of Bṛihaspati-sava the tradition never changed. Their *gotra*, Vishṇu Vṛiddha, is a Brahmin gotra, still surviving in the Maratha country.[2] Then, Vindhyaśakti is expressly called *dvija* or Brahmin [*dvijaḥ prakāśo bhuvi Vindhyaśaktiḥ*].[3] As to the place of their origin, the Purāṇic description—the 'Vindhyaka' or 'the Vindhyan' dynasty—limits the problem to the Vindhyan country, and their further localization fixes the exact spot. The Vindhyakas, i.e. the Vākāṭakas, arose on the river or in the country called Kilakilā (*Kilakilāyāṁ*). One might have thought of identifying this river with the *Kiyān*, the Ken of the maps, but no room for speculation is left, as my friend Rai Bahadur Hiralal has himself seen the Kilakilā—a small river near Panna—having a bad reputation for its unhealthy water.[4] We are thus brought to the very

1 Pargiter, P.T., p. 50, *n*. 35.

2 I am thankful to Professor D. R. Bhandarkar for this information.

3 A.W.S.R., Vol. IV, pp. 125 and 128 fn.—Plate LVII.

4 A full description of the river is now supplied to me by Mr. Śaradā

area, Ajaygarh-Pannā where the earliest Vākāṭaka inscriptions are found, that is the district of Ganj-Nachnā. The Bhāgavata Purāṇa, in describing the Vidiśā Nāgas and Pravīraka, calls the whole group 'the Kilakilā kings'—that is, it treats Eastern Malwā [Vidiśā] and Kilakilā as one tract, or Eastern Malwā as included in Kilakilā. The location of the dynasty in Bundelkhand is thus unanimous.

57. Let us now take up the history of the word *Vākāṭaka*. The phrase 'Vākāṭakānāṁ Mahārāja Śrī—so-and-so,' does not mean that the king so-and-so is the king of a people called Vākāṭakas, but only means the Mahārāja so-and-so 'of the Vākāṭaka Dynasty'. The plural form *Vākāṭakānāṁ* simply means 'of the Vākāṭaka dynasty',[1] as in the case of the Kadambas the expression *Kadambānāṁ* and in the case of the contemporary Pallavas, *Pallavāṇa*[2] (Pkt. 'of the Pallavas')—'*Bhāraddāyo Pallāvaṇa Sivakhaṁda-vamo*'—where 'of the Pallavas' stands quite independently.[3] This is, therefore, not a tribal but a personal dynastic name. The form *Vākāṭaka* means 'of the place "Vākāṭa" or "Vakāṭa",' as in Samudra Gupta's inscription, *Māhā-Kāntārakā, Kausalaka, Paishṭhāpuraka*, etc. signify ('of Mahakāntāra', 'of Kosala', 'of Pishṭhapura').[4] The dynastic name *Traikūṭaka* is an exact parallel. I found an ancient village called Bāgāṭ, in the northernmost part of the Orchhā State, 6 miles E. of Chirgaon of the British district of Jhansi. Its neighbouring village—a village called *Bījaur*—is often mentioned with Bāgāt, as *Bījaur-Bāgāṭ*. It is situated in the Ṭahraulī tahsil of Orchhā. It is between two rivulets, *Kaynā* and *Ḍugraï*, which fall into the Betwā. It is a large and ancient Brahmin village, mainly peopled by Bhāgaur Brahmins. The village is believed to be of Droṇāchārya, the famous military Brahmin mentioned in the Mahā-Bhārata.

Prasad of Satna, Rewah, from which I find that I crossed the river twice in its search without knowing its name. It runs through Pannā. One crosses it on the way from Nāgaudh to Pannā. It is a thin stream. [See p. 8, *n*.]

1 I.A., Vol. VI, p. 26.

2 E.I., Vol. I, p. 5.

3 In editing the Balaghat plates of Pṛithivisheṇa II, Kielhorn emphasized this point. E.I., Vol. IX, p. 269.

4 G.I., p. 234.

There are two large caves there which were described to me to be about 25 yds. × 30 yds., and I was told that there were also sculptures there, which from the description given to me would appear to belong to what we call the Gupta age. The place has never been visited by any archæologist. A thorough exploration may result in the find of inscriptions and other valuable relics.

57A. It seems that the Brahmin who according to the Purāṇas was the first anointed king and the founder of the dynasty and who assumed the appropriate appellation of *Vindhyaśakti*, adopted the name of his town as his dynastic title. That the town of Vākāṭa is of ancient origin is proved by a pilgrim's inscription at Amarāvatī where a common citizen, about 150 B.C., describes himself as a *Vākāṭaka*, i.e. as an original inhabitant of Vākāṭa.[1] The town might have borne even in those days the proud military tradition claiming association with Droṇāchārya, who, like the Vākāṭakas, was a Bhāradvāja Brahmin.

'Kilakilā Yavanāḥ' a wrong reading.

58. The older Purāṇas do not mention the caste of the Vindhyakas, but the Vishṇu Purāṇa has fallen into a confusion by a misreading of the Matsya text. The Matsya Purāṇa after closing the Āndhra list and giving the dynasties contemporary with the Āndhras, says in Chapter 272, verse 24,—*teshûtsanneshu Kālena tataḥ Kilakilâ nṛipāḥ*. With this line the Matsya closes its chronicles and then enters from verse 25 onwards on a description of the 'Yavana' rule, which means here the Kushan rule (*Yauna, Yauvan*[2]). The Vishṇu reads the first line of that description along with the Kilakilā kings, the next line of the Matsya being *bhavishyantīha Yavanā dharmato kāmato'rthataḥ*. The author of the Vishṇu paraphrases these two lines in these words—'*teshûchhanneshu Kailakilā Yavanā bhūpatayo bhavishyanti mūrdhābhishiktas teshām Vindhyaśaktiḥ*'. In this the Vishṇu is not followed by the Bhāgavata, and the commentator of the Vishṇu gives another reading and explains it correctly that Vindhyaśakti, according to that

[1] E.I., Vol. XV, p. 267 (Inscription No. 27).

[2] J.B.O.R.S., XVIII, 201.

reading, was a Kshatriya (*i.e.*, Hindu) chief. The other reading is thus given by the commentator—'*Vindhyaśaktir-mūrdhābhishikta iti pāṭhe Kshatriya-mukhya ityarthaḥ*'. This variant reading did not make Vindhyaśakti a member of 'the Kailakilā Yavanas'. The mistake is obvious, being caused by reading the word *Yavanāḥ* of the next line of the Matsya along with the *Kailakilāḥ*. It should be noted that it is not a consistent, but only an occasional, reading. The commentator did not find the statement that the Kailakilas were Yavanas in all the manuscripts of the Vishṇu Purāṇa. He found it omitted in some, as Mr. Pargiter has found it omitted in his *h.* Vs.[1] It seems that making the Kailakilas into Yavanas was a later emendation by some reviser of the text of Vishṇu who consulted the Matsya text. Evidently the original edition did not have *Yavanas* here, and it is a later addition.

Vindhyaśakti.

59. The Purāṇas in detailing the rise of Vindhyaśakti state that Vindhyaśakti arose from the Kilakilā kings. Here it is clear that the Purāṇas mean the Nāgas who at that time were prominently connected with Kilakilā, as their name changes from 'Vidiśā Vrishas' to 'Kilakilā Vṛishas', e.g. Vāyu:

tach-chhanena cha Kālena tataḥ Ḳilakilā-Vṛishāḥ
tataḥ K(a)ilakilebhyaś cha Vindhyaśaktir bhavishyati

* * * * *

Vṛishān Vaideśakāṁś chāpi bhavishyāṁś cha nibodhata[2]

The Bhāgavata similarly describes the later Nāgas, commencing with Bhūta Nandi, as the kings of Kilakilā:

Kilakilāyāṁ nṛipatayo Bhūta-Nando'tha Vaṅgiriḥ
Śiśunandiś cha tad-bhrātā Yaśo-Nandiḥ Pravīrakaḥ[3]

The Purāṇas treat Pravīra as coming in the line of the Kilakilā Vṛiskas, i.e. the Bhāraśivas of Eastern Bundelkhand and Baghelkhand.

[1] P.T., page 48, f.n. 82.

[2] Vāyu, verses 358–360; cf. Brahmāṇḍa, verses 178-179.

[3] Verses 32-33. The Bhāgavata omits the statement of there having been kings between Yaśaḥ Nandi and Pravīra.

The meaning of the statement that Vindhyaśakti arose from the Kilakilā kings is that he arose first as their recognized feudatory or a full-fledged member of their confederacy. That he was constitutionally in a subordinate position is proved by the fact that the official deeds of the Vākāṭakas omit him and begin the line of their independent kings with Pravarasena. It is only in the family history [*kshitipānupūrvī*] given in the Ajaṇṭā cave inscription [Cave no. XVI], that Vindhyaśakti is described as the founder of the *Vākāṭaka vaṁśa* (Vākāṭaka-vaṁśa-ketuḥ). From the description it appears that Vindhyaśakti, whose strength grew in great battles and who by the valour of his arms gained (a kingdom) and became the banner of the Vākāṭaka dynasty and who remained a strict Brahmin throughout his career (chakāra puṇyeshu paraṁ prayatnam), was primarily a general of the Kilakilā Vṛishas. His adoption of the name of his native town as his dynastic title shows that he had been an ordinary citizen and had no royal pedigree behind him. He takes patriotic pleasure in connecting himself with the Vindhyas and with Vākāṭa, his home. 'Vindhyaśakti' itself is obviously an assumed regnal name. He seems to have made large conquests in Andhra and Naishadha-Vidūra countries (§§75, 76A).

Capital.

60. The capital from which Pravarasena I ruled was Chanakā (§24), and the Purāṇas imply that it had been in existence already; he is not called its founder. It seems that it was founded by Vindhyaśakti, if not by the Nāgas [§ 24, *n.*]. I am inclined to identify the connected site of the ancient fortified town now known as *Ganj-Nachnā* with the *Chanakā* or *Kāñchanakā* of the Vākāṭakas. Its strategic position implies that it was built by a newly-founded power, and may justify the assertion conveyed by the name *Vindhyaśakti* that the V i n d h y a was really his strength. The position of Ganj-Nachnā as described by General Cunningham is as follows:

> 'The small village of Nāchna is situated 2 miles to the west of the town of Ganj, which is 25 miles to the S.-E. of Panna, and 15 miles to the S.-W. of Nāgodh .... The spot [Nachnā] is covered with bricks, and there are

many remains of brick buildings on the road from Ganj to Nāchna. The people say that Kūthara [the name of the fort at Nachnā] was a great city in former times, and that it was the capital of the king of the country. The site of Nāchna is still called Khās Kūthara .... There is said to be a tunnel from the fort of Kūthara to the Satna or Gorena-nala which flows past Nāchna, and joins the Kiyān or Ken river, 11 miles to the S. W. of Ganj.... .... The position in the entrance of a valley had the great advantage of offering a safe retreat into the recesses of the Vindhya Hills on the east, west, and south, in case of attack.'[1]

The site is distinguished by the two temples, described already, of Pārvatī and Chaturmukha, which have the figures of Gaṅgā and Yamunā on their doorways. Gaṅgā and Yamunā come to be peculiarly Vākāṭaka motifs inherited from the Bhāraśivas. The site is also known for three inscriptions of the reign of Pṛithivīsheṇa I. The temples are unique in the history of Indian architecture and sculpture, marking the beginning of what we call the Gupta Art. All these inscriptions are in Sanskrit.

VIII. Vākāṭaka Records and Chronology.

Vākāṭaka Coins.

61. From coins we get the names of the two Vākāṭaka emperors—Pravarasena I and Rudrasena I, grandson and successor of Pravarasena I (§§ 52 ff.). We do not find any coin of Vindhyaśakti, father of Pravarasena I. Vindhyaśakti was a subordinate king under the Bhāraśiva Nāga emperors, and probably no coins were struck by him. The coins of the two imperial Vākāṭakas, which have been identified here, had been missed before owing to their not having been read properly or not read at all. I have already discussed the coin of Pravarasena I (§ 30) which probably belongs to the Ahichhatrā mint. The successors of Rudrasena I came under the suzerainty of the Guptas, who, as a rule, did not allow any subordinate coinage.

[1] Cunningham, A.S.R., vol. XXI, p. 95. The correct spelling is *Nāchanā*, not *Nāchnā*.

But evidently there was an exception made in the case of Pṛithivī-sheṇa I, the son and successor of Rudrasena I, who got his son Rudrasena II married to the daughter of Chandra Gupta II. It seems that we have his coin—in the small, neat coin with a well-executed bull figure on the reverse, reproduced by Dr. V. Smith on plate No. XX, as fig. no. 4, in 'his *Catalogue of the Coins in the Indian Museum*'[1]. The obverse which bears the well-known tree of the Bhāraśiva coins (Kosam mint) and the representation of a mountain, has a Brāhmī legend. It was read by Dr. Smith (p. 155) as *Pavatasa*, 'of Pavata'. The first letter, however, is *Pṛi*, not *Pa*; the *ṛi* is at the bottom of the letter. The second letter is a conjunct with a [*v*] below a Guptan *th* (which has a clear dot in the middle); there are traces of *i*-mark on the top; it is to be read as *th* [*v*] *i*. The letter read by Dr. Smith as *ta* is *ś* with an *e*-matrā on the top The next letter is *ṇa*. The whole name seems to be:

Pṛith[*v*]*iśeṇa* = *Pṛithvīsheṇa*.

There is a figure at the right-hand bottom corner of the railing which reads as the figure 9, i.e. the coin is dated in the 9th regnal year. The *ṇ* is the hooked, i.e. the Gupta variety, which as well as the other letters all agree with the early Gupta forms.

In the same classification ('Coins of Kosam') Dr. Smith has illustrated another coin on the same plate (XX) as fig. no. 5. This has not been read by him. It has the same five-branched tree but in an idealized and conventionalized form, and has the same mountain representation as on the coin of Pṛithivīsheṇa I (fig. no. 4).[2] The mountain is evidently the Vindhya Hill. It has the same Vākāṭaka wheel which is inscribed on the Durehā pillar and on the Vākāṭaka inscriptions at Ganj and Nachnā and also on the coin of Pravarasena I of the year 76 (§ 30). The reverse has a lean bull facing a *dhvaja* or standard as on the Pallava seals (S.I.I., II, p. 521).[3]

[1] See also Plate III herein.

[2] This coin being larger, the mountain is larger but the shape is exactly the same as on fig. no. 4. [My reproductions of these coins are smaller than their original size.] I have used casts in reading them.

[3] The bull is walking to the standard, while the bull on the Pallava seal is recumbent; on the earlier Pallava seal in E.I. VIII, 144, the bull is standing and there is the *makara*-head standard.

Vākāṭaka Coins.

Coin of Pravarasena.

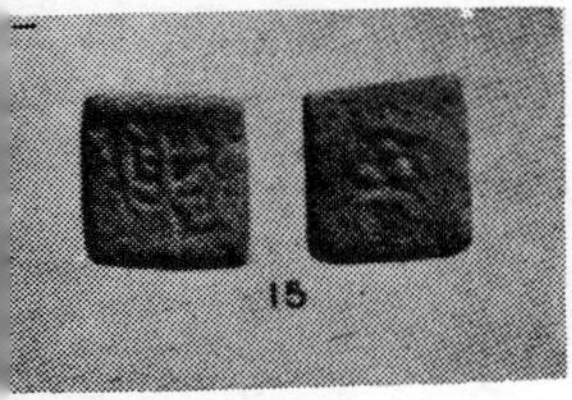

[C. I. M., Pl. XXII]

Coin of Rudra [Sena I.]

[C. I M. XX. 5]

Coin of 'Prithv[ī]sheṇa'

[C. I. M., Pl. XX. 4]

On the top of it, there is probably the bracket of a *makara*-head—the standard of the Ganges.[1] Above the bull, there is a figure with a halo on a pedestal, probably a representation of Śiva as in the Pallava seal. The obverse has a legend on the margin above the wheel It reads *Rudra*; the top of the *r* has a box-head and the head of *d* is thickened. To the right of the mountain there is the figure of 100. I take it to be the coin of Rudrasena dated in the year 100. It is allied to the coins of Pravarasena I and Pṛithivīsheṇa I by its date, the Gangetic symbols, the mountain, the tree, the bull, and the wheel (§ 30).

The other Vākāṭakas have no coins.

§ 61 A. For convenience of reference I note below all the Vākāṭaka inscriptions published up to this time, arranging them in their chronological order:—

Vākāṭaka Inscriptions.

Pṛithivīsheṇa I.—(*a*, *b*, *c*) Three short dedicatory inscriptions [same text] on stone pieces, to mark the erection of pious buildings at NACHNĀ and GANJ, by the donor Vyāghra-deva, under the reign of Pṛithivīsheṇa I. The donor was either a member of the family of Pṛithivīsheṇa or an officer or a feudatory of Pṛithivīsheṇa. The inscriptions bear the royal wheel-mark. —G.I., p. 233, nos. 53 and 54 at Nachnā, E.I., XVII, 12 (Ganj).

Regent Prabhāvatī Guptā.—(*d*) POONA Plates of the Regent Queen Prabhāvatī Guptā [daughter of Chandra Guptā II and of the *Mahādevī* Kubera-Nāgā], mother of *Yuvarāja* Divākara-sena, dated in the year 13th. The gift was made from Nandi-Vardhana, in the Nagpur District, C.P.—E.I., XV, 39.

Pravarasena II.—(*e*) CHAMAK Plates of Pravarasena II, son of Rudrasena II and Prabhāvatī Guptā, daughter

[1] I think, the bracket-shaped *makara* standard acquired the name *makara-toraṇa*. The 'bracket' is still called *toḍī* or torī (तोड़ी) in the United Provinces. The Patna Museum possesses an ancient miniature standard of *makara-toraṇa* in bronze, upholding a *chakra*. It was found near Buxar.

of Deva Gupta, dated in the 18th year, issued from Pravarapura. The plates were found at Chamak, in the district of Illichpur, Berar, and relate to Chamak (*Charmāṅka*) in the Bhojakaṭa kingdom.—G.I., p. 235.

(*f*) SEONI Plates, found at Seoni, C.P., of Pravarasena II, dated in the 18th year of his reign. It relates to a property in the Illichpur District—G.I., p. 243.

(*g*) (Second) POONA [1] Plates of the reign of Dāmodarasena Pravarasena (=Pravarasena II) of the year 19th, by Queen-Mother Prabhāvatī Guptā, *Mahādevī*, wife of Rudrasena II, mother of Mahārāja Śrî Damodarasena-Pravarasena. The gift was made at Rāmagiri (Rāmṭek, near Nagpur, C.P.)—I.A., vol. 53, 48.

(*h*) DUDIA Plates of Pravarasena II, dated in the 23rd year, issued from Pravarapura, found in the Chhindwara District, C.P.—E.I., vol. III, 258.

(*i*) PATNA MUSEUM Plates of Pravarasena II; fragmentary; no date; the plates came from Jabalpur, C.P., to Patna.—J.B.O.R.S., XIV, 465.

Pṛithivīsheṇa II.—(*j*) BĀLĀGHĀṬ Plates of Pṛithivīsheṇa II, son of Mahārāja Śrî Narendrasena, who was the son of Pravarasena II. Pṛithivīseṇa II's mother was the Mahādevī Ajjhitā Bhaṭṭārikā, daughter of the King of Kuntala (*Kuntalādhipati*). The plates are a draft ready for engraving a gift on the blank portion; no gift is recorded. They were found in the District of Bālāghāṭ, C.P.—E.I., IX, 269.

Devasena.—(*k*) Inscription in AJANTA CAVE TEMPLE, No. XIII (Ghaṭotkacha Cave) by Hastibhoja, minister of King Devasena, [inscribed] in the reign of Devasena Vākāṭaka [2] (*Vākāṭake rājati Devasene*). The minister was a southern Brahmin whose genealogy is given; he dedicated the cave-temple to Buddhist faith.—A.S.W.I., IV, 138.

[1] It should be called Riddhapur plates—see Hira Lal, *Inscriptions in C.P. and Berar*, 1932, p. 139. Riddhapur is 26 miles from Amaraoti.

[2] Bühler has wrongly ascribed a later date to this.

Harisheṇa.—(*l*) AJANTA inscription (No. 3 of Bühler) in CAVE TEMPLE no. XVI, of the reign of King Harisheṇa, son of Devasena who abdicated in favour of his son Harisheṇa. Devasena was the son of the son (name lost) of Pravarasena II. The first part of the inscription (verses 1 to 18) is the family history (*kshitipānupūrvī*), the '*ānupūrvī* (order of succession) of the Kings' of the Vākāṭaka dynasty, beginning with Vindhyaśakti. The second part (verses 19 to 32) is devoted to the pious foundation itself, the construction and gift of the Cave-Temple, a Chaitya, to Buddhist worship, by the minister (Varāhadevá), son of Hastibhoja who had been the minister of Devasena.—A.S.W.I., IV, 124.

(*m*) AJANTA CAVE TEMPLE inscription, no. 4 of Bühler, by a family of feudatory kings subordinate to King Harisheṇa. It gives their genealogy for 10 generations and records the construction of the Cave Temple (no. XVII) and its dedication to Lord Buddha. It is dated in the reign of Harisheṇa '*who did what was good for his subjects*' ['*paripālayati kshitīndra-chandre Harisheṇe hitakāriṇi prajānām*'].—A.S.W.I., IV, 130, *l*. 21.—A.S.W.I., IV, 128.

There are two more records—stone inscriptions—which I regard to be Vākāṭakan and which I shall discuss here later[1].

62. The Vākāṭaka genealogy, as constructed from inscriptions and the Purāṇas, stands thus [the members enclosed (in round brackets) did not succeed as Vākāṭaka kings]:—

Vākāṭaka Genealogy.

[1] One of them is the Durehā (Jāso) pillar; see the App. A (end). This expressly mentions the dynastic name, and is the earliest in script.

VINDHYAŚAKTI, king [mūrdhābhishikta].

PRAVARASENA I, the Pravīra, *Emperor*: ruled for 60 years.

(GAUTAMĪPUTRA) — (2nd son) (ruled as a sub-king) — (3rd son) (ruled as a sub-king) — (4th son) (ruled as a sub-king)

RUDRASENA I, the Infant, succeeding as a Bhāraśiva grandson and a Bhāraśiva king and ruling at Purikā under the guardianship of his paternal grandfather Pravarasena, and later on succeeding Pravarasena, at Chanakā, a contemporary of Samudra Gupta.

PṚITHIVĪSHEṆA I—contemporary of Samudra Gupta and Chandra Gupta II, conquered the king of Kuntala.

RUDRASENA II=(*m.*) Prabhāvatī Guptā, daughter of Chandra Gupta II and *Mahādevī* Kubera-Nāgā.

(DIVĀKARASENA, died as *Yuvarāja* in or after his thirteenth year)

DĀMODARASENA-PRAVARASENA [PRAVARASENA II], known to have ruled, from inscriptions, for at least 23 years at Pravarapura in the Central Provinces, evidently a new capital founded after his name.

NARENDRASENA [name lost at Ajaṇṭā—succeeded at the age of 8], name given in Bālāghāṭ plates as NARENDRASENA=*m.* Ajjhitā *Bhaṭṭārikā*, *Mahādevī*, daughter of the king of Kuntala; he was obeyed by the feudatory lords of Kosalā, Mekalā, and Mālava.

PṚITHIVĪSHEṆA II [rescued his 'sunken family']

DEVASENA, the ease-loving (*bhogeshu yatheshṭa-cheshṭaḥ*), handsome king, who abdicated in favour of his son Harisheṇa.

HARISHEṆA, conquered Kuntala, Avanti, Kaliṅga, Kosala, Trikūṭa, Lāṭa, Andhra............. whose minister Hastibhoja excavated the Cave Temple XVI at Ajaṇṭā and presented it to Buddhist monks.

The confusion respecting the succession of Devasena and his son Pṛithivīsheṇa II, caused by two records—the Ajaṇṭā inscription of cave XVI of the reign of Harisheṇa and the draft copper-plates of Pṛithivīsheṇa II, disappears on a proper construction of the words used in the plates which I have discussed under the history of the Later Vākāṭakas.

Veracity of the inscriptions.

63. Devasena's description in the inscription, incised during the reign of his son, marks the inscription with the stamp of truthful recording of fact by contemporary offi-

cers and composers. The handsome king, 'who was accessible to all his subjects like a good friend' was given to a life of ease and pleasure, he resigned kingship in favour of his son H a r i s h e ṇ a, saw him anointed king, and dedicated his life completely to pleasure.

Fixed Point in Vākāṭaka Chronology.

64. In the Vākāṭaka chronology the one fixed point according to the inscriptions is the contemporaneity of Chandra Gupta II with Pṛithivīsheṇa I and Rudrasena II. Another point, which we infer from the Allahabad inscription of Samudra Gupta, is that Pravarasena, the Emperor, had been dead and gone before Samudra Gupta launched on his imperial career, as we do not find his name there. Samudra Gupta made the kings of 'the Forest Country' adjoining the Gaṅgā-Yamunā *Doāb*, his own governors and servants,[1] which undoubtedly means that Bundelkhand and Baghelkhand passed under him. Who was, then, the Vākāṭaka king at the time whose feudatories in the Vindhya country were snatched away by Samudra Gupta? As his conquests are to be taken to have come after Pravarasena, and as the fourth Vākāṭaka king (Prithivīsheṇa I) ruled over the whole of the Vākāṭaka territory and his son was married to Chandra Gupta Vikramāditya's daughter, the Vākāṭaka contemporary of Samudra Gupta must have been the king succeeding Pravarasena and preceding Pṛithivīsheṇa, i.e., R u d r a s e n a I, whom we may identify confidently with R u d r a d e v a, the leading king of Āryāvarta in the list of Samudra Gupta (§ 139).

Purāṇic Data on Vākāṭaka Chronology.

65. But, we get more data and more help from the Purāṇas in the matter of the Vākāṭaka chronology. The Purāṇas give only 96 years to the dynasty of Vindhyaśakti, out of which they assign 60 years to the Infant and Pravarasena [Pravîra] together, and consequently 36 years would belong to Vindhyaśakti. In other words, with Rudrasena I they close the dynasty. We can, therefore, say with confidence, that Rudrasena came in conflict with Samudra Gupta and disappeared from the

[1] G.I., p. 13.

scene. The Vāyu and the Brahmāṇḍa give 96 years for the passing away of the empire (bhūmi).[1] The Vāyu uses the verb in the plural when it mentions the 60 years and thereby seems to refer the 60 years to both; its verb ['bhokshyanti'] instead of being in the dual, is in the plural, which is a Prakritism, as pointed out by Mr. Pargiter (P.T., p. 50, n. 31). The Bhāgavata does not mention and count the Infant at all. Samudra Gupta seems to have immediately on the death of Pravarasena started this campaign, and the imperial power of Rudrasena I was broken on the battlefield of Allahabad or Kauśāmbī which resulted in the death of the important members of his confederacy, viz. Achyuta, Nāgasena and also probably Gaṇapati Nāga.[2]

66. The Purāṇas thus close the Vindhyaka dynasty, while they regard the Guptas as still running by leaving them unnumbered and by not giving the total of their reign-period. Thus, by summing up the imperial Vākāṭaka rule, they place it before the rise of the Gupta Empire. The 96 years of the Purāṇas as the total of the Vindhyaka (Vākāṭaka) imperial period is confirmed by the Vākāṭaka inscriptions which mark off the reign of Pṛithivīsheṇa I by the statement 'who belonged to an uninterrupted succession of sons and sons' son, and whose treasure and means of government had been accumulating for one hundred years' (Fleet, G.I., p. 24). The coin of '*Rudra*' of the Kosam series, with the characteristic Vākāṭaka wheel, bears the year 100 [§ 61]. Rudrasena thus completed the 100th year of his dynasty, and had a reign of 4 years.

67. The Vishṇu and Bhāgavata give two totals, one of 100 years and another of an uncertain figure: 56, 6 or 60 (?), the reading being corrupt. The manuscripts of the Vishṇu read '*varsha-satam shaṭ varshāṇi*' and '*varsha-śataṁ shaś pañcha varshāṇi*', and the Bhāgavata reads '*varsha-śataṁ bhavisyanti adhikāni shaṭ*'.[3] It seems that after writing *varsha-śataṁ* something else was written which has become unintelligible. There was no reason to repeat the word *varshāṇi*

[1] Cf. Allahabad inscription where *pṛithivī* (l. 24) and *dharaṇi* mean 'India' and 'Empire'.

[2] See part III below (§ 132 ff.).

[3] P.T. 50, n. 30.

in the Vishṇu after *varsha-śataṁ*. The editors or copyists of the Vishṇu had two figures before them, one of sixty for Śiśuka-and-Pravīra, and another for the family of Vindhyaśakti, 100 years or 96 years. Ninety-six plus sixty, they made into '*varsha-śatāni shaś pañcha*' or '*shaṭ*', evidently, 100 and 56 or 100 and 60 were contracted into 106. It should be noted that they neither give the 60 of the Vāyu and the Brahmāṇḍa, nor the 96 of the Vāyu and the Brahmāṇḍa, and in place of these two they read 106 or 156. We, therefore, take 100 or 96 as the figure for the duration of the independent Vākāṭaka rule and 60 years for Pravarasena and Rudrasena. Rudrasena I by himself, as a king and not an emperor, seems to have had a reign of 4 years (100, '*varsha-śataṁ*', against the *96 years*, i.e. the difference between the different data of the two sets of the Purāṇas).[1]

68. The Purāṇas give another important chronological datum. They, after closing the rule of the Sātavāhanas about 238 or 243 A.D.[2] and their contemporaries the Muruṇḍa-Tukhāras (closing about 243 or 247 A.D.[3]) mention the rise of Vindhyaśakti. Taking, therefore, the start of Vindhyaśakti at 248 A.D., we get the following results from our combined data of the Purāṇas and the inscriptions :

1.	Vindhyaśakti	248–284 A.D
2.	Pravarasena I	284–344 A.D.
3.	Rudrasena I	344–348 A.D.
4.	Pṛithivīsheṇa I	348–375 A.D.
5.	Rudrasena II	375–395 A.D.
6.	Prabhāvatī Guptā as regent for—	
	(*a*) Divākarasena	395–405 A.D.
	and (*b*) Dāmodarasena-Pravarasena II	405–415 A.D.
7.	Pravarasena II (on majority) ..	415–435 A.D.
8.	Narendrasena (succeeded at the age of 8)	435–470 A.D.
9.	Pṛithivīsheṇa II	470–485 A.D.
10.	Devasena (abdicated)	485–490 A.D.
11.	Harisheṇa	490–520 A.D.

[1] Legally from one point of view the Vākāṭaka dynasty ended with Pravarasena I [§ 28, *n.*5].

[2] J.B.O.R.S., Vol. XVI, p. 280.

[3] Ibid., p. 289.

Corroboration from the early Gupta history.

69. The above chronology which is primarily based upon the Purāṇas, verifies itself with the known historical data we possess, namely, the reign of Chandra Gupta I and the reign of Samudra Gupta. Chandra Gupta captures Pāṭaliputra with the help of the Lichchhavis, both according to his coins and the *Kaumudī-mahotsava*. The reigning dynasty of Magadha which must have been a member of the empire of the Bhāraśivas, coming into existence about 250 A.D., is dispossessed by Chandra Gupta I. Chandra Gupta I strikes his coins in the name of the Lichchhavis from 320 A.D.,[1] that is, he defies the overlordship of the Bhāraśivas and their successor Pravarasena I. His coins have about 9 issues [in his two provinces—Kosala and Magadha] which will cover a rule of about 20 years. This again supports the statement of the *Kaumudī-mahotsava* that the child of Sundaravarman had escaped with his nurse to the Vindhyas and was recalled to Pāṭaliputra by the City Council of that Capital and was crowned king, which according to Hindu constitutional law, would take place after completing the twenty-fourth year. The *Kaumudī-mahotsava* and Samudra Gupta's inscription both prove that before the time of Samudra Gupta, the Gupta dynasty had been dispossessed of Pāṭaliputra. That there was a breach between the imperial coinage of Samudra Gupta and that of Chandra Gupta I is indicated by the fact that Chandra Gupta I's coins have never been found in association with the imperial Gupta coins. The period which Samudra Gupta occupied as a small rājā, living in Sāketa or between Benares and Sāketa, is determined by his coins of the Tiger type. On these coins he is described merely as '*Rājā Samudra Gupta*'. He had not yet adopted the Garuḍa standard or any of the figures which appear on his imperial coins. The reverse bears the figure of Gaṅgā standing

1 His previous coins, it seems to me, are found amongst the so-called Pañchāla coins illustrated by Cunningham in his CAI., Pl. VII, figures 1 and 2. These coins really belong to the Kosala series, as *Dhanadeva*, one of the kings of the series I have proved from the Ayodhyā inscription (J.B.O.R.S., X, p. 202 [204]) to be a Kosala king. The legend on the above coins [no. 1] reads *Chaṁdra-guptasya*, and not *Rudraguptasa* as Cunningham read it. The style is purely Hindu, unlike his Lichchhavi coins.

on a Gangetic dolphin (śiśumāra). Gaṅgā and Yamunā were the imperial marks under the Vākāṭakas. Gaṅgā is found on the Bhāraśiva coins and also on the coin of Pravarasena. It seems to have been adopted by Samudra Gupta in his feudatory capacity as an imperial Vākāṭaka mark, which is not repeated in his own imperial coinage. There are very few coins of the Tiger type, yet from the examples found, we are sure that there were at least two issues of this coin. In the Tiger type coins, Samudra Gupta has not assumed the imperial armour-robes like his father, which also shows that Samudra Gupta assumed the humbler rôle of an orthodox Hindu rājā of the United Provinces, quite in line with the other feudatories of the Vākāṭakas. Dating Chandra Gupta I *cir.* 320 to 340 A.D. and assigning 4 years to the two issues of the Tiger type coinage of Rājā Samudra Gupta, we arrive at 344 A.D., which was a critical date for Samudra Gupta. The death of the great Vākāṭaka Emperor, Pravarasena, who had evidently had a hand in curbing the ambition of Chandra Gupta I and in reinstating the Kota family whose prince had taken refuge at Pampā in the Vākāṭaka dominions, was the most appropriate opportunity in Samudra Gupta's calculation to make a bid for the recovery of Magadha and for an independent position, which had been the unrealized dream of the so-called *Mahārājādhirāja* Chandra Gupta I. We should recall here that the Tiger coins of Samudra Gupta are not struck with any affinity claimed with the Lichchhavis. The coins do not bear the Lichchhavi symbol of the goddess on the lion, nor the name of the Lichchhavis. At the same time, Samudra Gupta repeats in his inscriptions the fact of his being a Lichchhavi grandson. The constitutional significance of this is that Samudra Gupta lays claim to the independent position once established by the Lichchhavis and to the Lichchhavi dominions. Under his son Chandra Gupta II, the Lichchhavi capital became a provincial seat of a Gupta governor with the title of Mahārāja. The Lichchhavi Republic, therefore, had been suppressed and had gone before the grandson of the Lichchhavi became Emperor of India. And we do find that the Lichchhavi rulers migrated to Nepal where they founded a

Date of the dispersion of the Lichchhavis.

monarchy about 330–350 A.D.[1] The inference is irresistible that the Lichchhavis under whose protection the coins of Chandra Gupta I were struck, were defeated and dispersed by the Vākāṭaka emperor about 340 A.D. Samudra Gupta thus had a big legacy of political vendetta against the Vākāṭaka House and he missed no chance. The date 344 A.D. or thereabouts for the death of Pravarasena and the rise of Samudra Gupta thus fully agrees with the known facts.

IX. Vākāṭaka Empire.

Chandra Gupta II and the Later Vākāṭakas.

70. The Vākāṭaka chronology as proposed above, answers to the known dates of Chandra Gupta II. Chandra Gupta II initiated a policy of political marriages with the once enemy states, as a result of which he married his daughters to the Vākāṭaka ruler Rudrasena II and took a daughter of the Kadamba monarch to his own family.[2] He himself married a Nāga princess Kubera-Nāgā who was the mother of Prabhāvatī Guptā. Both Dhruva-Devī and Kubera-Nāgā are described as *Mahādevī* respectively in Gupta and Vākāṭaka documents; if Dhruvā Devī whose ancestry is not known, is not identical with Kubera Nāgā, he must have married her soon after coming to the throne, and she on the death of Dhruvā Devī would have succeeded to the position of the *Mahādevī*. An offspring of the Nāga princess going to the Vākāṭaka House, the successors of the Nāgas, put an end to the old Gupta-Vākāṭaka hostility. The Vākāṭakas again begin to rise and are given a measure of independence which no other state enjoyed under the Guptas. Soon after Prabhāvatī and on the fall of the Gupta Empire, under Narendrasena, they once more become a sovereign power in the Berar-Maratha country including Koṅkaṇa and up to Kuntala, in Western Malwā and Gujarat, and in Kosalā and Mekalā including Andhra. And under Harisheṇa the same limits are maintained. Narendrasena and Harisheṇa virtually succeed to the Gupta

[1] Fleet, G.I., Introduction, p. 135.

[2] *The Kadamba Kula*, pp. 21-22.

overlordship in the West and in the South up to the Kuntala country of the Kadamba kingdom. The significance of this large overlordship will become clear when we deal in detail with the Vākāṭaka government, fully described in the Purāṇas, and the Gupta conquest of the South and the reorganization thereof under Samudra Gupta which is also fully treated in the Purāṇas.

Vākāṭaka Imperial Period.

71. There are three main divisions of the Vākāṭaka Period: (i) the Imperial, (ii) the Guptan, and (iii) post-Guptan (from Narendrasena to Harishena and probably later).

72. The Vākāṭaka Empire begins from the reign of Pravarasena I and ends with the reign of Rudrasena I who had no time, on account of Samudra Gupta's first war (§ 132), to assume the imperial position of his Vākāṭaka grandfather. Emperor Pravarasena, whose coin bears the date 76, evidently counted the foundation of his state from the time of his father as he himself ruled for only 60 years. Samudra Gupta similarly in reckoning the 'Gupta-rājya' years[1] counted from the coronation of his father, and followed the example of Pravarasena I.

Vākāṭaka Imperial Organization.

73. The system of the Vākāṭaka imperial organization was to have sons and other relations as rulers over different provinces, a system borrowed from the Nāga Empire. The Purāṇas here are specially full. They say that four sons of Pravarasena became rulers and that there were three dynasties of relations by marriages and one dynasty of their descendants, over four centres—Māhishī, Mekalā, Kosalā and Vidūra.[2] Māhishī here is the Māhishmatī on the Narbada between the British district of Nimar and the Nimar zilla of the Indore State.[3] It was the capital of the province of Western

[1] Cf. G.I., p. 85, ... *abda-śate Gupta-nṛipa-rājya-bhuktau.*

[2] *Vindhyakānāṁ kulānāṁ te nṛipā vaivāhikās trayaḥ* (Br.). *Vaivahikāḥ* here has been misread in the text of the other Purāṇas as *vai vālhikāḥ* and *vai vāhikāḥ.* The mistake is curious, but easily understandable. *Vaivahikāḥ* was read as two words, *vai* and *vāhikā*, and *vāhikāḥ* was sanskritized into *Vālhikāḥ* and *Bālhikāḥ*!

[3] See J.R.A.S., 1910, p. 444 for its location.

Malwā. This division of the territories adjoining Berar is found to reappear in the Third Vākāṭaka Period as *Kosalā*, *Mekalā*, and *Mālava*.[1] For all these provinces the Purāṇas give the rulers and their totals, implying their end with the end of the Imperial Vākāṭaka period, i.e., by the conquest of Samudra Gupta.

Vākāṭaka Provinces: Mekalā, etc.

73 A. Out of the four provincial dynasties, the dynasty of Mekalā is expressly called in the Vāyu 'a dynasty of the descendants' of the Vindhyakas:

Mekalāyāṁ nṛipāḥ sapta bhavishyantīha santatiḥ.[2]

These subordinate kings of Mekalā, who were seven in number, are described by the Bhāgavata and several copies of the Vishṇu as the Seven Āndhras, i.e., the seven kings of the Andhra Country.[3] The Province of Mekalā evidently extended from the south of the present Maikal Range,[4] in a straight line, covering the modern State of Bastar wherein begins the Andhra country. To the east of it lay the Province of Kosalā, i.e., the area of the feudatory states of Orissa, and Kaliṅga. It should be noted here that the region from Raipur to Bastar is marked with the remains of Nāga settlements where inscriptions of later Nāga families from the tenth century onwards have been found in abundance. The tract formed a part of the Nāga Empire with the rest of the Central Provinces. The dynastic identity of this branch of the Vindhyakas or of Vindhyaśakti, I shall discuss under the Southern History when I deal with the Pallavas (§ 173 ff.). It is sufficient to notice here that the Vindhyakas were rulers of Andhra-deśa, that their province of Mekalā included Andhra, and that a branch line of the family was established there as a feudatory family who ruled for seven successions. The

1 Bālāghāṭ plates, E.I., Vol. IX, p. 271. Prof. Kielhorn who thought that the spellings '*Kosalā*', and '*Mekalā*' were wrong, substituted '*Kosala*', '*Mekala*'. But the Purāṇa text shows that the inscriptional forms are correct and represent the Vākāṭaka nomenclature.

2 P.T., p.5 1, *n.* 17. This is the reading in the majority of the MSS. [*ibid.*], and in all the copies consulted by Wilson and Hall [V.P., 4, pp. 214-215]. The variant *saitamāḥ* is a corruption and is meaningless.

3 P.T., p. 51, *n.* 16. 4 J.B.O.R.S., XVIII, 98.

ruling families of the other three dynasties came under the description '*the dynasties of relations by marriage* (*vaivāhikāḥ*)'[1]. The N a i s h a d h a province was under a dynasty who claimed to have descended from N a l a. Their capital was at V i d ū r a, which seems to be represented by *Bidar*, an ancient capital in the Nizam's Dominions; *Vaidūrya* is the Satpura. The M a h ī s h i n r u l e r s consisted of two sets, one of *Rājās* as the lord of the Mahīshins, and the P u s h y a m i t r a s with two more communities who are not called kings. These are included amongst the Mahīshins, that is, the people of Western Malwā which is called *M ā l a v a* in the later Vākāṭaka inscriptions. These republican Mahīshīs were evidently under this rājā, feudatory of the Vākāṭakas.

74. To take up the centres separately. One ruler of Mahīshī is named, '*Supratīka-nabhāra*' son of Śakyamāna.[2] He was king of the Mahīshins and lord of the land.[3] We have

Mahīshī and Three Mitra Republics.

[1] The Vishṇu misread the text of the Vāyu and made the groups from the Mahīshī rulers to the Mekalā kings, including the '*Vaivāhikāḥ*' (misreading it as '*Vālhikāḥ*') sons of Vindhyaśakti [*cf.* the commentator, '*tat-putrāḥ*, Vindhyaśaktyādīnāṁ *putrāḥ*']. The text of the Vishṇu is *tat-putrāḥ trayodaśaiva Vālhīkāḥ trayaḥ tataḥ Pushpamitra-Paḍhumitra-Padmamitrās trayo daśa* | *Mekalāś cha* | (Wilson, V.P., 4, 213). It applied the *santatiḥ* originally referring to the Mekalas and the figure *daśa* of the Traya-Pushyamitra group [§ 74] to the kings following Vindhyaśakti and coming before the Mekalās in the text of the Vāyu, i.e., the 'three' Vālhīkas (i.e., the Vaivāhikas) and the ten Pushyamitras-Paḍhumitras -Padmamitras. As the number 13 was thus completed, about the Mekalas [the real descendants] it said '*and also the Mekalas*'. The Bhāgavata following the Vishṇu was content with 13 sons. It is evident that the Vishṇu found *santati* after and with the Mekalas.

The number *sapta*, seven, the Vishṇu reads with Kosalā—'*sapta, Kosalāyāṁ*' (a reading attested by the commentator and supported by Wilson's MSS. See J. Vidyasagara's ed., p. 584; Wilson, IV, 213, 214). In the preface the [e] Vāyu Purāṇa designates it '*pañcha-Kosalāḥ*'- 'the Five-Kosalas' [*Vaidiśāḥ pañcha-Kosalāḥ*, while it mentions '*Mekalāḥ Kosalāḥ*' separately [Pargiter, PT., p. 3). With these two the seven provinces of the '*Sapta-Kosalā*' would be complete. In the *M-Bh.* also, there are two units in this region with the name *Kosala*; *Sabhā*, XXXI, 13 ['the King of Kosala, the King of Veṇa-taṭa, the Kāntārakas, the King of the Eastern Koṣalas'].

[2,3] Supratīko nabhāras tu samā bhoksnyati triṁśatim | Śakya-māna bhavo rājā Mahīshīnāṁ mahīpatiḥ|| [PT., 50-51 *ns.* 6–10].

coins of this ruler. The coins read :—*Mahārāja Śrī Prat (i) kara.* Prof. Rapson who published his coins [1] pointed out that they belong to the series of the Nāga coinage.[2] The Purāṇic name seems to be *Su-Pratīkana Bhāra* (=Bhāraśiva), as spelt in the present manuscripts. The letter *na* here is a misreading for *ra*, like the misreading of *paurā* for *maunā* which is pointed out by the commentator of the Vishṇu Purāṇa.[3] The correct reading was *Su-Pratīkara-bhāra.* To him 30 years are given. In the same area, i.e. under the centre Mahīshī, there were three communities whose names ended in *Mitra.* The Vishṇu gives them as *Pushpa-mitra-Paḍhumitra-Padmamitrās trayaḥ.* The Vāyu and the Brahmāṇḍa name only two, *Pushpamitrāḥ* and *Paṭumitrāḥ.* But the Brahmāṇḍa adds *trimitrāḥ.* The Bhāgavata calls 'Pushyamitra' [i.e., the President] a '*rājanya*', which is the technical term for a type of republican president.[4] In view of the datum of the Vishṇu Purāṇa, naming the three communities and that of the Brahmāṇḍa mentioning tri-mitras,[5] we have to take that their state was divided into three sections, and that they had ten successions, and the expression *trayo daśa* of the Vāyu is to be taken as meaning that the three states had ten rulers or ten successions of presidents. The other reading in the manuscripts [in place of *trayo daśa*] *tathaiva cha* [6] would indicate that they were also given 30 years as given to the main rulers of Mahīshī. They are assigned no separate location, and consequently I take that they were in Western Malwā. They, in the next period, i.e., the Guptan, are described as 'Āvantyas' who were under or in the confederacy of the *Ābhīras* (§§ 145 ff.). It is well-known that the Pushyamitras rose to such a height of power in the reign of Kumāra

1 J.R.A.S., 1900, p. 116, Pl. figs. XVI and XVII.

2 He read it as *Mahārāja Śrī Prabhākara.* I read as '*t*' the letter which he read as '*bh*'. In coin legends '*i*'-strokes are generally omitted. The difference between '*bh*' and '*t*' of that period is slight and confusing.

3 Vidyāsagara's ed., p. 584.

4 See, Jayaswal, *Hindu Polity*, vol. I, pt. 1, page 40.

5 षट्स्त्रिमित्राः *Shaṭs trimitrāḥ* of the Brahmāṇḍa is to be taken as a misreading for पटु-त्रिमित्राः, Paṭu-trimitrāḥ (Paṭu, 'the Tri-Mitras', the Three Mitras).

6 Wilson, V.P., 4. 214; Pargiter, P.T., 51, *n.* 14.

Gupta that they attacked the Emperor with great severity. As the successions here are of republican presidents, their number ten means that each president's office lasted for three years. This province of Malwā seems to have been an acquisition of the Vākāṭakas about 300–310 A.D.

75. In Mekalā, there flourished seven rulers in seventy years,[1] i.e., from about 275 A.D. to 345 A.D. It seems that this portion was acquired in the time of Vindhyaśakti. The rulers of Mekalā who were a branch of the Vindhyaka dynasty, were kings of Andhradeśa.[2] The history of Andhra, which is discussed below under Southern India, fully corroborates the period we get from the Purāṇas for these rulers.

Mekalā.

76. The Kosalā rulers under the Vākāṭakas numbered nine successions [according to the Bhāgavata, seven]. They were called Meghas. They might have been the descendants of the Chedis of Orissa and Kaliṅga, i.e. the Chedis of the family of Khāravela who were called *Mahāmeghas* in their imperial days. Their nine or seven successions would carry them back to the time of Vindhyaśakti, the time of the conquest of Andhra, or earlier, to the Bhāraśiva times. According to the Vishṇu there were seven territorial units of Kosalā [Sapta-Kosalā]. These rulers are described in the Purāṇas as '*very powerful*' and '*very wise*'. The Meghas reappear under the Guptas as governors of Kauśāmbī where two of their inscriptions have been found.[3]

Kosalā.

76A. The Province of Berar (Naishadha) with its capital at Vidūra (Bidar, Northern Hyderabad) was under the Nala dynasty, who were 'brave' and 'very strong'. Their number is not noted by any authority except probably the Vishṇu, of which the majority of manuscripts would give them also nine successions.[4] Their beginning or end is described in this way—*bhavishyanti ā-Manukshayāt*: 'they will be until

Naishadha or Province of Berar.

[1] Taking the reading *saptatiḥ* of the Brahmāṇḍa.

[2] P.T., 51, *n.* 16.

[3] E.I., 1925, p. 158.

[4] The reading *tāvanta eva* ('that much') alternates with *tata eva* ('after').

their destruction by the (dynasty of) Manu', the alternative meaning being 'they will be since the destruction of the Manus'. In the latter case, their rise is dated with the end of the Manus, i.e., the Hāritīputra *Mānavyas*, i.e., the dynasty called in modern text-books the *Chuṭu* Dynasty (see Part IV, § 157 ff.), in other words, since about 275 A.D. In the former case, the meaning would be that the Berar family was destroyed by the *Mānavya Kadambas*, which would be about 345 A.D. Both interpretations equally suit the known chronology of the Chuṭus (see Part IV, below) and that of the Vākāṭakas and the Guptas. Taking the reading of the *e* Vāyu[1] we have to prefer the first interpretation—that the Nalas arose on the destruction of the Chuṭu Mānavyas. This will coincide with the conquest of Andhra in Vindhyaśakti's time. Vindhyaśakti as a general of the Bhāraśivas seems to have put an end to the kingdoms which had arisen on the fall of the Sātavāhanas. The end of the Naishadha family came with the conquest of Samudra Gupta. Whether they had lasted for nine successions or less is not certain.

Purikā and Vākāṭaka Dominions.

77. Probably under Purikā was comprised the government of Nagpur, Amaraoti and Khandesh. Pravīra was the ruler of both Purikā and [Kāñ]Chanakā, i.e., both Western C.P. and Bundelkhand were under the direct Home Government. The province of Malwā was under the Nāga family stationed at Māhishmatī; Eastern and Southern Baghelkhand, Sirguja, Balaghat and Chanda were under the Mekalā rulers, and the territory to the West of Orissa and Kaliṅga was under the rulers of Kosalā. If the above map of provincial governorships is compared with Harisheṇa's list (Kuntala-Avanti-Kaliṅga-Kosala-Trikūṭa-Lāṭa-Andhra .[2]. . . . . .) it would become evident that Kuntala was a later addition, the overlordship of which had been asserted and re-asserted from the time of Pṛithivīsheṇa I onwards. Lāṭa might have been included under Māhishmatī in the early Vākāṭaka period; at about 500 A.D. it was certainly under them.

[1] Pargiter, P.T., 51, *n.* 24, *bhavishyanti Manu-(k)shayāt.* [2] § 61A (*l*).

The Yādava dynasty of Siṁhapura.

78. In the Eastern Punjab there was the feudatory '*Dynasty of Singhapura*' (Siṁhapura) who were the '*kings*' of *Jālandhara*'. This Siṁhapura was an ancient fortified city which is known to the Mahā-Bhārata.[1] An inscription [2] of their family recorded at Lakkhāmaṇḍal, on the Upper Jumna, in the district of Dehra Dun, proves that their jurisdiction in the Gupta times extended up to the Siwaliks. The family, as feudatory rulers of the '*Singhapura rājya*', seems to have been founded about 250 A.D., as 12 generations of theirs are given in the inscription.[3] Their date shows that they must have come into existence in the latter part of the Bhāraśiva time or in the beginning of that of the Vākāṭakas. They were *Yādavas*, and the inscription says that they had been in that part of the country since the beginning of the Yuga (Kali Yuga). This receives corroboration from the history of the migration of the *Yādavas* from *Mathurā* as recorded in the Sabhā Parvan, Chapter XIV, verse 25 ff. The *Śālvas* and *Kuniṇdas* had migrated along with and at the same time as the Yādavas from Mathurā [Śūrasena] and its neighbourhood, and settled in the Punjab. The *Ṭakkas*, who later migrated into Malwa from the Śālva country, the *Siṁhapura Yādavas* and the *Mathurā Yādava-Nāgas* thus seem to have all belonged to the great Yādava stock, which explains their special patriotism for Mathurā. The Siṁhapura family was thus a family allied to the Bhāraśivas. It was kept on by the Vākāṭakas. The '*Siṁhapura-rājya*' seems to have been a bulwark erected by the Nāga emperors to

[1] It is placed among the Trigartas, Abhisāra, etc. *Sabhā*, Ch. XXVI, 20.

[2] E.I., i, 10. I endorse the date of the inscription as given by Rai Bahadur Daya Ram Sahani, viz., the Sixth Century A.D. (E.I., Vol. XVIII, p. 125) as against the Seventh Century proposed by Bühler (E.I. Vol., i. 11).

[3] Their genealogy stands thus:—(1) Senavarman, (2) Āryavarman, (3) Dattavarman, (4) Pradīptavarman, (5) Īśvaravarman, (6) Vṛiddhivarman, (7) Singhavarman, (8) Jala, (9) Yajñavarman, (10) Achalavarman Samaraghangala, (11) Divākaravarman Mahighanghala, (12) Bhāskara Ripughanghala (E.I., i, 11). Nos. 1 to 11 are related as father to son; No. 12 is brother to No. 11.

throw back the Kushans. The early Siṁhapura kings are noted in the inscription for their Hindu orthodoxy (*Ārya-vratatā*) and bravery. They were, like the Bhāraśivas, Śaivaites. Their kingdom lasted, at least, down to the time of Yuan Chwang (631 A.D.) who has noticed it. The Guptas evidently allowed them to continue, probably in view of the importance of their family and the part which they must have played in pushing back the Kushans from northern Āryāvarta during the Bhāraśiva time. They are not registered in the Purāṇas as they formed part of the Āryāvarta dominions of the Vākāṭakas which they inherited from the Bhāraśivas. The kings of Siṁhapura, i.e., of Jālandhara, never struck coins of their own. The Madras were to the west of the kingdom of Siṁhapura.

Kushans in Vākāṭaka Period.

79. The Kushans about 280 A.D. were placed between two fires. Varahrān II. who reigned on the Sassanian throne from 275 to 292 A.D., subjugated Seistan. It may be assumed that Pravarasena I, who undertook four *aśvamedhas* and must have launched at least four campaigns, carried on the Bhāraśiva policy of weakening and destroying the Kushan power. Between 301 and 309 A.D. the Kushans seek the protection of Hormazd II, who marries the daughter of the king of Kabul, that is, the Kushan king. This is just the time of the vigour of Pravarasena I, and at this juncture the Kushan king gives up India, which no more remains his 'imperial' seat. He withdraws himself into Afghanistan, outside India proper, for his safety, and throws himself completely into the arms of the Sassanian king. Whatever territory still lingered in the Western Punjab was due to that protection. And the protection required could be only against Pravarasena I, the Hindu *Samrāṭ*.

Vākāṭakas and Eastern Punjab.

80. When Samudra Gupta comes on the stage and defeats Rudrasena, the whole Empire of the Vākāṭakas including the Mādrakas in the north, he wins at one stroke. The ready submission of the Mādrakas without a fight is an indication of the fact that the Mādrakas had been within the empire and a part of the empire of the Vākāṭakas. That the

Vākāṭaka Empire covered the Eastern Punjab explains the rise of the new house of the Yādavas in Jālandhara. It also explains the intercourse between the Mādraka country and Eastern India in the later Bhāraśiva and the Vākāṭaka period. The Guptas who reach Bihar about 250–275 A.D. were, as we shall see (§ 112), from the Madra country. And this connection with the Madra country is responsible for the Kushan type of coinage at the distant Pāṭaliputra under Chandra Gupta I, which has caused so much puzzle to a numismatist (Mr. Allan) that he refuses to believe that Chandra-Gupta I's coins could have been struck by him and comes to the conclusion that they were posthumously struck by his son after the conquest of the Punjab.[1] Considering the revival of the Mādraka coinage in the Bhāraśiva period and the facts noted above bearing on the history of the Kushan and the foundation of the kingdom of Jālandhara, there can be little doubt that the Vākāṭaka Empire included the Mādraka country.

Rajputana, and Gujarat: no Satrap there.

81. The same has to be said about Rajputana and the States in Gujarat. The inscription of Samudra Gupta places the Ābhīras at the head of the group of the republican communities of Western and Eastern Malwā, and the Mālavas at the head of the group of the Mālavas-Ārjunāyanas-Yaudheyas-Mādrakas. The Mālava-to-Mādraka group extends from S. to N., i.e., from southern Rajputana, one above the other, reaching the Punjab; while the Ābhīra group, beginning in Surāshṭra and coming to Gujarat includes the region next to the south of the Mālavas. in a straight line from west to east (§145). This is exactly

[1] Allan, *Catalogue of the Coins of the Gupta Dynasties*, p. lxiv ff. It should be noted, in connexion with the theory of Mr. Allan, that no Hindu would ever think of celebrating the marriage of his father and mother. The coins, whereon Chandra Gupta I is caressing his wife, could only have been struck by Chandra Gupta I himself.

Chandra-Gupta I's pre-Pāṭaliputran coins, as pointed out above, are those illustrated in Cunningham, C.A.I., pl. VII, figs. 1-2. They were struck when he was subordinate to the Bhāra-Śiva-Vākāṭaka Empire. The coins bear *Triśūla*, which was a Bhāraśiva emblem. Cunningham read the legend as *Rudra-Guptasa* (p. 81). But the first letter is *cha* which s confirmed by the anusvāra dot on *cha*. The last letter is *sya*, not *sa*.

the position which the Purāṇas assign to the Ābhīras of Surāshṭra-Avanti in the beginning of the next period (the Gupta Empire), which we shall see in the next part of this book. There were no Śaka-Satraps left in Kathiawar or Gujarat in the Vākāṭaka period. They had been ousted from there, and according to the Purāṇas they remained in Cutch and Sindh only [Part III, § 148]. The Republican India, which re-struck coins in the Bhāraśiva period, accepted, without any war, Samudra Gupta as emperor. It was the case of recognizing a settled fact; when the Gupta Emperor succeeded to the position of the Vākāṭaka Emperor, the Republican India naturally accepted the Gupta, as it had accepted the Vākāṭaka, as their *Samrāṭ*.

South.

82. The history of Southern India of the time is treated separately in this book (Pt. IV), but it is necessary to anticipate a few facts at this point to understand the Vākāṭaka and the Gupta history and its relation with the South. The Vākāṭaka Empire under their direct rule bordered on the frontiers of Kuntala. This is evident from the frequent clashes which occur on the subsequent rise of the strong Kadamba kingdom of Kuntala-Karṇāṭa. To be a neighbour of Kuntala, the direct Vākāṭaka government must cover Koṅkaṇa and the area of the Southern Maratha States, i.e., their sway must have penetrated to the other side of the Bālāghāṭ Range. The territory to the east was occupied by 'the Āndhras' who were within the Vākāṭaka zone; Kaliṅga and Kosalā also being under the Vākāṭaka overlordship. Before the time of Pravarasena I, almost contemporaneous with Vindhyaśakti, the Pallavas established in Andhra-deśa a seat for themselves. The Pallavas, like Vindhyaśakti, were Brahmins of the Bhāradvāja gotra. They, about the time of Pravarasena I, like him, perform *Aśvamedha*, *Vājapeya* and other Vedic sacrifices and try to succeed to the imperial throne of the Sātavāhanas, the Emperors of Dakshiṇāpatha. Here history was being repeated as in the time of Pushyamitra Śuṅga and Śātakarṇi [I] Sātavāhana. The Pallavas are described in the Purāṇas under the designation 'the Āndhra Kings'—'the kings of

Andhradesa', as ruling over Mekalā with Andhra, and are specified as 'the descendants (*santati*) of the Vindhyakas, i.e., Vindyaśakti (§ 176). A dynasty which lasted for about three generations preceded the Pallavas. They were the Ikshvākus who, on the heel of the extinction of the Sātavāhana line, try to succeed the Sātavāhanas, announcing their intention by an *aśvamedha*. Their capital was at Śrī Parvata which is now called Nāgārjuni koṇḍa in the Guntur district. They are known from the inscriptions of their relations at the newly discovered stūpa at Nāgārjunī koṇḍa and from inscriptions at Jaggayya-peṭa. The Ikshvākus disappear at the rise of Vindhyaśakti and the Pallavas. The Pallavas were Brahmins and the Sātavāhanas had been Brahmins. There was a great Brahmin tradition of imperialism in the South, and it was so strong that the moment the Pallavas were defeated by Samudra Gupta, the Kadamba feudatory of the Pallavas, Mayūra-śarman, and his son Kaṅga, who were Brahmins, not accepting the abolition of the Southern Empire, declared the re-establishment of the Southern Empire. This was not, of course, suffered by Samudra Gupta and Pṛithivīsheṇa Vākāṭaka.

Need for an All-India Empire.

83. The main feature of the history of the time as between the North and the South is that the North is trying to establish an Empire for All-India. This was the result of the experience which the Hindus had gained during the last empire of the Sātavāhanas. They found that a Southern power could not cope with the invaders against India who always came from the north. To have two emperors in one India appeared to them as a source of great weakness. This seems to be the moral motive for Pravarasena I's becoming the universal Indian Emperor or *Samrāṭ*[1] and

[1] The Pallava [Śiva] Skandavarman I, though a *Dharma-mahārājādhirāja* of the South, never struck any independent coin, and his son and descendants remained '*Mahārājas*', i.e., Mahārājas to the Vākāṭaka *Samrāṭ*. '*Mahārāja*' denoted a feudatory position at the time. Śivaskandavarman's descendants describe him only as a '*Mahārāja*' in their copperplates. The title of [*Dharma*] *Mahārājādhirāja*, was short-lived and was intended as against the Cholas, etc., i.e., the South.

for his successor Samudra Gupta expressing satisfaction at uniting the whole of India between his two arms. The need for this was apparent, both from the past experience of the Kushan Empire and the new necessity from the rise of the powerful Sassanian Empire next-door to India, born in the time of Vindhyaśakti. That need stood specially punctuated in the time of Pravarasena I, when by about 300 A.D., the Kushan Empire was practically merged into the Sassanian Empire. The Vākāṭaka king performed four *aśvamedhas*. On the analogy of the Mahā-Bhārata digvijaya in four sections, we may infer that Pravarasena I had his digvijaya divided into four sections, one of which would have been in the South. Although we have not yet discovered any contemporary account of the digvijaya of the *Samrāṭ* Pravarasena, and that the chronology of the Tamil literature mentioning the Āryas and the Vāḍukas, i.e., their invaders from the North, is extremely uncertain, yet it seems certain that the early Vākāṭakas having reached and occupied the territory on the other side of the Bālāghāṭ and the Andhra country, had become the next-door neighbours of the states of the Tamil-land, and a digvijaya over them was made easy by the success of the Pallavas who could and did occupy Kāñchī, the capital of the Cholas, the leading state of Tamiḻagam. The issue having been already settled with the Ikshvāku successors of the Sātavāhanas who had transmitted only a lost prestige and a discredited name as the imperial defenders of India, Pravarasena I could rightfully declare himself to be the *Samrāṭ* of the whole of India.

The Achievements of the Vākāṭakas.

84. The Bhāraśivas had made the Gaṅgā and the Yamunā free, but it was left to the vigorous Pravarasena I, son of a soldier and himself a great soldier, to push the Kushans out of India. In his time, the Kushan king became the king of Kabul, while up to 240 or 245 A.D., according to Chinese authorities, the king who sent Yüeh chï horses to a Hindu king in Indo-China was the Muruṇḍa 'King of India',[1] that is, he was still regarded as the Emperor of India

[1] Jayaswal, '*The Muruṇḍa Dynasty*', the Mālavīya Commemoration Volume, p. 185. *Muruṇḍa* was the royal title of the Kushans [J.B.O.R.S., XVI, 203].

and was reigning in India, although he had left the Antarveda of the Yamunā-and-Gaṅgā.

Three great contributions: All-India Imperial Idea; Revival of Sanskrit; Social Revival.

85. There were three great contributions of the Vākāṭaka Emperor. His father Vindhyaśakti for about forty years of the last portion of the Bhāraśiva imperial rule was the real fighter and empire-builder of the Bhāraśivas. Inheriting his energy and ideal, Pravarasena I evolved a clear political thesis. (1) His thesis was a Hindu Empire for the whole of India and enthronement of the śāstras. (2) A great literary movement in favour of Sanskrit begins about 250 A.D. and in fifty years reaches a pitch at which the Guptas take it up. We have the drama Kaumudī-mahotsava, written about 340 A.D., where the whole literary movement is cinematographed. It was written at the Court of a feudatory of the Vākāṭaka Emperor by a woman, at practically one sitting, to whom Sanskrit Kāvya was as facile a subject as to Bhāsa and Kālidāsa. Classical Sanskrit had become her vernacular. It had become the Court language. Expressions and forms had become set, and everyone in the official circle talked and wrote in Sanskrit. The earliest Vākāṭaka inscriptions found near or at their capital are in Sanskrit. In the South at that time,—a generation after Śivaskandavarman—Sanskrit begins ruling in royal documents. The set genealogical form in the Vākāṭaka documents, repeated generation after generation, shows that in the time of Pravarasena I, Sanskrit drafting must have come into vogue. Samudra Gupta and his successors follow exactly the system of Vākāṭaka drafting. At the Court of another feudatory, Gaṇapati Nāga, vernacular literary tradition is converted into Sanskrit classical poetry where the verses written for the Nāga-rāja in the *Bhāva-sataka* remind one of the [Prakrit] *Gāthā-śaptaśatī*. (3) The *Kaumudī-mahotsava* gives us an insight into the Social Revival. Revival of *Varṇāśrama dharma* and Hindu orthodoxy is emphasized very pointedly; it was the cry of the time. The society under the Vākāṭaka imperialism was seeking to purge

the abuses crept in under the Kushan rule. It was a Hindu Puritan Movement which was greatly fostered, and which received a wide imperial implication under Pravarasena I.[1]

Revival of Art.

86. We find the figures of Gaṅgā and Yamunā become royal and national symbols in architecture. The Matsya Purāṇa which embodies the text on architecture up to the Sātavāhana period, as observed above, knows nothing of the figures of Gaṅgā and Yamunā as essential or otherwise, to be associated with the temple of Śiva or Vishṇu or of any other god. Their adoption is essentially a political motif. The association of the Bhāraśivas with the Ganges was a vital moral force in the Bhāraśiva period. The Bhāraśivas liberated the Gaṅgā and brought her in the sphere of art as on their coins. They also brought the Yamunā within the compass of their art, as Bhūmarā and the Nāga-canopied figures of the two river-goddesses at Deogarh would indicate. But the Vākāṭakas made them their 'imperial symbols', from whom they were transmitted to the Chālukyas and became their '*Imperial Symbols*'[2] (§ 101 A). The Pallavas —the branch line of the Vākāṭakas—used them.[3] And the people were always conscious of the political meaning of this symbolism —'the Empire' ('the Empire of Āryāvarta').[4] In the Nāga-

1 Long and repeated Vedic sacrifices [agnishṭoma, aptoryāma, ukthya, shoḍaśin, ātirātra, vājapeya, Bṛihaspatisava, sādyaskra and Aśvamedhas] [G.I., 236] must have been occasions for big gatherings and missionary propaganda.

2 See S.I.I., Vol. I, p. 54, where *Gaṅgā* and *Yamunā*, *Makara-Toraṇa*, *Kanaka-Daṇḍa*, etc. are called the dynastic imperial insignia (*Sāmrājya-chinhāni*) of the Chālukyas. See also I.A., VIII, 26.

3 See the seal of the Velurapalaiyam plates, S.I.I., Vol. II, p. 521, where in the second row the figure of Yamunā is in relief with a tortoise below, and the figure of Gaṅgā with two pitchers at her feet is in the middle. There is a serpent-hood canopy on the head.

4 I.A., XII, 156, 163. The Rāshṭrakūṭa copperplate of Waṇi (Baroda) described the triumph of Govind-Rāja II in capturing the banners bearing the figures of *Gaṅgā* and *Yamunā* in these words: '*Govinda-Rāja, the personification of fame, taking from his enemies the Gaṅgā and the Yamunā, charming with their waves, acquired at the same time that* supreme position of lordship (which was indicated) by (those rivers in) *the form of a visible sign*'—cf. Fleet, I.A., XX, 275, who attributed them to have been

Vākāṭaka idolisation of Gaṅgā and Yamunā. there is the idolisation and idealisation of the land of the Gaṅgā-and-Yamunā where they re-established orthodoxy. The elegant moulding of the river-goddesses at Bhūmarā and Nachnā are a mirror of the Nāga-Vākāṭaka culture. The Vākāṭakas themselves were a line of handsome men. The (*e*) Vāyu manuscript notes that the four sons of Pravīra were *sumūrtayaḥ*, handsome, statue-like.[1] The Ajaṇṭā inscription especially notes the handsomeness of Devasena and Harisheṇa. Under the Vākāṭakas the art of sculpture and the graphic art of Ajaṇṭā which lay under their direct government, were vivified. The tradition was kept up in the later Vākāṭaka period. The credit of this revival of Hindu art which had been universally attributed by the present-day writers wholly to the Guptas, like the credit of Sanskrit revival, really belongs to the Vākāṭakas. The seed of all architectural modes which reach their full development at Eran, Udaygiri, Deogarh and Ajaṇṭā and even later, are all to be found in the Vākāṭaka temples at Nachnā—the perforated window, the *gavāksha* balcony, the sikhara, the entwined serpent, the sculptured and ornamented door-frame, the bulging shape of the sikhara, the square temple in the residential style, etc. [On the age of the Nachnā temples, see App. A at the end.]

Coinage.

87. Their non-adoption of a spectacular coinage like that of Chandra Gupta I is not due to any want of artistic capacity[2], but is due to their conservatism and partiality for the past. They would not imitate the coinage of the Kushans whom they regarded as the enemy of the nation and as low Mlechchhas. Its adoption by Chandra Gupta I would have been looked down upon by them as an act of denationalization. Under the Vākāṭaka influence Samudra Gupta himself had to revert, in his feudatory stage, to a type of coinage which was national[3].

derived by '*some means or another from the Early Guptas*.' [The Nāga-Vākāṭaka symbolism had not been discovered in his time.]

1 P.T., p. 50, *n*. 38.

2 See the bull on the coin of Pṛithivīsheṇa I, § 61 above; C.I.M., Pl. XX, fig. 4.

3 His tiger-type (which is in gold), bearing the Imperial Vākāṭaka symbol of Gaṅgā.

88. The system of the Vākāṭaka administration was borrowed from the Bhāraśivas and in its turn it was borrowed by Samudra Gupta. But both had introduced certain modifications of their own. The Vākāṭaka system consisted of a large central state under their direct rule with two capitals and a number of hereditary sub-rulers, and an imperial confederacy of free states. In the Bhāraśiva system the imperial keystone existed almost as an equal brick of the state-arch, while in the Vākāṭaka one it became a prominent piece.

Vākāṭaka administration.

89. The Vākāṭakas established subsidiary dynasties of their relations. According to the Purāṇas, Pravarasena I's four sons were rulers. Mahārāja Śrī Bhīmasena who has left a painted inscription in a cave-temple on the Ginjā hill, about 40 miles to the south-west of Allahabad, dated in the 52nd year, was evidently the governor of Kauśāmbī and probably a son of Pravarasena.[1] Important subordinate families (e.g. of Gaṇapati Nāga, Su-Pratīkara), as well as the members of the Empire (the Republics), were allowed to mint their own money. In the Gupta system, in Āryāvarta, the only ruling relation was the Vākāṭaka who was practically independent. The Guptas preferred to have servants as governors and practically stopped the coinage of all subordinates. Both allowed their subordinate rulers to employ the title of *Mahārāja*, after the fashion of *Mahākshatrapa*, avoiding of course, that term. The Vākāṭaka emperor, however, did not translate the *Shāhānushāhi* as *Mahārājādhirāja*, as the Guptas did, but went back to the time-honoured Vedic imperial title *Samrāṭ*.

Subordinates and Empire.

90. The faith of the Vākāṭakas was strict Śaivaism.[2] It changed only for one generation in the time of Rudrasena II, under the influence of his wife Prabhāvatī and father-in-law,

Religious Faith and Sacred Remains.

[1] A.S.R., Vol. XXI, p. 119, Plate XXX; E.I., Vol. III, page 306. See here below § 103.

[2] The Vākāṭaka inscriptions record it; their coins have Nandi. Up to the time of Rudrasena I, *Mahā-Bhairava* was the royal deity; Pṛithivīsheṇa adopted *Maheśvara* [which form is a compromise between Vishṇu and Śiva]. G. 1. 236. Nachnā has Mahā-Bhairava [See App. A].

Chandra Gupta II, who were both ardent Vaishṇavas. But when Chandra Gupta's influence was gone, the family atonce reverted to their Śaivaism. Temples and remains of the Vākāṭaka period are prominently of the martial Śiva—the temples at Nachnā, and the Bhairava liṅgams at Jāso [1], which differ from the [Bhāraśiva] Ekamukha liṅgams at Bhūmarā and Nakṭi [illustrated by Mr. Banerji; Arch. Memoirs, No. 16, Pl. XV; ASWC., 1919-20, Pl. XXIX].[2] All these liṅgams artistically belong to one school, though the deity-aspects differ. Although there is no great fundamental difference between these and the Guptan art, yet in aim and spirit they belong to a distinctive school. The great guide to distinguish the Vākāṭaka from the Gupta remains—which all have been described as Guptan, though Cunningham has put in the caution—'*Although it is probable that the earliest specimen of this kind of temple belongs to a period shortly preceding the Gupta rule*' (A.S.R., Vol. IX, p. 42),—is the distinguishing faith. Śaivaism is peculiar to the Nāga-Vākāṭakas and Vaishṇavism to the Guptas. Eran and the existing Vaishṇava remains at Deogarh should therefore be taken as Guptan, while those at Nachnā, Jāso and mostly (if not wholly) the remains at Tigowa are undoubtedly Vākāṭakan.

X. Appendix on the Later Vākāṭaka Period [348 A.D.–550 A.D.] and the Vākāṭaka Era [248-249 A.D.].

Pravarasena II and Narendrasena.

91. The period of Pṛithivīsheṇa I [348 A.D.–*c.* 375 A.D.], with his conquest of Kuntala [*c.* 360 A.D.[3]], is more allied to the former period. The later Vākāṭaka period begins with Rudrasena II [*c.* 375–395 A.D.] which is uneventful, except for his change of faith to Vaishṇavism, under the influence of his father-

[1] See Appendix A at the end.

[2] The Ekamukha lingam at Nakṭī near Khoh. It is a youthful face as prescribed in Matsya, 258. 4.

[3] Pṛithivīsheṇa I defeated Kaṅgavarman Kadamba about 360 A.D. See Part III, below.

in-law, Chandra Gupta II. After him the rule of his widow Prabhāvatī Guptā as Regent to her minor sons extends for about 20 years, probably a year or two beyond that of Chandra Gupta II. Her son Pravarasena II was a contemporary of Kumāra Gupta and seems to have died not at a very ripe age, as the son of Pravarasena II succeeded at the age of eight. According to the Ajaṇṭā inscription, the son of Pravarasena II 'ruled well' which is rendered in the Bālāghāṭ plates[1] as '*he who took upon himself* (the responsibility of) *the dynastic majesty, on account of the special qualities he had acquired by his previous training* [pūrvvādhigata-guṇa viśeshād[2]-apahṛita-vaṁśa-śriyaḥ]. Having succeeded at the age of 8, in his Yauvarājya he 'acquired' (*adhigata*) the necessary qualification and he shouldered the burden of government himself (taking it over from the regency). In this sense *apahṛita* is well-known in the Gupta literature, e.g. *paśchātputrai-rapahṛitabhāraḥ* (Vikramorvaśî, Act 3) where *apahṛita* does not denote taking by force.[3] The Ajaṇṭā inscription which makes the son and heir of Pravarasena II come on the throne at the age of 8, leaves no room for a rebellion by a younger prince. His name is lost in the Ajaṇṭā inscription but is preserved in the Bālāghāṭ plates as Narendrasena. That the prince ruled well is corroborated by the Bālāghāṭ inscription where

1 The Bālāghāt plates are merely a draft kept ready to engrave on the blank plates an order of a land-grant when made. It therefore has no gift, no donee, no date, no endorsement of registration (like '*dṛishṭam*') and no seal cut. Kielhorn under a mistaken notion of the date of the Deva Gupta of the Vākāṭaka plates, who was taken to be a later Gupta as proposed by Fleet, dated this as well as the Dudia plates of Pravarasena II wrongly in the 8th century (E.I., IX, 270, 269; E.I., III, 260). Bühler's dating proved to be correct.

2 Kielhorn read with doubts *viśvāsāt*. I think, what was intended was *viśeshāt*. An expression like *guṇa-viśvāsāt* will be meaningless in Sanskrit, *guṇa* must be present, and here it had already come from culture. No question of '*confidence*' arises. This *adhigata-guṇa-viś (esha)* corresponds to *guṇaviśesa-kusalo* in the Hathigumpha Insc., line 17 (E.I., XX, 80).

3 *apahṛita* having been wrongly interpreted by Kielhorn as '*took away the family's fortune*', it was supposed that there was a disputed succession.

Narendrasena is described to have kept his feudatories of K o s a l ā, M e k a l ā and M ā l a v a obedient to him. The overlordship on K u n t a l a or a strong political alliance therewith is inferable from the fact of the marriage of Narendrasena with Lady A j j h i t ā, daughter of the King of Kuntala. Narendrasena, according to the chronology proposed above, flourished about 435–470 A.D. The king of Kuntala with whom he had his political alliance through his marriage with the Princess Ajjhitā at that time was K ā k u s t h a, the Kadamba, who according to the Kadamba inscription on the Talagunda pillar (E.I., VIII, p. 33; cf. Moraes, *Kadamba Kula*, pp. 26-27) contracted political marriages with several great families including the Guptas. This monarch reached the zenith of the Kadamba power (c. 430 A.D.). Kākustha, as the Yuvarāja, in the reign of his brother used the Gupta era (§ 128 *n.*). On account of the marriage alliance his position improved. The Gupta marriages put the Kadambas and the Vākāṭakas on more or less an independent status. By or in the reign of Kumāra Gupta I Narendrasena's position must have been greatly strengthened as against his own feudatories and neighbours by his putting an end to the family feud with the Kadambas.

Trial for Narendrasena.

92. Narendrasena, about 455 A.D., passed through most troublesome days, which were troublesome both for the Gupta Emperor Kumāra Gupta, his maternal uncle, and for himself. The powerful P u s h y a m i t r a Republic, to whom were allied the Republics of the P a ṭ u m i t r a s and P a d m a m i t r a s, rose and attacked the Imperial power. They had been subordinate to the Vākāṭakas and were somewhere in Western Malwā, near Māndhātā. Just about that time, evidently connected with that movement of rebellion or attempt at freedom, was the attempt of the T r a i k ū ṭ a k a s, a dynasty which had been newly founded under that designation about that time by D a h r a s e n a.[1] Dahrasena Traikūṭaka was in A p a r ā n t a[2] between the Tapti-

[1] E.I., X, 51.

[2] Raghuvaṁśa, iv, 58, 59; Rapson, C.A.D., p. clix. See also the inscription of Vyāghrasena, son of Dahrasena, of 490 A.D., E.I., XI, 219, where they are described as the rulers of A p a r ā n t a.

western Khandesh-Kanheri and the sea (above Bombay). Like his sovereigns or overlords the Vākāṭakas, Dahrasena adopts a dynastic designation ('*Traikūṭaka*') after a place-name and a name-ending *-sena*, although his father who was a commoner was Indra-*datta*. Without any conquests he performed an *aśvamedha* in advance and struck his coins. But he was soon brought back under Narendrasena's control, as he is found using the Vākāṭaka Era in 456 A.D. (see §§ 102–106). The Pushyamitras before 456 A.D. were defeated by the Imperial power. Narendrasena had the support of his father-in-law's kingdom situated next to Koṅkaṇa [Aparānta] and at that time either under Kākustha or Kākustha's son Śāntivarman who too was a very strong monarch.[1]

Pṛithivīsheṇa II and Devasena.

93. Narendrasena seems to have had two sons. The elder Pṛithivīsheṇa II succeeded him and was followed by Devasena, who on his abdication was followed by his own son Harisheṇa. Devasena preferred a life of ease and pleasure to the duties of kingship. Pṛithivīsheṇa II found it necessary on the break-up of the Gupta Empire to make a heroic effort to raise his family from a 'sunken' condition, and he succeeded, for we find the next king in possession of all the Vākāṭaka Empire including Kuntala, Trikūṭa and Lāṭa. The trying period in the reign of Pṛithivīsheṇa II (470–485), on the chronology proposed above, coincides with the second Hun invasion, *c.* 470 A.D. His family must have 'sunk' along with the Guptas. Great credit is due therefore to Pṛithivīsheṇa II for its rehabilitation. Within twenty years or so, while the Huns were still powerful, we find the Vākāṭakas next-door to them and stronger than before, having under their sway Kuntala, Avanti, Kaliṅga, Kosalā, Trikūṭa,[2] Lāṭa and Andhra, that is, the whole of the Vākāṭaka dominions in the south, the Central Provinces and Western India up to Koṅkaṇa and Gujarat. A new dynasty just then founded by a Maitraka general at Valabhī covered the next territory of Surāshṭra.

[1] See *Kadamba Kula*, p. 28.

[2] Vyāghrasena was the king of Aparānta [Trikūṭa] at the time [E.I., XI, 219], whom we find using the Vākāṭaka era (§ 102 ff.).

The Maitrakas who had been evidently generals to the Guptas, as they used the Gupta era, probably arose from one of the Mitra Republics (Pushyamitras, etc.). They must have been feudatories to the Vākāṭakas, the next-door power. The Vākāṭakas thus acted as the bulwark in the Central Provinces and Western India against the Huns in 470–530 A.D.

Harisheṇa.

94. Thus with the end of the Gupta overlordship the fortunes of the Vākāṭaka family took a different turn. Pṛithivīsheṇa II rescued the family fortunes in the days of the disruption of the Gupta Empire. Harisheṇa, son of Devasena, succeeded to the whole of the Vākāṭaka territory, both their home provinces and feudatory dominions. He showed great vigour and re-established the Vākāṭaka Empire. From the time of the death of Skanda Gupta, the Vākāṭakas become a wholly independent power. At this period they seem to exhibit great recuperating capacity and hold their own in a period of revolution and political changes in the Empire of India. All the three princes Narendrasena, Pṛithivīsheṇa II and Harisheṇa were capable and successful rulers. Harishena's rule ended about 520 A.D. The later history of the Vākāṭakas is lost.

Extent of the Second Vākāṭaka Empire.

95. Harisheṇa, about 500 A.D., had to subjugate some of the old feudatories of his house, including the Traikūṭas. This seems to be evident from the Ajaṇṭā inscription and the inscriptions of the Traikūṭakas. Dahrasena, the Traikūṭaka, had once declared his independence about 455 A.D., i.e. the year of the Pushyamitra War of Skanda Gupta, and was brought back by Narendrasena under his control (§ 92). But we find again his son Vyāghrasena [*c.* 490 A.D.] issuing coins, and then the family disappearing, which is to be dated in the reign of Harisheṇa. After 494 A.D. no trace of their family is found.[1] It should be noticed that the Traikūṭakas use the era which, as we shall presently see, was the

[1] The Pardi plates of Vyāghrasena are dated in the year 241 [489-490 A.D.] and the Kanheri plates are dated in 245 (E.I., XI, 219; *Cave Temples of W.I.*, p. 58).

era of the Vākāṭakas. It seems that this feudatory dynasty was finally abolished in or after the reign of Harisheṇa.

96. A great proof of an effective sway of the Vākāṭakas over Koṅkaṇa, wherein Trikūṭa was situated, is an inscription published in the Journal of the Royal Asiatic Society, Vol. IV, p. 282, where a fortress named after the political home of the Vākāṭakas, the *Kilakilā*, is mentioned as 'Kilagilā' which was the capital of Koṅkaṇa at the date of the inscription (1058 A.D.). Trikūṭa was at the western end of the Vākāṭaka Province of Berar and Khandesh. Harisheṇa made obedient to himself Kuntala and Lāṭa with Avanti, which were at each end of Aparānta. Kaliṅga, Kosala and Andhra brought the Vākāṭaka Empire from Trikūṭa and the western sea to the eastern seaboard. All these had been parts of the Vākāṭaka Empire before. Lāṭa was next-door to the Vākāṭaka kingdom and was the old seat of the Ābhīras. Avanti had been under the Pushyamitra group. In the time of Narendrasena it is included in the term Mālava. In the time of Pravarasena II or Prabhāvatī Guptā, this was probably transferred back to the Vākāṭakas by the Guptas. The subjugation of Lāṭa by Harisheṇa means the final extinction of the Ābhīras and the Pushyamitras, if they had not already disappeared under Skanda Gupta who had established a governorship of Surāshṭra immediately after the Pushyamitra War. The addition of Lāṭa to the Vākāṭaka Empire was a result of the fall of the Gupta Empire.

Prosperity and Art under the Later Vākāṭakas.

97. The Second Vākāṭaka Empire was so rich that even a minister of Harisheṇa could excavate and decorate with paintings a beautiful chaitya-building at Ajaṇṭā, Cave No. XVI, adorned, as the donor himself with a rightful pride says,

> 'with windows, spires, beautiful terraces, ledges, statues of the nymphs of Indra and the like, supported by lovely pillars and stairs'—'a lovely chaitya-building'.

A member of the same ministerial family cut the Cave No. XIII, which is called the Ghaṭotkacha Cave, wherein the donor gives his family history. The family was of Malabar Brahmins who married both Brahmin and Kshatriya wives. Hastibhoja was the minister when the Vākāṭaka Devasena ruled (' *Vākāṭake rājati Devasene* '). The wealth of the empire of the later Vākāṭakas is further illustrated by the inscription in Cave-temple No. XVII, which was cut as a Vihāra by a Vākāṭaka feudatory in the reign of King Harisheṇa. His family had existed for nine generations, which evidently arose under the reign of Pravarasena I. They were probably a Gujarat family, which is suggested by their names. They proudly describe this piece of architecture ' *the Chaitya of the King of Ascetics* ' ' as a piece of gem in monolith ' (*ekāśmakaṁ maṇḍapa-ratnam-etat*) where the donor placed a reservoir ' *charming to the eyes* '. These donors were fully alive to a keen sense of æsthetics and their art was highly conscious. The architectural motifs of the pillars are not repetitions ; every piece is an individual conception. The ' Aśokan ' polish is used on the walls of Cave No. XIII [1], but the artistic sense seems to have forbidden its employment on any art moulding of the Ajaṇṭā caves.

98. Some of the most famous Ajaṇṭā paintings, e.g., Buddha's return to his father's palace, the scene between Yaśodharā-Rāhula and the King of Ascetics, and the Ceylon Battle, are to be found in the two Vākāṭaka caves, Nos. XVI and XVII. The caves are pre-eminently of the Āryāvarta Nāgara variety.

[1] Dr. Vincent Smith took Cave No. XIII, to be a B.C. Century Cave (*History of Fine Art in India and Ceylon*, p. 275) on account of its polish. But the art of ' Maurya ' polish was not forgotten. It was discredited in the Śuṅga and Sātavāhana period and was revived in the Vākāṭaka-Gupta period. In the sculptures of the Chandragupta Cave at Udaygiri and also on several sculptures at Khajurāho I have personally seen the polish. The method was not lost up to the eleventh century when some of the broken parts of sculptures at Khajurāho bear it as an act of repair. Some artistic reason was at the bottom of the discontinuance of the polish. At Kuajurāho, the outer sculptures are never polished. It seems to me that the polish interfered with light and shade and tended to obliterate their natural lines. The chisel protested against the veneer. The history of the so-called Maurya polish before the Mauryas is carried back by polished prehistoric vajras, made in imitation of bones, found in Chota Nagpur, which are in the Patna Museum [the polish on these is artificial and not the result of constant handling].

99. The Vākāṭaka territory was the meeting ground of the North and the South. The Vākāṭaka minister Hastibhoja and his family were from the Southern country. And also, the Pallavas themselves were a branch of the Vākāṭakas ; constant intercourse between the two kingdoms would have been a natural sequence. This explains the occasional introduction of the Pallava motifs in the Vākāṭaka cave-temples. The Dravidian features in some of the sculptures are also similarly explained.

100. It should be noticed that we possess the written history of three caves only. But we can safely say that the caves which are called Guptan, should be all attributed to the Vākāṭakas, as the direct Gupta rule never reached Ajaṇṭā, and Ajaṇṭā continued to remain throughout in Vākāṭaka possession.

100 A. The later Vākāṭakas, though not Buddhists themselves, allowed their subjects full liberty of conscience to follow Buddhism.

Vākāṭaka Horse.

101. The Vākāṭakas seem to have been strong in horse which is noted in the Ajaṇṭā inscription dealing with the military greatness of Vindhyaśakti. Here seems to lie the key to the military strength of the Vākāṭakas. Only a power strong in cavalry can successfully operate in the Vindhyas. The horse of the Bundelās became famous in later history. The cavalry tradition of Bundelkhand is probably ancient.

The end of the Vākāṭakas, c. 550 A.D.

101 A. The Chālukyas must have extinguished the Vākāṭakas. Pulakeśin I performed his *Aśvamedha* about 550 A.D. at Vātāpi (Bijapur district).[1] This should be taken as marking the close of the Vākāṭaka kingdom. The imperial symbols of *Gaṅgā* and *Yamunā* would thus be taken over by the Chālukyas from the Vākāṭakas (§ 86) at this period, which in later times would naturally be regarded by the Chālukyas as their own hereditary symbols coming down from the very foundation of the family.[2] Hariseṇa had under him either

[1] E.I., VI, 1. [2] E.I., VI, 352-353; S.I.I., i. 54 [Chellur grant].

Jayasiṁha or Raṇarāga [the grandfather and father of Pulakeśin I]. Harisheṇa is recorded to have subjugated or made obedient to himself (.....*svanirdeśa*.....) the rulers which had been feudatories of the Vākāṭakas with the new addition of Andhra.

> Hari-Rāma-Hara-Smar-Endra-kāntir
> Harisheṇo hari-vikrama-prāptaḥ (17)
> sa-Kuntal-Âvanti-Kaliṅga-Kosala-
> Trikūṭa-Lāṭ=Āndhra..............
> ....pi svanirdeśa........(18)
>
> —A.S.W.I., IV., 125.

Evidently the new family of the Chālukyas arose in the Andhra country, in the immediate vicinity of Berar. Pulakeśin's son Kīrtivarman conquered the Kadambas and the small rulers of Aparānta, and Maṅgaleśa conquered the Kāṭachchuris, before which the Vākāṭakas had evidently already disappeared. The Vākāṭakas, therefore, must have ended with the *Aśvamedha* of Pulakeśin I. The '*Rājā Jayasiṁha Vallabha*' who in the Aihole inscription is said to have founded the Chālukya family (E.I., Vol. VI, p. 14) is not credited with any conquest, nor is his son Raṇarāga. After Pulakeśin I his sons and grandson established their empire over the same territories which had been under the Vākāṭakas (Lāṭa, Mālava, Gurjara, Mahārāshṭra, Kaliṅga, etc.), which means that they were the political successors of the Vākāṭakas and were laying their claim as such. This also explains their clash with the Pallavas, and their permanent enmity with them, the Pallavas being blood-relations [a junior branch] of the Vākāṭakas. The description of the 'Rājā Jayasiṅha Vallabha' (E.I., VI, 4, verse 5) shows that Jayasiṁha had been a *Vallabha* or revenue officer of the king of the former government, i.e. the Vākāṭaka. It seems that after Harisheṇa, in the reign of one of his descendants, probably a grandson, or on the failure of the Vākāṭaka line, Pulakeśin I stepped into the shoes of the Vākāṭakas and claimed their imperial dignity and position. Their inscriptions silently pass over the Vākāṭakas.

The Era of 248 A.D.

Dates on Vākāṭaka coins.

102. We have three dated records of which two certainly, and one presumably, are Vākāṭaka. The coin of Pravarasena I is dated 76 (§ 30). The coin of Rudrasena is dated 100 (§ 61). There cannot be any doubt as to these two being Vākāṭakan. Then, there is the inscription of the Mahārāja Bhīmasena dated in the 52nd year (§ 89). Pravarasena I himself ruled for 60 years. The dates on his coins and on that of his successor, therefore, are to be referred to a reckoning started from the previous rule, that is, the time of the coronation of his father, which on the known chronology of the Guptas and its correspondence with the Vākāṭakan, must have taken place in the middle of the third century. The chronology adopted by us above, places the latter's rise in 248-249 A.D. If we can find this era which was certainly used by Pravarasena I, used in any part of the Vākāṭaka Empire in later centuries, we can identify it with the *Chedi Era*, which is called, wrongly, by some writers as *Traikūṭa Era*.

Ginjā inscription.

103. About the Ginjā inscription of the Mahārāja Śrī Bhīmasena, General Cunningham who discovered it remarked that the 'characters of the inscription are of the earliest Gupta forms; but the opening is worded in the well-known style of all the shorter Indo-Scythian inscriptions'.[1] He assigned the inscription to the pre-Gupta time. The style is certainly the same as that of the Kushan inscriptions found at Mathurā. It reads :—

> *Mahārājasya Śrī Bhīmasenasya saṁvatsare*
> *50.2 grīshmapakshe 4 divase 10.2* (etc.).[2]

The name Bhīma-*sena*, the style of dating and the early character of the letters warrant our assigning Bhīmasena's inscription

[1] A.S.R., Vol. XXI, p. 119, Plate XXX; and E.I., Vol. III, p. 302, Plate facing page 306.

[2] I have given the reading from the tracing of this painted inscription reproduced in the Epigraphia Indica which is better than the one lithographed by Cunningham. I am giving the reading of the necessary portion only.

to the same era in which are dated the Vākāṭaka coins. Their value would be: year 52=300 A.D.

„ 76=324 „

„ 100=348 „

The years, except the last one, fall within the reign of Pravarasena I.

Gupta Era and the Vākāṭakas.

104. For the period after Pravarasena I, we have one solid fact bearing on the question in that the Vākāṭakas, as already noticed, never used the Gupta era, even when Prabhāvatī Guptā was the regent.

Area of the Era of 248 A.D.

105. The existence of an era beginning in 248 A.D. next-door to Bundelkhand was contended for by Dr. Fleet[1]: two contemporary kings of the Gupta time date their records, one in the named era of the Guptas and the other in an unnamed era: the Parivrājaka Mahārāja Hastin has the dates 156, 163 and 191 of the Gupta Era in his documents, while his contemporary the Mahārāja Śarvanātha of Uchchakalpa, along with whom the former fixed up a boundary pillar at Bhūmarā in the Nagaudh State, has the years 193, 197, 214 of an unspecified era in his documents. The two rulers, on the boundary pillars, used neither of these eras but a neutral reckoning the *Mahā-Māgha saṁvatsara*. Dr. Fleet contended that by referring the years of Śarvanātha to the era beginning with 248-49 A.D. we get 462-63 A.D. for Śarvanātha and 475 A.D. for Hastin. Dr. Fleet, however, in 1905 (J.R.A.S., page 566) gave up this contention and referred both sets of dates to the Gupta Era, on the ground that the era of 248 A.D. was not known in or near Bundelkhand or Baghelkhand, and that it was known in 456 or 457 A.D. in Western India as employed by Dahrasena, the Traikūṭaka king. It was, however, recognised by him that the era could not have originated with the Traikūṭakas:

> '*But there is nothing to stamp the era as the Traikūṭa era and still less to prove that it was so founded*' (p. 657).

1 I.A., Vol. XIX, p. 227.

Similar is the view of Prof. Rapson.[1] To the association of the era with the Kalachuris in the twelfth century nobody has attached any importance, and this, for the simple reason, that there is no room in history for the Kalachuris to have started an era in 248 A.D. in the Chedi country or elsewhere. Fleet hesitatingly suggested that the founder of the era might have been the Ābhīra king Īśvarasena who dealt a blow at the Sātavāhana power. Fleet also pointed out that the era is somehow connected with the fall of the Sātavāhanas about 248 A.D. Prof. Rapson remarked on this:[1]

> 'But the foundation of an era must be held to denote the successful establishment of the new power rather than its first beginnings or the downfall of the Andhras.'

And Prof. Rapson stressed that it was impossible to connect the Ābhīras and the Traikūṭas as belonging to the same dynasty or even to the same race for total lack of evidence. Moreover, the Ābhīras who rose against the Western Śakas arose much earlier than 248 A.D.—i.e. *cir.* 188-190 A.D.[2]

106. The Traikūṭakas who were feudatories of the Vākāṭakas, by using the era used by Pravarasena I, prove their subordinate position and submission to the Vākāṭakas. The Traikūṭakas employ the feudatory title of *Mahārāja.* The appearance of the era in the western portion of the Vākāṭaka Empire shows that the era was in vogue amongst the feudatories of the Vākāṭakas. The use of the regnal years of individual kings from the time of Prabhavāti Guptā to Pravarasena II is in a period when the Gupta influence is at its zenith at the Vākāṭaka Court.

107. The only objection of Dr. Fleet that there was no connection visible between Trikūṭa where the era is found in use in the fifth century A.D. and Chedi (Bundelkhand and Baghelkhand) with which the Era of 248 A.D. is associated, now disappears in the light of the data on the Vākāṭaka history. We find the era in vogue in the Chedi country in the time of Pravarasena I. Fleet's former view that Śarvanātha's

[1] *Coins of the Andhra Dynasty*, page clxii.

[2] V. Smith, *Early History of India*, p. 226, *n.*, citing Dr. D. R. Bhandarkar.

years are in the Era of 248 A.D. seems to have been sound. There is not the slightest doubt that the Mahārāja Hastin was a Gupta feudatory and that there was a necessity to fix a boundary pillar between the Vākāṭaka dominions under Mahārāja Śarvanātha and the Gupta dominions under Hastin. Both Śarvanātha and Hastin were feudatories and Hastin avowedly a Gupta feudatory. Śarvanātha, therefore, could only be a feudatory to the Vākāṭaka king, whose capital or town at Nachnā lay within a few miles of Uchchakalpa or Uchahara (Nagaudh State).

§108. There are two facts which establish the Era of 248 A.D. to be the Vākāṭaka Era. The Purāṇas, after the fall of the Sātavāhanas register the rise of Vindhyaśakti as the next great power or as the imperial power succeeding the Sātavāhanas. An era will be naturally counted from the rise of a new power whether at once or subsequently—e.g. the Gupta Era does not come into force until the last years of Samudra Gupta or the reign of Chandra Gupta II [the forged copper-plates of Samudra Gupta (Gaya and Nālandā plates), which were imitated from some genuine copperplates, are dated in regnal years]. Then the second fact to take note of in this connection is that Pravarasena I became Emperor and the previous Emperors, i.e. the Kushans, had in fact an imperial era. To start an era had become a chief symbol of imperial position. Samudra Gupta did the same, and he also, like Pravarasena, counted the era from the coronation of his father. It is apparent that he followed the Vākāṭaka precedence and his example helps us here like a reflex action.

We would therefore call the era of 248-49 which began on the 5th of September, 248 A.D.[1], the Vākāṭaka Era of Chedi.[2]

[1] Kielhorn, E.I., Vol. IX, p. 129.

[2] The dates of Jayanātha, Mahārāja of Uchchakalpa, being taken to be in the Era of 248 A.D. his Kārītalāī plates dated '174' fall in 422 A.D., and his father Vyāghra could very well have been a younger contemporary of Pṛithivīsheṇa I, if we take the interval to be that of 45 years or so, and he could have endowed pious foundations in the capital of his king and might be identical with the Vyāghradeva of the three inscriptions at Ganj and Nachnā. But the identity by no means could be established on the present materials. If they are identical, Jayanātha's dates must be in the Era of 248 A.D.

PART III.

Magadha (31 B.C. to 340 A.D.) and the Gupta India at 350 A.D.

'Rājādhirājaḥ pṛithivīmavitvā
Divaṁ jayaty-aprativārya-viryaḥ'.

'*The King of Kings of irresistible prowess, having protected the Country (thereby) wins Heaven*'. [Aśvamedha Coin of Samudra Gupta.]

ā-Samudra-kshitīśānām =ā-Nāka-ratha-vartmanām [Kālidāsa].

XI. History of Magadha from 31 B.C. to 250 A.D. and the Rise of the Guptas [275 A.D. to 375 A.D.].

Āndhras and Lichchhavis at Pāṭaliputra.

109. Magadha, after the fall of the Kāṇvas, according to the Purāṇas, passed on to the Āndhras [Sātavāhanas]. This statement is corroborated by the find of Sātavāhana coins in the excavation of Bhīṭā [Allahabad District]. I read one Sātavāhana coin excavated in my presence by Dr. Spooner at Kumhrār [Patna]. The Sātavāhanas, however, could not have been for more than fifty years at Pāṭaliputra and in Magadha after the fall of the Kāṇvas (31 B.C.). The Nepal inscription of Jayadeva II of the Lichchhavi dynasty, dated in Śrī-Harsha Saṁvat 153 (=758 A.D.),[1] states that 23 successions before Jayadeva I, his ancestor Supushpa Lichchhavi was born at the city of Pushpapura. The date of Jayadeva I is about 330 A.D. to 355 A.D. as worked out by Dr. Fleet.[2] Now, giving an average of about 15 years to this long list of 23 kings we may place Supushpa in the beginning of the Christian Era. The Lichchhavis in occupying Pāṭaliputra might have taken a mandate for doing so from the Sātavāhana Emperor, or they might have independently captured the capital, which they had aspired to do for centuries. The

1 I.A., Vol. IX, p. 178. Fleet, G.I., Introduction, pp. 184-185.

2 Fleet, G.I., Introduction, 135, 191; I.A., XIV, 350.

disturbance caused to the Sātavāhana Emperor by the appearance of Kadphises and Wema Kadphises in Northern India afforded an ample opportunity to the Lichchhavis to fill up the vacuum at Pāṭaliputra. We may also take it that their occupation of Pāṭaliputra would have ended with the advance of Vanaspara, viceroy of Kanishka, to Magadha about the close of the century.[1]

Kshatriya dynasty of Kota.

110. The Lichchhavis, having once occupied Pāṭaliputra for about a century, must have felt a sort of claim to re-possess Magadha on the liberation of the Gangetic valley by the Bhāraśivas. But when the Bhāraśiva reorganisation comes into play, we find Magadha not in the possession of the non-Brahmanical Lichchhavis but of an orthodox Kshatriya family. This family is called 'the Magadha family' in the Kaumudī-mahotsava, and by Samudra Gupta it is called 'the Dynasty of Kota' (*Kota-kula*). The founder's name seems to have been Kota; the descendant of Kota who was a contemporary of Samudra Gupta and whose name is lost in the earlier part of the Allahabad inscription, is called *Kota-kulaja*. The names of these Magadha kings ended in *varman*.[2] This family must have come into existence about 200–250 A.D.

Gupta and Chandra.

111. The Guptas appear about 275 A.D. somewhere in Magadha. Gupta, the first Rājā,[3] rises as a feudatory prince. As later, we find the early Guptas connected with Allahabad [Prayāga] and Oudh [Sāketa], *Mahārāja* Gupta's fief seems to have been near about Allahabad. His son was Ghaṭotkacha, and Ghaṭotkacha's son was the first prince who turned the name of his ancestor *Gupta* into a dynastic title. His name was Chandra. At the time of the rise of Chandra, called by the Prakrit name *Chaṇḍa-sena*[4] in the Kaumudī-mahotsava, the king

[1] See Part I (§ 33) above.

[2] See in Bhandarkar Annals, 1930, XII, pp. 50 ff., '*Historical data in the drama Kaumudī-Mahotsava*' by the present author.

[3] Prabhāvatī Guptā [Poona Plates, E.I., xv] appropriately calls him *ādirāja*.

[4] For *Chandra* becoming *Chaṇḍa* in Prakrit see the inscription of *Chaṁḍasāti*, the Sātavāhana king, published in E.I., Vol. XVIII, p. 317.

of Magadha at Pāṭaliputra was Sundara-varman, ruling from his palace called *Su-Gāṅga*. This palace is named in the inscription of Khāravela as the *Su-Gaṁgîya* and in the Mudrā-Rākshasa as the *Su-Gāṅga*. The capital city of Pāṭaliputra thus came down with its ancient palace intact to the period of king Sundara-varmā and Chandra. King Sundara-varman was an old man, having a child of a few years of age yet in charge of a nurse. Chandra or Chandra-sena had been adopted as his son by the king of Magadha, evidently before the birth of the young prince. Chandra regarded himself as the heir, being the elder, though a *Kṛitaka* son. He entered into a marriage alliance with the Lichchhavis who are described as the enemy of the Magadha dynasty in the same drama Kaumudī-mahotsava.[1] The Lichchhavis with a large army and Chandra laid a siege to Pāṭaliputra. A battle was fought in which the old king Sundara-varman died. The young prince Kalyāṇa varman was carried away to the Kishkindhā hills by the faithful ministers. Chandra founded a royal dynasty (*rāja-kula*). The angry authoress of the drama calls the Lichchhavis 'Mlechchhas' and Chaṇḍa-sena a Kāraskara, implying a casteless or a low-caste man, not fit for royalty.[2]

112. Before we enter on the subsequent history of the fortunes of Chandra Gupta I, let us see if we can find out the caste of the Guptas which has remained a mystery up to this time. The data which we obtain from the contemporary inscriptions are :

Origin of the Guptas.

(*a*) that nowhere they disclose their origin or caste status, as if they have purposely concealed it; and,

(*b*) that their caste sub-division was *Dhāraṇa*.

and coins of Śri Chandra Sāti where 'Chandra' becomes '*Chaṁḍa*' —Rapson, *Coins of Andhras*, p. 32. For the dropping of *sena*, cf. the case of *Vasanta-sena* and *Vasantadeva* of the same king (G.I., Introduction, p. 186 ff.); *Dahrasena* on his coins adopts the style *Dahra-gaṇa* (C.A.D., p. clxiv).

[1] The drama is published in the Quarterly Journal of the Andhra Research Society, Vols. II and III.

[2] कहिं एरिस-वंसस्स से राअसिरी ?—K.M., Act. IV, p. 30.

From the inscription of the Gupta Princess, Prabhāvatī Guptā[1] we know that she belonged to *Dhāraṇa* gotra. She is evidently giving here her father's gotra, as her husband's gotra was different (*Vishṇu Vṛiddha*). Our knowledge, however, is expanded by the Kaumudī-mahotsava which gives the caste of Chandra as *Kāraskara*. The Kāraskaras are mentioned by Baudhāyana as a low community, to whom the Brāhmaṇas should not go and on return from whom they should perform a ceremony of purification.[2] The Kāraskaras in Baudhāyana are joined with the Punjābī community *Āraṭṭas* [which literally means—'the republicans']. Their exact location is given by Hema-chandra, who in explaining the Sālvas calls them the people of the Kāra valley.[3] The place Kārapatha or Kārāpatha was at the foot of the Himalayas.[4] The *Sālvas* were a division of the *Madras* and were at Sialkot where their name as *Siāl*, derived from *Sālva* which is also spelt as *Sālya*[5], survives. The Kāraskaras were therefore a Punjab people, a subdivision of the Madras. We know that the *Madras* were called Vāhīkas and *Jārtikas*[6]. The Madraka[7] community was thus made up of several subdivisions, comprising Sālvas, Yartris or Jārtikas [whom we call to-day Jāṭs] and others. Now, we may recall here the grammatical illustration of Chandra-gomin: '*the Jārta (king) defeated the Hūṇas.*' This is pre-eminently referable to Skanda Gupta[8]. We have thus evidence from different sources converging at one point, that is, that the Guptas were

1 E.I., XV, 41; *cf.* ibid., p. 42, *n*.

2 Baudhāyana, Dh. S., I, i. 32.

3 Hemachandra, A-Ch. IV, p. 23 (*Sālvās tu Kāra-kukshīyāḥ*).

4 Raghuvaṁśa, XV, 90. Wilson's Vishṇu Purāṇa, Vol. III, p. 390.

5 Wilson and Hall, V.P., Vol. V, p. 70.

6 Rose, *Glossary of Punjab Tribes and Castes*, i. 59; Grierson, L.S.I., IX., Pt. 4, p. [illegible]; *n.* 8. *M. Bh., Karṇa P.*, (verse 2034).

7 *Cf.* on '*Madraka*', my *Hindu Polity*, i, pp. 120-121. It means 'one owing allegiance to the Madra State'.

8 G.I., 54 (*l.* 15), 59 (*l.* 4). The two inscriptions (Bhītarī and Junāgarh) describe a decisive and famous battle; while Yaśodharman's was a mere raid into Kashmir (G.I., 147, *l.* 6) and the Hūṇas' submission to Yaśodharman was practically without a war.

Kāraskara Jāṭs—originally from the Punjab. *Kakkaṛ* Jāṭs[1] in my opinion are the modern representatives of the original community of the Guptas. Amongst the Kāraskaras the particular subdivision to which Guptas belonged was evidently *Dhāraṇa*. The word *gotra* in Prabhāvatī Guptā's inscription (Poona Plates) would mean a caste-subdivision. *Dhaṇri*, the Jāṭ clan found in Amritsar,[2] may be compared with the Sanskrit *Dhāraṇa* of Prabhāvatī Guptā. The Kaumudī-mahotsava is in full agreement with and is in fact supported by Chandra-gomin, who is undoubtedly a Gupta author.

113. The position of the Madraka Jāṭs was probably not very low at the time, for had it been very low, King Sundara-varman would not have thought of making Chandra-sena his adopted son. His original intention seems to have been to bequeath the kingdom to Chandra. And it was only due to the birth of Kalyāṇa-varman from some younger queen (Kalyāṇa-varmā is said to have several step-mothers—'*mātaraḥ*') that the breach between the adoptive father and the adopted son occurred. The real cause of the opposition from the public, which was very pronounced, seems to be a dislike for the social system of the Kāraskaras who were not subject to the fourfold-varṇāśramism of the orthodox system. It is the same dislike which is expressed in the Mahā-Bhārata against the Madrakas. They had one caste amongst them with social equality and freedom, which did not agree with the settled rules of the Gangetic society. The compliment was mutually exchanged: the Kaumudī-mahotsava taunted at the Kāraskara caste as rulers; the Guptas replied—' we shall abolish the Kshatriyas '.

114. Now we know from the Purāṇic history that in the reign of Kanishka (and probably also of his successor), Vanaspara imported some Madrakas for administrative purposes. But the Punjab military dress of Chandra Gupta I on his coins would suggest that the family had migrated recently in the Bhāraśiva

[1] *Cf.* Rose, *Glossary*, ii. 363, *n*. The name is pronounced as *Kakkar* also.

[2] *Glossary of Tribes and Castes of the Punjab and N.-W. Frontier*, Vol. II, p. 235.

period after the liberation of the Madraka country by the latter. Very likely a Bhāraśiva king gave Gupta a fief, having border-land between Bihar and Kauśāmbī, for it was to suppress a rebellion of the Śavaras that Chandra Gupta I had gone to his frontier when the City Council of Pāṭaliputra pronounced a decree of deposition against him.

Expulsion of Chandra Gupta I.

115. Chandra Gupta I having his caste against him and being somewhat of a usurper, was disliked by the Magadhans of his day, particularly as he failed to adapt himself to the traditional Hindu way of government. He showed a hostile, repressive attitude to the people of Magadha. The Kaumudī-mahotsava records that Chaṇḍa-sena [1] had put leading citizens into prison. The people of Magadha looked down upon him as something like a parricide. Chandra Gupta I had thus several elements arrayed against him. A cry was raised that he was not a Kshatriya, he had practically killed his aged adoptive father on the battlefield, he had called in the aid of the hereditary enemies of Magadha—the Lichchhavis, he had married a lady who was neither a Magadhan nor a Brahmanical Hindu. To this we should add that he had defied the imperial authority of the Brahmin Emperor Pravarasena I.

116. With the aid of the Lichchhavi power and protection he trampled upon the liberties of the people of Magadha and put the leading citizens into prison. Alberūnī therefore recorded a true and historical tradition when he said that the king or kings associated with the Gupta-*kāla* [-era] were cruel and wicked. The Hindus had the constitutional law laid down in their codes to destroy the king who acted as a tyrant or whose hands had the marks of the blood of his parents.[2] They planned and rose, called in Prince Kalyāṇa-varman from the Vākāṭaka territory (Pampāsara) and crowned him

[1] There are other known examples, as cited above, of new kings changing the second member of their name on coming to the throne. *Chandra-sena* similarly changed his name into *Chandra Gupta*. But the hostile contemporaries persisted in calling him by his original, humbler name, and insisted on the vernacular pronunciation for its obvious pun [*Chaṇḍa*=' *fierce* '].

[2] *Hindu Polity*, ii, 50, 189.

king at the Su-Gāṅga Palace at Pāṭaliputra. The authoress of the Kaumudī-mahotsava exultantly said—'*the law of Varṇa is restored · the royal family of Chaṇḍa-sena is abolished.*'[1] This happened while Chandra Gupta was on his campaign somewhere between Rohtas and Amarkantak fighting the rebellious Śavaras. The outlandish monarch was ousted in or about 340 A.D., for Kalyāṇa-varmā was of full age to receive Hindu royal coronation at the time.[2] In the year of his coronation Kalyāṇa-varmā was married to the daughter of the king of Mathurā.

Guptas in Exile and their Moral Transformation.

117. The years 340 A.D. to 344 A.D., the period of exile of the Guptas from Bihar was not very long but it was full of consequence and future, which produced entirely a new history—a new history not only for Bihar but for the whole of India. It turned the Guptas from outlandish usurpers into a dynasty of the Hindu of Hindus, Magadhan, and protectors and upholders of the Dharma, Brahmin and cow, literature and sculpture, language and law, national culture and national civilisation of Hindu India. Beginning as a feudatory ruler under the Vākāṭakas with their imperial insignia of the goddess *Gaṅgā* on his coin and the title of *Rājā* only and with no marks of royalty on his person (as portrayed on his Tiger-type coin), Samudra Gupta ended with a proud satisfaction as recorded on his imperial gold coins marked with his *Garuḍadhvaja*, a satisfaction which is a rare luck of a king in history: on his coins which he published after he had built up his empire, he registered the realisation of the ideal of Hindu hero and Hindu king that he after winning the whole country governed it so well that he won the heaven thereby (p. 112). He made Sanskrit, after the fashion of the Vākāṭaka Emperor, his court language; he undertook and performed aśvamedhas, having made good his restoration to the imperial throne of Pāṭaliputra.

1 प्रवर्तित-वर्णाश्रमपथमुन्मूलित-चण्डसेनराजकुलम् ।—K.M., Act V.

2 Taking the capture of Pāṭaliputra at 320 A.D., and the coronation age being 25, the prince having lived in exile for about 20 years, the date of restoration would be *c.* 340 A.D.

Ayodhyā and its influence.

117 A. Chandra Gupta I who was dying either of wounds or of a broken heart on his expulsion from Pāṭaliputra, addressed Samudra Gupta, one of his younger sons, with tears in his eyes, and with the tacit consent and approval of his Council of Ministers,—'you now, my noble sir, be the king ("protect the kingdom"),' and expired.[1] The death must have taken place on the other side of the Ganges, in the territory of his relations, the Lichchhavis. As a Lichchhavi subordinate and relation, his son at this moment would have obtained the province of Sāketa, i.e. the adjoining territory of Oudh. where at Ayodhyā we find in the next reigns the Gupta Emperors residing as at their second and favourite capital. It was a centre of culture. Ayodhyā had been the home of the poet Aśvaghosha, the Kālidāsa of the preceding epoch. To Ayodhyā belonged the great scholar Śikhara Svāmin who became the Prime Minister of Rāma Gupta and Chandra Gupta II.[2] Ayodhyā had the orthodox imperial tradition of Rāma's name, a name which was given to the eldest son of Samudra Gupta,[3] a name which embodied the whole of the past Hindu civilisation. Samudra Gupta fully imbibed that tradition. Hindu learning became a part of the political cult of Samudra Gupta and his descendants. The *rājasa* (kingly) *bhakti* in Vishṇu moulded their national actions and their political character. Like Vishṇu they stood solidly to support the kingdom of India. Their *bhakti* (faith) is intense. They think of Vishṇu and they think in Vishṇu. Samudra Gupta and Chandra Gupta II become practically one with their God. Any one who has seen the Vishṇu image enshrined by Samudra Gupta at Eran, would be reminded of Samudra Gupta himself and see the King's figure and dress in that statue. One who would see the Vishṇu-Varāha at the Chandra Gupta Cave at

[1] G.I., p. 6. [2] J.B.O.R.S., XVIII, 37.

[3] The popular name *Rama-pāla*='*Rawwāl*', retained by the Arab author Abu Saleh (J.B.O.R.S., XVIII, p. 21) may be compared with the *Rājāvali* names of the Guptas which Cunningham found at Ayodhyā. They end in *pāla* instead of °*gupta*, e.g. *Samudra pāla, Chandra pāla*, etc. A.S.R., Vol. XI, p. 99.

Udayagiri will be reminded of Chandra Gupta II himself rescuing Dhruva-devī.[1] Without understanding the spiritual and religious currents of the time which bring about royal and national rebirth, one cannot truly appreciate any political reformation. It is for that reason that a proper appraisement of the Gupta cult becomes here necessary.

118. You would never be able to decipher the dedication of their victories to Vishṇu, e.g. at Bhîtarî and at Mehraulî, and at the same time the magnificence and munificence conveyed by the aśvamedhas and the *Garuḍmadaṅka* coins, without that key. You would not be able to unlock the mystery of these Hindu Moghuls minus Moghul cruelty and debauchery. You will not get the secret how could Chandra Gupta II abolish capital punishment,[2] how he could raise the majesty of Hinduism to the very pinnacle of glory, and how he drew the limits of good government which no sceptre could extend further.

Old Faith and New.

119. From the Bhāraśivas up to the Vākāṭakas there was the rule of that God of social asceticism, that aspect of the Almighty which undertakes destruction, the God who though a giver, keeps no wealth, possesses no material splendour, the God who is austere and sombre. But, on the other hand, the second Gupta king and the first Gupta Emperor—Samudra Gupta—invokes that aspect of God whose function is royal and *rājasa*, who wears gold, not ashes, who builds and reigns, protects and rejoices in plenty, who is the traditional God of Hindu sovereignty. Vishṇu is the king amongst gods, is magnificently dressed, stands erect and solid and upholds the kingdom of His men, is a hero and conquering lord in battle—whose emblem is *Chakra*—the symbol of Empire—which irresistibly destroys the forces of evil against that Empire of Lord Vishṇu. There is the conch in one of His hands for announcing battle and for announcing triumph. There is, in the third, the sceptre of rule, and finally there is the lotus in the fourth, the symbol of prosperity, growth and rejoicing for His subjects. The belief in the God-in-royalty, Samudra Gupta made the belief of his dynasty and the belief

[1] *Cf.* J.B.O.R.S., XVIII, 35. [2] *Fa-Hien*, ch. XVI.

of his country. His devotion to Vishṇu is so great that his personality almost merges in Him:

साध्वसाधूदय-प्रलय-हेतु-पुरुषस्याचिन्त्यस्य भक्त्यवनतिमात्रग्राह्यमृदुहृदयस्य[1]

is a description in the language of the Bhagavad-Gītā, and a description which, according to the literary practice of the age, has to give a double meaning. The devotee and his God are both described by the same language. This might appear to a non-Hindu reader or to a reader who has not entered into the Hindu mystery of *bhakti* as a blasphemous assumption of God's attributes. But it is not so; there is in the cult of *bhakti* its highest doctrine that there should be unity (*ananyatā*) between the deity and the devotee. The devotee begins to partake of the nature of his deity until he is spiritually fully transformed and finally become one with the deity. He becomes the missionary and the agent of the Lord. He works as the medium, and all his works are dedicated to his Lord. The Guptas felt and believed that they were Vishṇu's servants and agents, that they had a mission from Vishṇu, that like Vishṇu they should conquer the unrighteous and rightless sovereigns, and that like Vishṇu they should rule in full sovereignty and bring happiness promised by the lotus in Vishṇu's hand, to the people of India. They fully executed this mission and Samudra Gupta felt the consciousness that he had executed that mission well and won the Heaven thereby. Like Vishṇu, Samudra Gupta and his successors filled their kingdom of India with gold and plenty, with propserity, elegance and culture.

XII. POLITICAL INDIA AT 350 A.D. AND SAMUDRA GUPTA'S EMPIRE.

Rich details in Purāṇas about the 350 A.D. States.

120. We have no doubt that the Allahabad pillar inscription of Samudra Gupta which is his imperial biography written and published in his life-time,[2] gives details of the kingdoms and rulers which existed at the time

[1] G.I., p. 8, *l.* 25.

[2] It is not posthumous as Fleet wrongly supposed. See Bühler, J.R.A.S., 1898, p. 386. It was published before his *aśvamedha* or *aśvamedhas*. [Fleet's mistake misled many including myself.]

of the foundation of the Gupta Empire. Yet we have probably a richer description of political India at the period in the Purāṇas. They, in fact, give us a complete picture of Samudra Gupta's India with which they close their chronicles. As their details have not been studied and the significance of this part of the Purāṇic history has been entirely missed, it is necessary to have an analysis of the Purāṇic materials which, as we shall see, are very valuable.

121. The Vāyu and the Brahmāṇḍa continue the threads of Indian history where the Matsya stops, i.e. at the fall of the Āndhras, which, according to their calculation, happened in or about 238 A.D. (J.B.O.R.S., XVI, p. 280).[1] The Vāyu and the Brahmāṇḍa take up the imperial history again and begin it with Vindhyaśakti of the Vindhyaka dynasty. They, parenthetically under Vindhyaśakti—to explain the rise of the dynasty of Vindhyaśakti and particularly his son Pravīra—give the history of the Vidiśā Nāgas and their successors, the Nava Nāgas,[2] i.e. the Bhāraśivas. Then they give a full account of the Vākāṭaka ('*Vindhyaka*') empire, with its component parts, giving the number of the rulers and their totals. In other words, they treat the history up to the reign of Vindhyaśakti's son Pravīra along with the Nava Nāgas, whose period they give as past history. And then they begin contemporary history: from the Guptas onwards they neither give the number of rulers nor their rule-periods. From the Guptas onwards, the families were still ruling and those families were therefore contemporaries with the Guptas. As we shall presently see, the Purāṇas undoubtedly imply that they were subordinates and component parts of the Gupta Empire. To this they make a few exceptions, i.e. they note also those contemporaries who were not integral parts of the Gupta Empire. Their details are accurate and territorially specific. They are, therefore, invaluable to the history of the period. And as they stop at that, they are to be treated as a

[1] Their contemporaries the Tukhāra-Muruṇḍas, etc. close about 243 or 247 A.D.—J.B.O.R.S., XVI, 289.

[2] Alternative spelling: *Nava Nāka*. Does Kālidāsa intend a double meaning by his *ā-Nāka°* in the verse cited at p. 112? If *ā-Samudra°* refers to the Guptas, *ā-Nāka°* will refer to the Nākas, i.e. Nāgas.

contemporary record, contemporary with the empire of Samudra Gupta. The Purāṇas have taken up the Gupta line as an imperial dynasty as coming after Pravīra the son of Vindhyaśakti. Up to and including the Vākāṭakas, they have dealt with only imperial lines. The Vishṇu and the Bhāgavata here give some data which are exclusive to them. Here they seem to have preferred some independent materials.

Vishṇu on the rise of the pre-imperial Guptas.

122. The Vāyu and the Brahmāṇḍa place the beginning of the Guptas after closing the Nāgas who were rulers in Bihar up to Champāvatī or Bhagalpur, but the Vishṇu places their beginning in the period of the Nāgas whereby it implies the rise of Gupta and Ghaṭotkacha:

नवनागाः पद्मावत्यां कान्तिपुर्यां मथुरायामनुगङ्गाप्रयागं मागधा गुप्ताश्च भोक्ष्यन्ति ।

which means, that while the Nava Nāgas ruled at Padmāvatī, Kāntipurī and Mathurā, the Māgadha Guptas ruled at Prayāga-on-the-Ganges. This shows that their first fief was in the district of Allahabad and that at that time they were considered to have been natives of Magadha. The plain meaning of this datum is that the Early Guptas were rulers at Allahabad, not on the Jumna side but on the Ganges side, i.e. on the side of Oudh and Benares. The Vishṇu reads *anu-Gaṅgā-Prayāga* as one word, which it gives as the name of a capital like *Padmāvatī*, *Kāntipurī* and *Mathurā*. It is not *anu-Gaṅgā* by itself, an indefinite regional term. Neither the Bhāgavata nor the Vishṇu mentions here Sāketa. The Vishṇu by putting the plural form 'the *Guptas*' and qualifying them with the adjective the 'Magadhan', refers to a period when the Guptas had been dispossessed from Magadha, the pre-imperial years of Samudra Gupta.

Purāṇas on Gupta Empire.

123. The other Purāṇas, on the other hand, give another set of facts about the Gupta dynasty. The Vāyu and the Brahmāṇḍa say that the descendants of the Gupta dynast (*Gupta-vaṁśajāḥ*), i.e. the Guptas later than the founder of the family, will rule (*bhokshyante*):

(*a*) the provinces of Anu-Gaṅgā-Prayāga,[1] Sāketa and the Magadhas;[2]

(*b*) [will rule, *bhokhyante*, or 'will rule over', *bhokhyanti*] the Maṇidhānya provinces of the Naishadhas, Yadukas, Śaiśitas and Kālatoyakas;[3]

(*c*) [will rule *bhokhyante*, or 'will rule over', °*nti*] the Kosalas, Āndhras, ('Oḍras', *per* Vishṇu) Pauṇḍras, the Tāmraliptas with the sea-coast people and the beautiful capital of Champā protected by Deva (*Deva-rakshitāṁ*);[4]

(*d*) [will rule] the Guha provinces (*Guhān*, Vishṇu), the provinces of Kaliṅga, Māhishika and Mahendra,[5] [or, 'Guha will be governor (*pālayishyati*, as against *bhokshyati*) of Kaliṅga, Mahisha and Mahendra.[6]]

That the last three Imperial Provinces were under the governorships respectively of a Maṇidhānyaka (Vishṇu) or a Maṇidhānyāja [a descendant of Maṇidhānya (Brahmāṇḍa)], Deva, and Guha is proved by the Vishṇu's treatment which makes them rulers respectively of these Provincial Governments. In the Vāyu and Brahmāṇḍa text which was here one and the same, they are all put in the accusative, the nominative being the *Gupta-vaṁśajāḥ*; the name of the sub-rulers are taken to be qualifying the provinces, viz. *Maṇidhānyajān* (Br.), *Devarakshitāṁ* [qualifying Champā], and *Guhān* [which survives in the Vishṇu].

1 Or, '*Anu-Gaṅgā and Prayāga*' [अनुगङ्गं प्रयागं च, P.T., 53, *n.* 5.]

2 अनुगङ्गं प्रयागं च साकेतं मगधांस्तथा ।
एतान् जनपदान् सर्वान् भोक्ष्यन्ते गुप्तवंशजाः ॥

3 नैषधान् यदुकांश्चैव शैशितान् कालतोयकान् ।
एतान् जनपदान् सर्वान् भोक्ष्यन्ते [˚न्ति, Vāyu] मणिधान्यजान् ॥
[Brahmāṇḍa.]

4 कोसलांश्चान्ध्र-पौण्ड्रांश्च ताम्रलिप्तान् स-सागरान् ।
चम्पां चैव पुरीं रम्यां भोक्ष्यन्ते [˚न्ति] देवरक्षिताम् ॥ [Vāyu.]

5 कलिङ्गमाहिषिक-माहेन्द्रभौमान् गुहान् भोक्ष्यन्ति । [Vishṇu.]

6 कलिङ्गा महिषाश्चैव महेन्द्रनिलयाश्च ये ।
एतान् जनपदान् सर्वान् पालयिष्यति वै गुहः ॥ [Br., Vā.]

Independent States. 124. Then the following contemporaries are given who are not under the Gupta dynasty:

(A) The dynast called **Kanaka** ruling **Strīrāshṭra, Bhojaka** (Br.), **Trairājya** (Vishṇu) and **Mūshika** (Vishṇu).

(B) The **Ābhīras** of **Surāshṭra** and **Avanti**.

(C) The **Śuras**.

(D) The **Mālavas** of the **Arbuda**.

B, C, and D, according to the Bhāgavata, were non-sacramental, though twice-born, Hindus (*vrātyā dvijāḥ*), and their national rulers (*janādhipāḥ*) were '*almost Śūdras*' (*śūdra-prāyāḥ*).

(E) **Sindhu** [the Indus valley] and the **Chandrabhāgā**, **Kauntî** (Cutch), and **Kashmir** were under the **Mlechchhas** who were non-Brahmanical Śūdras [or according to some manuscripts, *antyāḥ* or the lowest, untouchables]. They were *Mlechchha Śūdras*, i.e. those Mlechchhas [e.g. Śakas] who according to Hindu Law had acquired the status of Śūdras but were Mlechchhas all the same, i.e. foreigners (§ 146 B). The Purāṇas are here distinguishing these Mlechchha Śūdras from the Hindu Śūdras. The Vishṇu Purāṇa actually calls them '*the Mlechchha-Śūdras*'.[1] The Vishṇu Purāṇa adds after **Sindhu-ṭaṭa** 'the *Dārvîka* **country**', i.e. Eastern Afghanistan which is now inhabited by the **Darveshkhel** and the **Dauras**, from the Khyber Pass westwards. Instead of *Dārvīka*, we have the form *Dārvīcha* in the Mahā-Bhārata.[2]

Gupta Provinces. 125. There were, thus, apart from the provinces in Āryāvarta, three imperial provinces, according to the Purāṇas, constituted by the Guptas which they caused to be ruled by their governors. The last two (*c*, *d*, p. 124) were in 'Southern' India. And the second (*b*) was also below the Vindhyas, just at its gate in the West. From the Hindu point of view this was also situated in Dakshiṇāpatha, to the south of the Vindhyas, but following the modern

[1] P.T., 55, *n.* 30.

[2] Hall, Wilson's *Vishṇu Purāṇa*, II, 175. *n.*

terminology we shall call it here (1) the Deccan Province. The Vishṇu Purāṇa mentions it as the third province amongst the provinces ruled through governors, while the Vāyu and the Brahmāṇḍa place it as the first amongst the three provinces. The Vishṇu Purāṇa begins with (2) the Province of Kosala-Orissa-Bengal-and-Champā, while the other two Purāṇas place the Province of Kosala, etc. as the second. And the next, according to all the authorities, is (3) the Province of Kaliṅga-Māhishika-Mahendra. The Bhāgavata stands by itself. It does not give the three provinces, and originally it seems to have included the whole empire in the words *medinî*: '*Goptā bhokshyanti medinîm*,' 'the descendants of Gupta (*Goptāḥ*, Pkt. for *Gauptāḥ*) will rule the Earth.' The Purāṇas in general employ the word *medinî*, *mahî*, *pṛithivî*, *vasundharā* or any other synonymous word for the Earth, when they mean an empire.[1] If we follow the order given in the Vishṇu we almost follow the Allahabad inscription. *Kosala-Oḍra-Pauṇḍra*, *Tāmralipti*, and *Samudrataṭa* would correspond to the inscriptional *Kosala* and *Mahā-Kāntāra* on the one hand[2] (line 19) and *Samataṭa* on the other [in line 22]. It seems that a province was constituted by Samudra Gupta, the capital of which was at Champā and which extended from the south-east of Magadha, through Chota-Nagpur, the tributary states of Orissa and Chhattisgarh, right down to Bastar and the Chanda District. Both the Vāyu and the Brahmāṇḍa place Andhra next to Kosala. To the old Vākāṭaka province of Kosalā and Mekalā was added by Samudra Gupta Orissa and Bengal and the government thereof was

1 This use is confirmed and made clear by Samudra Gupta's use of *pṛithivī* and *dharaṇī* for 'All-India' in his Allahabad inscription (line 24). It means 'the Country', 'the whole Country'. In the present text of the Bhāgavata, however, [अनुगङ्गामाप्रयागं गोप्ता भोक्ष्यन्ति मेदिनीम् ।] *anu-Gaṅgā* stands as if qualified by *medinī*, Probably the intention was to signify that the Guptas who were rulers originally of anu-Gaṅgā Prayāga, enjoyed the whole empire or enjoyed anu-Gaṅgā-Prayāga *and* the Empire.

2 The Mahā-Bhārata locates the State of the Kāntārakas in the direction from *Bhojakaṭa-pura* [Berar]-to-E. *Kosala*, beyond the kingdom of the *Veṇā valley* [Waingaṅgā] and before '*Eastern Kosala*' [Southern text: *Prākoṭaka*]—*Sabhā*, 31,13. *Kāntāraka* corresponds with Kanker and Bastar. The other Kosala [*Southern Kosala*] covered Chanda District.

controlled from Champā, from which the routes to Bengal and Kosala emanated and also the river-highway was available to go right down to Tāmralipti. *Champā* is qualified as '*Devarakshitā*' which probably signifies that it was under Prince Deva (*Deva* was the pre-coronation name of Chandra Gupta II, J.B.O.R.S., XVIII, p. 37). Chandra Gupta II on the Mehraulî pillar is credited to have conquered the Vaṅgas, which may mean that as the Viceroy of the East-South he had to wage a war. Samataṭa seems to have been annexed by Samudra Gupta soon after his expedition.

126. The Province of Kaliṅga-Māhishika[1]-Mahendra (or, -*Mahendrabhūmi*) was made into one unit, according to the Purāṇas. This corresponds with the inscriptional divisions in line 19. After Mahā Kāntāra, Kaurāḷa, which is '*the Kaunāḷa water*' of Pulakeśin II, is the Kolleru lake to the south of Piṭhāpuram between the rivers Godāvarī and Krishnā.[2] Pishṭapura, Mahendragiri and Koṭṭūra are the hill-fortresses in Ganjam.[3] This corresponds roughly with what we now call the Eastern Ghats or the Northern Circars of the E. I. Company, i.e. the territory between the river Kṛishṇā and the Mahānadī. Pishṭapura was the capital of Kaliṅga, as noted in almost a contemporary inscription of 'the Magadha dynasty' ruling at Pishṭapura and Siṁhapura.[4] One of the earliest rulers of this Magadha dynasty was Śaktivarman and probably the next ones were Chandravarman and his son Vijayanandivarman. Vijayanandi-varman changed the dynastic name from 'the Magadha family' into 'the Śālaṅkāyana dynasty'. This must have happened in or after Skanda Gupta's time. We find a successor of Vijayanandi-varman

The 'Magadha Dynasty' of Kaliṅga.

[1] One copy of the Vishṇu, in place of *Māhishika*, gives 'the banks of (the river) *Mahā*' (*Māheya-kachchha*). This was probably 'the valley of the Mahānadī.'

[2] E.I., Vol. VI, p. 3. '*Kolanu*' in Telugu means a 'lake'.

[3] V. Smith, E.H.I., p. 300 [4th ed.].

[4] E.I., Vol. IV, 142; Vol. XII, p. 4; Vol. IX, p. 56 and I.A., Vol. V, p. 176.

(Vijayadeva-varman) even performing a horse-sacrifice, i.e. declaring his full independence. It is almost certain that the later Vākāṭakas, when they conquered Kaliṅga, were asserting their rights as relations or successors of the Guptas, as well as their old right of overlordship over this part of the country, and their assertion must have been against the Śālaṅkāyanas. This '*Magadha kula*' was evidently the ruling feudatory family set up by Samudra Gupta or his successor. They were Brahmins taken from Magadha. Their early kings issue their charters in Sanskrit. The name of the first ruler must have been *Guha* which the Vāyu and the Brahmāṇḍa give. Its form as *Guhān* or *Guham*, [given in the Vishṇu Purāṇa] is a remnant of the original accusative which is here lost in the Vāyu and the Brahmāṇḍa. That a ruler over Kaliṅga with the name *Guha* ('*Guha Sīva*') was a feudatory under the Emperor of All-India and beyond (Jambudvîpa) ruling from Pāṭaliputra, who was Brahmanical in faith, is described in the legendary *History of the Tooth Relic* of Ceylon [1], which is believed to belong to the fourth century A.D. It seems to have its foundation in the fact of Guha's governorship under Samudra Gupta.

The Deccan Province of the Gupta Empire.

§ 126 A. The third unit of the Gupta Empire was the tract to the south of the Vindhyas, consisting of the Naishadha, Yaduka, Śaiśika and Kālatoyaka provinces. *Śaiśika* was next-door to Māhishmatī.[2] Taking *Naishadha* to be Berar, and *Yaduka* to be Devagiri (Daulatabad), we may fix this imperial province as being between the Bālāghāt range and the Sātpura, the valley of the Tāptī river. *Kālatoyā* is placed in the Mahā-Bhārata between the Ābhīras (Gujarat) and Aparānta.[3] The ruler of this province, which was created at the cost of the Vākāṭaka Empire, was a Maṇidhānyaka, a son or a

1 *Dāṭhā-vaṁso*, J.P.T.S., 1884, p. 109, verses 72–94 ff. "*Guha-Sīvâhvayo rājā*" (72); "taththa rājā mahātejo Jambu-dîpasya issaro" (91); "tuhyaṁ sāmanta-bhūpālo Guha-Sîvo panâdhunā, nindato tādise deve chhavatthiṁ vandate iti". The complaint was made to the Emperor at Pāṭaliputra that his feudatory of Kaliṅga was worshipping a piece of 'dead bone', and reviling Brahmanical gods!

2 Wilson, Vishṇu Purāṇa, Vol. II, pp. 166, 167.

3 *Ibid.*, Vol. II, pp. 187, 188.

descendant of Maṇidhānya.[1] The province thus created was probably handed over to Pṛithivīsheṇa on conclusion of better relations, for Pṛithivīsheṇa must be ruling over this portion to be in direct contact with the king of Kuntala, whom he conquered.[2] We find in the reign of Chandra Gupta II the Vākāṭakas ruling in and from Berar.

Southern Independent State.

127. Then follows a unit in the South, the ruler of which is a man named K a n a k a, which like G u h a is a personal name and not that of a dynasty:

"Strīrāshṭraṁ Bhojakāṁś chaiva bhokshyate K a n a k ā h-vayaḥ" (V. and Br.).

King 'Kanaka.'

'The ruler of the name of K a n a k a will rule[3] S t r ī-rāshṭra and the B h o j a k a s.' The provinces here are more fully set out by the Vishṇu:

"Strīrājya-Trairājya-Mūshika-janapadān Kanakâhvayaḥ bhokshyati."

Mūshika is the country of the M ū s ī river which flows by Hyderabad to the south. *Bhojaka* seems to be a part of the Southern Maratha country. *T r a i r ā j y a* is the well-known group of the three traditional countries of the South.[4] Strīrājya which is always placed in the Purāṇas next to the Mūshika country and in association with Vanavāsa, I take to be identical with Karṇāṭa or Kuntala.[5]

Identification of Kanaka or Kāna.

128. Now, who could this great ruler be, who is the overlord of the three Tamil kingdoms at the time and who is causing his rule from the Mūshika country up to the Southern Koṇkan? Who is this man called Kanaka? The Pallavas are

[1] Vāṭadhānya and Maṇidhānya were neighbours according to the Mahā-Bhārata—Wilson, V.P., Vol. II, p. 167. [*Vāṭadhāna=Pāṭahāna =Pāṭhāna*].

[2] E.I., Vol. IX, p. 269; A.S.W.R., Vol. IV, p. 125.

[3] According to the Vishṇu, *bhokshyati* 'will make others rule' or 'rule over'.

[4] See Fleet, J.R.A.S., 1905, p. 293—'*Chola-Pāṇḍya-Kerala-dharaṇī-dhara-traya*'.

[5] *Strīrājya* and *Kuntala* are probably translations of Tamil words.

evidently superseded at this moment by this new dynast. This Kanaka, according to the Purāṇic description, is nearly the emperor of the South. The only ruling family to whom the description can refer was the newly founded Kadamba dynasty. Mayūraśarman, the Brahmin general of the Pallavas, had got a feudatory state from the Pallava Emperor [*Pallavendra*]. On the defeat of the Pallavas of Kāñchī, who were the leading power of the South, at the hand of Samudra Gupta, Mayūraśarman probably declared his independence. His son Kaṅga-varman seems to have defied Samudra Gupta to be the Emperor of both the North and the South. The date of Kaṅga-varman is about 350 A.D.[1] According

1 In the *Kadamba Kula* [pp. 13–18] dates are given on the assumption that Mayūraśarman began his rule as a result of Samudra Gupta's southern conquests. But this is not correct. Mayūra, according to the Talagunda record, started his career as a political bandit and was given a fief by the 'Pallava Emperor' whose service he entered as a general and who anointed him as his *Sēnāpati* [*paṭṭa-bandha-saṁpūjāṁ*, E.I., VIII, 32. Senāpatis received *paṭṭabandha* ('pagree'-binding ceremony), according to the *Rājá-Nīti-mayūkha*]. No aśvamedha by him is recorded in the Talagunda inscription of his great-grandson. It was probably in his last years that he assumed kingship. *Cf.* A.R.S.M., 1929, p. 50. His son Kaṅga was the first to assume the royal designation ° *varman*. Mayūraśarman's time should be regarded as 325–345 A.D. and that of his son Kaṅga, 345–360 A.D. This is confirmed by the date of Kākusthavarman on his plate which he issued as *yuvarāja*. It is dated in the 80th year. The Kadambas never founded any era of their own. We do not find there the era in which the 80th year is given, before or after any more. Pṛithivīsheṇa conquered the king of Kuntala, i.e. the Kadamba king who could be no other than Kaṅga. Pṛithivīsheṇa himself at the time was under Samudra Gupta, and Kākustha gave a daughter in marriage to the Guptas. The era used by the *Yuvarāja* Kākustha must be the Gupta era. In 400 A.D. [80 G.E.] Kākustha was the Yuvarāja to his elder brother Raghu. The time of his great-grandfather would thus be about 320–340 A.D. or 325–345 A.D.; that of Kaṅga who abdicated, about 340–355 or 345 to 360 A.D.; and of Kākustha, about 410–430 A.D. The dates proposed by Mr. Moraes in his *Kadamba-Kula* for the Early Kadambas should go higher up by some 20 years.

See on Mayūraśarman's newly discovered Chandravalli (Chitaldrug) lake inscription where he is registered merely as '*Kadaṁbāṇaṁ*' (without any title) [A.S.R. Mysore, 1929, 50], and a corrected reading of the inscription, App. B (below). There is no '*Mokari*', '*Pāriyātrika*' or '*Saka*' in the insc.

to the Talagunda inscription [E.I., 8, 35] K a ṅ g a performed '*lofty great exploits in terrible wars and his diadem was shaken by the Chauris of his provincial feudatories*'. K a ṅ g a was defeated by the V ā k ā ṭ a k a king P ṛ i t h i v ī s h e ṇ a I and he abdicated.[1] *Kanaka* here seems to be a Sanskritisation of the Tamil *Kaṅga*. Another reading of the Purāṇic name, in the Vishṇu, is *K ā n a*.[2] It seems that on assumption of imperial power he was by Pṛithivisheṇa, who was at that time a feudatory of Samudra Gupta, brought to book, and his abdication was evidently a consequence of his imperial ambition and failure.

§ 129. The Purāṇas help us to fix the period of the rise of Kāna or Kanaka, i.e. Kaṅga. Let us see what is the exact point of time at which the Purāṇas are describing here the Guptas and their contemporaries. This is the last section of their chronicles. The M ā l a v a s, the Ā b h ī r a s, the Ā v a n t y a s and the Ś ū r a s [=Yaudheyas][3] had not yet come under the imperial sway. They are mentioned as independent states by the Bhāgavata; the Vāyu and the Brahmāṇḍa do not give them in their list of Samudra Gupta's provinces. Nor do they include the Punjab. They assign, in Āryāvarta, only the valley of the Ganges, Oudh, and Bihar to the Guptas. With their definite date—100 years from Vindhyaśakti—the Purāṇas take **3 4 8–3 4 9 A. D.** as the landmark for the close of their chronicles, that is, the date of the d e a t h of R u d r a d e v a or R u d r a s e n a V ā k ā ṭ a k a as their exact point of time. The way the Purāṇas show fullness about the Nāga history, the Vākāṭaka Empire, and its successor, the Empire of Samudra Gupta [covering the same area of Kosalā, Mekalā, Andhra, Naishadha, etc.], indicates that this part of the chronicles closing with the death of King Rudrasena was composed in the Vākāṭaka kingdom and with the help of the Vākāṭaka royal records. The death of Rudrasena—348-349 A.D., being the date of the Purāṇic history of G u p t a I n d i a, it naturally does not give a full

The Date of the Purāṇic data and the rise of Kāna or Kanaka.

[1] *Kadamba Kula*, p. 17.

[2] Wilson's Vishṇu, Vol. IV, p. 221, note by Hall.

[3] See § 146 below.

picture of Samudra Gupta's empire, and it records the Śakas or Yaunas still ruling in Sindh the Western Punjab and Afghanistan. The date of the rise of Kaṅga therefore will also be c. 348-349 A.D.

Samudra Gupta and Vākāṭaka Empire.

130. Samudra Gupta after his first war in Āryāvarta was really going over the empire of the Vākāṭakas, commencing his campaign from Bihar via Chota Nagpur to Kosala, etc., the South-Eastern parts of the Vākāṭaka Empire and then back into Āryāvarta. At this moment it would be convenient to trace and follow the course of Samudra Gupta's conquests. We would, therefore, put off the discussion on the Republics and the Mlechchha State of Sindh, Kashmir and Afghanistan, and take up in the next chapter the wars of Samudra Gupta.

XIII. Samudra Gupta's Wars in Āryāvarta and in the South.

Three Wars of Samudra Gupta.

§ 131. According to the Allahabad inscription, Samudra Gupta's wars in Āryāvarta were in two parts—one before the Southern expedition and the other after the Southern expedition. The result of these wars was the Gupta Empire as portrayed in the Purāṇas, almost with exactitude, in the shape of its three imperial provinces (§ 125) along with the home province of Anu-Gaṅgā-Prayāga-Sāketa-and-Magadha.

The Battle of Kauśāmbî.

132. The first act of Samudra Gupta, which turned the scales of his political fortunes in his favour, was a pitched battle at some place where he defeated two, or rather three, kings—Achyuta, Nāgasena and Gaṇapati Nāga. The immediate result of this was that the Prince of the family of Kota (whose name is not given in the verse) was captured by his armies, and Samudra Gupta had the pleasure of re-entering Pushpapura. The verse 7, lines 13 and 14, of the Allahabad pillar inscription describes this as follows:

udvelodita-bāhu-vīryya-rabhasād-ekena yena kshaṇād
unmūly-Āchyuta-Nāgasena-Ga......
daṇḍair grāhayat-aiva Kota-kulajaṁ Pushp-āhvaye kṛiḍatā,
sūrvvene.... ṭaṭa.........

The letters after *Ga* are lost but probably the name of *Gaṇapat*.... was there which is suggested by the remaining letter त and the requirement of the metre. This we can gather from the grouping in line 21 which is in prose and which begins the *Nāgasena-Achyuta* group with *Gaṇapati-Nāga*:

Gaṇapati-Nāga-Nāgasena-Achyuta-Nandi-Balavarma—The most important personality of the group is Gaṇapati Nāga. The great result of the battle being avowedly an easy capture of Pāṭaliputra and of the Prince of the family of Kota, the battle must have been intimately connected with the question of the recovery of Magadha. Samudra Gupta himself did not capture 'Kota's descendant' who was the ruler of Pāṭaliputra at the time. We may take it, therefore, that one army had attacked or laid siege to Pushpapura, and that Samudra Gupta gave battle to Nāgasena and Achyuta and also probably to Gaṇapaṭi aṭ a place other than Pāṭaliputra, and at some distance from Pāṭaliputra. Now, we know from coins and from the *Bhāvaśataka*, a work written under the reign of Gaṇapati Nāga (§ 31) that Gaṇapati Nāga was the ruler of Malwā (*Dhārâdhīśa*) with his capital at Padmāvatī and probably a second capital at Dhārā. The name of Achyuta Nandi as set out in full in line 21, and the coin of 'Achyuta' found at Ahichhatra which has the same symbols as on the Nāga coins of Padmāvatī and also has the same fabric, suggest that he was a scion of the Nāgas. Nāgasena was probably the son of Kīrtisheṇa of Mathurā,[1] father-in-law of Kalyāṇavarman king of Magadha and Pāṭaliputra.[2] As Kalyāṇavarman who had dispossessed Chaṇḍasena of Pāṭaliputra was related to the king of Mathurā and thus belonged to the confederacy of the Nāga-Vākāṭakas, we find Nāgasena and Achyuta Nandi, in all probability led by Gaṇapati who was a noted soldier and the leader of the Nāgas according to the

[1] This Nāgasena is to be distinguished from the Nāgasena of Padmāvatī, a member of the Nāga family, mentioned by Bāṇa in the *Harsha-Charita*, for the latter had met with his end not on a battle-field, but on account of some political intrigue at Padmāvatī. No coin of his is found. He seems to have been a Gupta subordinate.

[2] *Kaumudî-mahotsava*, Act IV.

Bhāvaśataka, meeting Samudra Gupta in a pitched battle. They might have been on their way to the relief of Pāṭaliputra. The convenient place upon which the kings or rulers from Ahichchhatra, Mathurā and Padmāvatī could have converged was Kauśāmbī or Allahabad, more likely the former, as the old royal route to Pāṭaliputra lay through Kauśāmbī. The proclamation of this victory on the Kauśāmbī Pillar seems to convey that meaning. The *praśasti* was meant to be engraved on this very pillar, as line 30 expressly mentions:

bāhurayam-uchchhritaḥ stambhaḥ.

All the three rulers or sub-kings were killed in one day (*kshaṇāt*) on the battlefield.

133. This war may be dated in or about 344-45 A.D. immediately after the death of Pravarasena I, the Vākāṭaka Emperor. This war gave the large tract of the Gangetic valley to Samudra Gupta. From Oudh which already belonged to him and had been his base, his territory extended up to Hardwar and the Siwalik, and to the east, from Allahabad up to Bhagalpur at least, if not up to Bengal which seems to be included by the Purāṇic reference to Pauṇḍra. Leaving probably the valley of the Yamunā for the time being, Samudra Gupta consolidated his power in Magadha and decided upon attacking the south-eastern end of the Vākāṭaka empire. It was far from the centre of the Vākāṭaka seat of power which, up to that time, was in the Kilakilā region. To Samudra Gupta it was nearer from Chota Nagpur. The Vākāṭakas evidently governed their provinces of Kosalā-Mekalā through and from the Central Provinces. Samudra Gupta, therefore, could cause successfully, apart from other military considerations, not only confusion but almost helplessness to the Vākāṭaka Emperor by attacking the Vākāṭakas in Kosalā, Mekalā and Andhra. The Pallavas who occupied an important position in the South at the time were in subordinate alliance with the Vākāṭaka Emperor, being their branch. The four Aśvamedhas of the late Vākāṭaka *samrāṭ* had given him dominion over all the four quarters of India. In the South Samudra Gupta had a policy more of conciliation than of aggression. He captured rulers and released them, and except

Next step.

for the territories which were integral parts of the Vākāṭaka Empire—Kosalā and Mekalā—he did not annex any southern territory. In Kaliṅga he set up a new feudatory. His progress, consequently, in the South must have been swift. At the same time it was very profitable. The whole of Northern India was soon flooded with gold presumably imported from the South. Samudra Gupta coined only gold money, and at his aśvamedha at a later stage, he struck gold coins to such a volume that he could distribute them to an unprecedented extent.

Southern Conquest.

§134. It cannot be entertained that the enumeration of the names of the Southern kings and chiefs in the Allahabad record is made at random. The writer Harisheṇa, who was one of Samudra Gupta's marshals and a man intimately associated with the emperor and who held the portfolio of the Minister of Peace and War, must be expected to follow an accurate record of his master's conquests. He was composing history which was intended to be published on an Aśokan pillar for all ages to come. He divided the conquests and submission of All India into Southern, Northern, Western and North-West groups, where he was following a geographical plan with accuracy. The string of names could not have been put in by haphazard. Further, we may assume that the composition must have found approval of the Emperor who was alive when the record was published.[1] Kāñchī, Āva-mukta, Veṅgī and Palakka are one division. Palakka as Palakkada appears several times in Pallava inscriptions[2] which refer to grants in the Guntur District, and also to *Veṅgorāshṭra* which here corresponds with Samudra Gupta's *Veṅgī* between the Godāvarī and the Kṛishnā.

135. This Southern or the 'Dakshiṇāpatha' campaign was not undertaken, as generally supposed, as a *digvijaya*. It was a military move against the Vākāṭaka power,

[1] *Ante*, p. 121, *n*. 2. See Bühler's opinion, J.R.A.S., 1898, p. 386, with which I fully agree.

[2] I.A., Vol. V, pp. 51, 52, 155, consult also E.I., Vol. VIII, p. 159 [*kada*='place', p. 161.]

necessitated by the result of Samudra Gupta's first battle in Āryāvarta in which Gaṇapati Nāga, Achyuta Nandi and Nāgasena fell. The second centre of the Vākāṭaka power was rooted in the Andhra country, where, from the capital Daśanapura[1] the junior branch of the Vākāṭakas had been ruling as 'the Pallava emperors' ('*Pallavendra*'[2]) of the South, and had penetrated as far south as Kāñchī, the capital of the Cholas—the most important Tamil State. Samudra Gupta's sole objective in the South was the Pallava army. If, to avenge the destruction of the Vākāṭaka military leaders (Gaṇapati Nāga and others) in the North, the Pallavas with their generals and feudatories from the South and Rudrasena from Bundelkhand invaded Bihar, Samudra Gupta would have been placed between two fires. To avoid this junction, Samudra Gupta would have thought of taking them and dealing with them in detail. He descended swiftly via Chota Nagpur, Sambhalpur and Bastar straight into Veṅgī, the original seat of the Pallavas, and reached the battlefield on the Colair Lake. It is the old route which takes one direct into Andhradeśa. Samudra Gupta did not follow the East-Coast route, as none of the lower Bengal and Orissa towns is mentioned by his secretary Harisheṇa. The Colair Lake in the seventh century again became the arena of a sanguinary fight in the time of Pulakeśin II.[3] If we consider the list of the rulers enumerated by Samudra Gupta's secretary and prince-marshal, we see at once that all these rulers belonged to the regions of Andhra and Kaliṅga lying within the range of the Kurāḷa or Colair Lake. They were all, evidently, assembled together (§ 135 A) and a decisive battle was fought,[4] and owing

[1] E.I., I, 397, where it is described as *adhishṭhāna*, 'capital'; see Fleet, I.A., V, 154. In the latter inscription it is again called 'capital' —'Vijaya-Daśanapura'.

[2] This is the title by which they are designated both by the Gaṅgas and the Kadambas, their feudatories. E.I., XIV, 331; VIII, 32.

[3] E.I., VI, pp. 3, 6.

[4] The list is (line 19): (1) *Kausalaka* Mahendra; (2) *Mahākāntāraka* Vyāghrarāja; (3) *Kaurālaka* Maṇṭarāja; (4) *Pishṭapuraka-Mahendra*;

to some clever movement and strategy on the part of Samudra Gupta all the leaders were enveloped, a debâcle followed and they surrendered. Samudra Gupta restored them to liberty on terms. Samudra Gupta returned from this place —the region between Bezwada and Rajahmundry. He had no necessity to go to Kāñchī. Nor was he interested at the time in any other Southern state either on the East Coast or the West Coast. He hurried back to Bihar, having defeated and generously and diplomatically won over the Pallava group and having detached them from the Vākāṭaka allegiance. When back, he marched against Rudra Deva who fought bravely as every one of his northern subordinates did, and was killed with them on the battlefield, probably at Eran (§ 137).

Battle of Colair Lake.

135 A. Samudra Gupta passed through Kosala on his Sambhalpur route, and then Mahākāntāra which on the evidence of the Mahā-Bhārata we have identified with Kanker and Bastar. Next he came to Kurāḷa. He must have passed Veṅgī[1] but the ruler of Veṅgī is placed next to the ruler of Pishṭapura, the capital of Kaliṅga, which was in the Godavari District. This ruler (Svāmidatta) had also two districts in Ganjam round the hill-fortresses of Mahendragiri and Koṭṭūra. Eraṇḍapalli was a town in Kaliṅga, in the district of Ganjam, in the neighbourhood of Kaliṅganagara (Mukhalingam) which is mentioned in the copperplate of Devendra-varman, found at Siddhantam near Chicacole (E.I., XIII, 212). This district must have been under Svāmidatta of Pishṭapura, and Damana of Eraṇḍapalli must have been a 'rājā' or ruler of the status of a district officer. Next to him is Vishṇugopa, the ruler of Kāñchī, who at the time was the Yuvarāja to his brother Siṁhavarman I, or probably the guardian of

girika-Kauṭṭūraka Svāmidatta; (5) *Eraṇḍapallaka* Damana; (6) *Kāñcheyaka* Vishṇugopa; (7) *Āvamuktaka* Nîla-rāja; (8) *Vaiṅgeyaka* Hastivarman; (9) *Pālakkaka* Ugrasena; (10) *Daivarāshṭraka* Kubera; (11) *Kausthalapuraka* Dhanañjaya (prabhṛiti-sarvva-Dakshiṇāpatha-rāja-, *etc.*).

[1] For its location near Ellore in the Godavari District, see E.I., IX, 56.

his son Siṁhavarman II of Kāñchī. From Eraṇḍapalli to Kāñchī is a big jump. This can be consistent only on the hypothesis that they were together at one and the same spot. Then comes the ruler of Āvamukta or Avamukta. The Āva country or people had their capital Pīṭhuṇḍa near the Godavari. Āva and Pīthuṇḍa are noted in the Hathigumpha inscription.[1] After him comes the ruler of Veṅgī, a tract which Samudra Gupta had already passed on his way from Mahākāntāra to Kurāḷa. It was not possible for Samudra Gupta to go to Kāñchī, if he went there, without meeting the ruler of Veṅgī on the way: this is another proof that all these fighters were at one place. Palakka, as already pointed out, is the same place wherefrom several grants in the district of Guntur and near about Bezwada were made by the early Pallavas. In the grants the name appears as *Palakkada*. It was situated in the Andhradeśa nearabout the Krishnā. Devarāshṭra, which figures next in the person of its ruler, fixes again the location of all these 'rājans' at one and the same place. It was a district (*vishaya*) in *Elmañchi-Kaliṅgadeśa* (modern *Yellamanchilli*) according to a plate of Chālukya Bhīma I[2] whose another plate was discovered at Bezwada. Kusthalapura must have been similarly some district-place in the same region, though we have not yet recovered its name in any other record. Probably except the rulers of Kosala and Mahākāntāra, all these military chiefs—from the rank of kings, e.g. Svāmidatta and Vishṇugopa, to that of district magistrates [against whom no conqueror would take the trouble of marching]—must have been together and must have fought at one and the same battlefield. The order in which they are mentioned probably represents the order of the battle-array or the order of their surrender. Their importance is as fighters and military leaders, not as rulers. They seem to have been grouped under two chief leaders: [the numbers before the names denote their order in the Allahabad inscription. See footnote[4] to § 135, pp. 136-137.]

[1] E.I., XX, 79; line 11; J.B.O.R.S., XIV, 151.

[2] Madras Report on Epigraphy, 1909, pp. 108-109.

I		II
(3) MAṆṬA-RĀJA of KURĀḶA leading	and	(6) VISHṆUGOPA of KĀÑCHI leading
(4) Svāmidatta and		7. Nīlarāja of Āvamukta,
(5) Damana of Eraṇḍapalli.		8. Hastivarman of Veṅgī,
		9. Ugrasena of Palakka,
		10. Kubera of Devarāshṭra, and
		11. Dhanañjaya of Kusṭhalapura.

The main army was under Vishṇugopa, who was supported on flanks by the Kaliṅga forces. The battle might be called the '**Battle of Kurāḷa**'. By this battle there was achieved the conquest of the Vakāṭāka provinces of Kosalā, Mekalā and Andhra. Samudra Gupta returned by the same route of Kosala, as no other countries are noted by Harisheṇa. We may date it about 345-346 A.D. It must have followed soon after the battle of Kauśāmbī (344 A.D.). Like Khāravela, Samudra Gupta's campaigns might average one in two years [344 A.D. to 348 A.D.]. Starting after the rains he could have returned to Patna the same year.[1]

Second Āryāvarta War.

136. Samudra Gupta on his return now invaded the real Vākāṭaka centre, the home-province of the Vākāṭakas in Āryāvarta between the Yamunā and Vidiśā, or to adopt the modern geographical name—the land of Bundelkhand. This Āryāvarta War gave to Samudra Gupta dominion over '*the Āṭavī rulers* [of Āryāvarta]', i.e., the Vindhyan principalities of Baghelkhand and Eastern Bundelkhand. The war was waged, therefore, in the Vindhyan regions of Āryāvarta, that is, in or about Bundelkhand. To operate in the hills of Pannā is a difficult venture which military leaders would avoid. To

[1] The easy march according to Kauṭilya (ch. 130) was one *yojana* (7 miles) a day for an ordinary army; for a better one, 1½ yojanas, and for the best 2 yojanas a day. [The value of yojana to be 7 miles is well ascertained by Cunningham.] The campaign of Samudra Gupta must have been swift.

the south-west, Bundelkhand is bounded by the districts of Bhilsa [Vidiśā] [Eastern Malwā]. And Bundelkhand is much more accessible from Eastern Malwā, to which there was and has been a good plain road from the Gangetic valley across the Betwa or the Chambal. Samudra Gupta would have attacked the province of the Kilakilā-Vidiśa from the plain country now lying mostly in the Gwalior territory—the passage-land of the Marathas to Hindustan. The battle seems to have been fought at Eran. The reasons for this conclusion are as follows.

Battle of Eran.

137. As Samudra Gupta built his monuments at Eran which was in the heart of the Vākāṭaka home-province, it is definite that he had a triumphant march into the Vākāṭaka country. In the reign of the next Vākāṭaka king, Pṛithivisheṇa I, we find Bundelkhand still under the Vākāṭakas. Immediately to the south of Eran and also to its east there were the Republics (§ 145). Samudra Gupta's founding a Vishṇu temple at Eran, which was not in the territory under his direct administration, is suggestive. In the Eran inscription, where the king has not yet assumed the title of *Mahārājādhirāja*, and where the set genealogy is yet unknown, lines 21 to 26, verses 6 and 7, show that after a military victory, Samudra Gupta raised a war memorial, like the one raised later by his grandson at Bhitarī. The inscription is earlier than the Allahabad pillar inscription. The word '*Antaka*' is emphasised in this inscription; a whole lot of kings (*pārthiva-gaṇas sakalaḥ*) are noted to have been overthrown and deprived of their sovereignty, and the king is said to have taken a consecration[1] and is described to have become one whose valour had become '*irresistible*'—a title afterwards adopted on his coins. His action in war is given prominence, in line 21, which made his enemies fear him even in sleep. To mark the glory, he established (line 26) a foundation, which is evidently the Vishṇu Temple, still existing. On the freeze of the temple a funeral-scene is depicted,[2] which is unusual, and is to be interpreted as the cremation of the Vākāṭaka king,

[1] '*Abkisheka*'.

[2] A.S.R., Vol. X, p. 85.

defeated and slain. The town from that day became a direct, personal possession of the Gupta Emperor—which is the real meaning of the term '*svabhoga-nagara*'.

Eran a natural Battlefield.

138. **Eran** is at the gate of Bundelkhand on one side and Malwa on the other. The whole of Malwa, both eastern and western, was under republics who submitted, without any fight, to Samudra Gupta. It seems that at this place, which had been a strategic point and had an ancient fort and which with a vast stretch of plain country is designed by nature to be an excellent battlefield, the action with the Vākāṭaka king was fought. It became a battlefield again in later Gupta times, as we have the memorial given here to a Gupta general (Goparāja) who fought and died here in the time of the Huns, where 'his devoted wife in close companionship' accompanied him on to the funeral pyre.[1]

Rudradeva.

139. **Rudradeva** was defeated and killed on the battlefield by Samudra Gupta. Rudra is the only king whose name is coupled with 'deva' in the inscription of Samudra Gupta, and we may take it to be intentional. **Rudrasena** was the biggest monarch in India at the time, having succeeded his grandfather who had been a true Emperor of All-India. '*Sena*', in *Rudrasena* is really not a part of the name: as pointed out above we may compare the dropping of *sena* in the Nepal inscriptions where the Lichchhavi king **Vasantasena** is sometimes described as *Vasanta-sena* and sometimes as *Vasantadeva*. *Deva* is more dignified and stood for full royal dignity. The chronology proposed above makes Rudradeva succeed in 344 A.D., and Samudra Gupta's conquests are unanimously dated about 345 to 350 A.D. The **Rudradeva** of the inscription is thus contemporaneous with and identical with **Rudrasena** I (§ 64).

Āryāvarta Kings.

140. The Āryāvarta kings defeated by Samudra Gupta were:

Rudradeva, Matila, Nāgadatta, Chandravarman, Gaṇapati Nāga, Nāgasena, Achyuta Nandi, and **Balavarman**.[2]

[1] Fleet, G. I., p. 92. [2] G. I., p. 12.

This list is divisible into two parts. (1) From Gaṇapati Nāga to Balavarman are the names of the kings already defeated in the first Āryāvarta War; the battle of Kauśāmbī accounting for the three, the last one, Balavarman, might have been the ruler of Pāṭaliputra captured by Samudra Gupta's army who is left unnamed in verse 7. If so, Balavarman, was the second or the *abhisheka-* [the coronation-] name of Kālyāṇavarman. The other group must therefore consist of the kings and rulers defeated in the Second War or in a probable continuation of the Second War.[1] Of these Nāgadatta is to be identified with the Nāgadatta, father of the Mahārāja Maheśvara Nāga—a Nāga sub-king whose seal bearing the *lāñchhana* of a cobra was found at Lahore and has been edited by Fleet in his *Gupta Inscriptions*, which according to its script belongs to the fourth century A.D. (G. I., page 283). Matila ruled in the district of Bulandshahr, whose seal with another Nāga emblem was discovered.[2] We do not know who this Chandravarman of Samudra Gupta's inscription was,[3] but we know that a Yādava dynasty of feudatories had been set up about 250 A.D. at Siṁhapura in the Jālandhara Doab [§§ 78 and 80]. This house must have been feudatory to the Vākāṭakas. Their names ended in 'varman'. Although in the list of the Simhapura rulers we do not find any name as Chandravarman yet it is possible that he might have been a younger cadet who came to the battlefield to fight for Rudrasena, or *Chandravarman* was a second name of some king of the line. The sixth king who would have been a contemporary of Samudra Gupta and whose name is Vṛiddhivarman, is described as '*Chandra*'

[1] Very likely a little later, another expedition was undertaken to the west of Mathurā in the Srughna country and up to Jālandhara.

[2] I.A., XVIII, p. 289. It is the symbol of the Nāga *Śaṅkhapāla*. There is a conch and a serpent. The shape of the serpent is round and rays (ābhā) come out of its body, i.e. from its body rays emanate. A *dhyāna* of Durgā describes Saṅkhapāla thus: *dāhottīrṇa-suvarṇābha*,° used as a *kaṅkaṇa* (bracelet) by the Goddess.

[3] Once V. Smith proposed to identify the *Chandravarman* of Samudra Gupta with the *Chandravarman* of the Susunia inscription (J.R.A.S., 1897, p. 876). But the script of the latter (E.I., XIII, p. 133) is much later.

in verse 7 of the Lakkhā Maṇḍal inscription [E.I., Vol. I, 13]. Chandra-varman, according to the Allahabad inscription, was a neighbour of Nāgadatta who must have been a ruler beyond Mathurā and whose successor's seal was found at Lahore. There is no room for Nāgadatta between Ahi-chhatra and Mathurā. The grouping—*Rudradeva-Matila-Nāgadatta-Chandravarman*—is made up in a geographical order: Matila was next to Rudradeva, Nāgadatta was further west and Chandravarman, furthest, in the Eastern Punjab.

140 A. Now the question is whether all these three rulers fought on the side of Rudradeva in one battle or separately. Nāgadatta and Chandravarman were not in the neighbourhood of Rudrasena, but we know from Indian History that kings and allies travelled from long distances to fight pitched battles; it is not unlikely that the three feudatories fought along with Rudradeva in one and the same battle, which must have been expected. This must have been the biggest battle of Samudra Gupta, as he notes that all the Āṭavika kings became his servants after his war with these kings, which means that the rulers of Bundelkhand and Baghelkhand took part in this battle and changed allegiance to the Gupta conqueror on the fall of their sovereign lord. But as to the two western kings or rulers it seems more likely that there was a subsequent engagement to the west of Mathurā. The Purāṇic (Va. and Br.) description of Samudra Gupta's empire at the date of the death of Rudrasena [§129], which does not include the Punjab, would also indicate it. There was thus, more likely, a Third War in Āryāvarta, a year or so later.

Date of Āryāvarta Wars.

141. The enveloping movement of Samudra Gupta against the Vākāṭaka Empire was practically a continuation of his First Āryāvarta War. The three big battles form really one continuous campaign. The campaign, therefore, must have been carried through quickly. Under a generalship which was so perfect that it never met with a reverse or check, the campaigns would have been finished easily in three fighting seasons—October [Vijayādaśamî] to April each year. Following the chronology adopted above we may date the First Āryāvarta Battle about 344-345 A.D.,

the Second Āryāvarta War in or about 348 A.D., and the probable Third War *c.* 349 or 350 A.D.

XIV. THE SUBMISSION OF THE FRONTIER RULERS AND THE HINDU REPUBLICS, AND THEIR PURĀṆIC DESCRIPTION, AND THE SUBMISSION OF FARTHER INDIA.

Frontier Kingdoms.

142. After the [Third] Āryāvarta War ending with the fall of Nagādatta and Chandravarman, Samudra Gupta's period of war ended. The Allahabad inscription (line 22) is clear on the point. There were only five main states on his frontiers and they became part of his empire. (1) Samataṭa, (2) Ḍavāka, (3) Kāmarūpa, (4) Nepāla and (5) Kartṛipura paid 'all' imperial 'taxes' and their kings presented themselves in person.[1] This line of 'the Frontier Kings' runs from the mouths of Ganges through the Lushai-Manipur[2]-Assam to the Himalayan Mountains covering what we call now Bhutan, Sikkim and Nepal, and thence onwards to the Simla Hills and Kangra (Kartṛipura), i.e. the hills above Bengal [*Pauṇḍra*], the United Provinces, and up to the E. Punjab [the Mādraka country]. The inclusion of Kartṛipura implies that the result of the [Third] Āryāvarta War was the inclusion of the Eastern Punjab. This is probably also inferable from the Bhāgavata Purāṇa which does not note the Madraka State in its list of the free republican states (§ 146). In the next reign we find the Gupta Era in the year 83 [=403 A.D.] dominant up to Shorkoṭ (old *Śivipura*) near the eastern bank of the Chenab[3]. In Nepal, Jayadeva I, the new Lichchhavi king of Nepal, was a relation of Samudra Gupta and his submission meant practically the submission of the whole group of the Himalayan States on the Indian side. The Gupta Era was introduced in Nepal in the reign of Jayadeva I.[4] The relationship was evidently a great factor in avoiding a mountain

1 Allahabad Pillar Insc., l. 22, G.I., p. 8.

2 Col. Gerini, *Ptolemy* (pp. 55–61) identifies *Ḍavāka* with Upper Burma.

3 E.I., XVI. 15.

4 Fleet, G.I., Intro., p. 135; I.A., XIV, 345 (350).

expedition. Samudra Gupta seems to have, later on, annexed Samataṭa to the Province of Champā, to have a natural frontier up to the sea, which was a matter of necessity for an easier access to and the administration of Orissa and Kaliṅga, and the sea-trade with Further India (§ 150).

Kashmir and Daivaputra group and their submission.

143. We should note here that the Empire of Samudra Gupta ending with Kangra, leaves out Kashmir and the plains below it. This becomes clear from the Bhāgavata, the original text of which was completed before the submission of the Daivaputra-group whom the text describes as richly deserving suppression. Line 23 of the Allahabad inscription registers the 'tranquil fame' of Samudra Gupta 'pervading the whole land' and his re-establishing many dynasties 'fallen and deprived of sovereignty'. The result of this policy of peace is immediately given as the submission of the *Daivaputra-shāhi-shāhānu-shāhi-Śaka-Muruṇḍas*—which completes the imperial geography of the North-West and Kashmir. This was the Mlechchha State of the Bhāgavata and the Vishṇu. The Shāhānushāhi made his submission in person, for the inscription gives the forms of submission which the Daivaputra group and others made respectively, and the order of their enumeration proves his personal submission. The first member of the group is the Daivaputra Shāhi-shāhānushāhi. The words *Daivaputra* and *Shāhi* qualify *shāhānushāhi*, which were probably necessary to distinguish the Kushan emperor from the Sassanian emperor who was at that time the next neighbour of the Gupta Empire. The first form of submission was that of offering themselves (*ātmanivedana*) and the second consisted of two things: presenting (*upāyana*) unmarried girls and giving of daughters in marriage (*kanyādāna*). The third was the request [*yāchana*] which consisted of two matters: asking for charters for the currency of the Garuḍa coinage within the jurisdiction of their own territories and an application to enjoy the governments of their own respective countries ['*garutmadaṅka-svavishaya-bhukti-śāsana-yāchana*:' asking for charters (*śāsana-yāchana*) for the use

of the Garuḍa-coin (*garutmadaṅka-bhukti*) and for the government of their own territories (provinces or districts, *svavishaya bhukti*)]. We know from the Pālada or Shālada and the 'Shāka' coins of the Kushan subordinate kings of the Western Punjab, that they accepted the Gupta coinage.[1] They printed the effigy of Samudra Gupta and his name on their coins, and it was continued up to the reign of Chandra Gupta II when we find his effigy and name also similarly stamped. As to the identity of these Gupta kings there cannot be any doubt, for the kings wear ear-rings or *kuṇḍala* on these coins, while the Kushans never used them. These coins, have been already described by numismatists as coins allied to the Gupta coinage.[2] The *kanyā-dāna*, 'giving in marriage' (*dāna*, as opposed to *upāyana*, 'presenting') of 'a *kanyā*' should refer to the Kushan Emperor, looking at the system current at the time, that, as a rule, it was a big rival ruler who bending his head offered a daughter in marriage to the conqueror.

Sassanian Emperor and Kushan subordination.

144. The Sassanian emperor at the time was Shapur II (310–379 A.D.) who was the suzerain of the Kushan king. The Kushans at this time issued from Afghanistan the 'Kushāno-Sassanian' coins with the title *Shaonano-shao*.[3] The protection of the Sassanian Emperor and the close alliance with him could not prevent a virtual annexation of the Indian territories of the Kushans (to the east of the Indus) by the Gupta emperor. The Kushan subordinates of Kashmir, Rawalpindi and Peshawar were practically transferred to the Indian Empire by their adopting the Gupta imperial coinage. The personal submission of the Kushan Shāhānushāhi naturally prevented Samudra Gupta from pursuing a policy of aggression. But the enemy was left with potential power of mischief, for, soon after the death of Samudra Gupta the *Śakādhipati* raised the banner of revolt, probably with the support of the Sassanian Emperor Shapur II. The ignominy of having to offer a Kushan royal princess

1 J.B.O.R.S., XVIII, 208-209.
2 J.B.O.R.S., XVIII, 208-209.
3 Vincent Smith, Catalogue of Coins in the Indian Museum, p. 91.

suffered in the time of Samudra Gupta was now sought to be avenged by the demand for Dhruva-Devī, which led to the final destruction of the Kushan king and Kushan power by the march of Chandra Gupta II up to Balkh, the farthest seat and centre of the Kushans.[1]

Republics and Samudra Gupta.

145. The republics of the Mālavas, Āryunāyanas, Yaudheyas, Mādrakas, Ābhīras, Prārjunas, Sahasānīkas, Kākas, Kharparikas and others were not on the frontiers of Samudra Gupta's empire as wrongly supposed by Dr. Vincent Smith, for, in line 22 (Allahabad Pillar Inscription) where 'the frontier kings' are mentioned, they are expressly excluded from that category. They were internal States and had become part of the Gupta empire by agreeing to pay all kinds of imperial taxes and obeying imperial orders. In the enumeration of the tributary republics there is a territorial scheme. The Mālavas, Āryunāyanas, Yaudheyas and Mādrakas are counted from the direct Gupta territory—say, from Mathurā. The first state is the Mālava. Nāgara or Karkoṭa-Nāgara which is situated in the modern State of Jaipur was the capital of the Mālavas whose thousands of republican coins—'*as thick as shells on the sea-shore*'—have been found there (§§ 42, 46). The Bhāgavata calls them the Arbuda-Mālavas and the Vishṇu locates them in Rajputana (*Marubhūmi*). They were thus decidedly in Rajputana from Mount Abu up to Jaipur. The territorial designation Māḷwār (माळ्वार) seems to me to be based on their name.[2] To their south, there was the Nāga territory, and with the Nāga coins their coinage bears affinity.[3] They were, like the Nāgas, followers of Nāga worship. Their capital was dedicated to Karkoṭa Nāga. Immediately north to them were the Yaudheyas, stretching from Bharatpur

[1] J.B.O.R.S., XVIII, 29 ff.

[2] *Mārwār* of our maps is pronounced in the Punjab as *Mālwār*. In Rājputana ḷ is pronounced as in the South. *Mālava=Māḷava+vāṭaka* will be the equivalent of *Māṛwār*. For *Vāṭa=wār*, 'division,' see Hira Lal, *Inscriptions in C.P.*, pp. 24, 87; E.I. VIII, 285; Both *Vāṭaka* and *Pāṭaka* occur with geographical names for 'division'.

[3] Rapson, I.C., sec. 51; V. Smith, C.I.M., 162.

[where their republican inscription of a time anterior to Samudra Gupta has been found at Bijaygarh] right up to the lower course of the Sutlej on the border of the Bhawalpur State where Johiyāwār still bears the stamp of their name. This was the biggest republican state also in the time of Rudradāman [c.150 A.D.]; the Yaudheyas were his neighbours, that is, reaching Lower Sindh. Between the Mālava and the Yaudheya States there was the small State of the Āryunāyanas whose exact location is not known but whose coins indicate that they were near Alwar and Agra. The Mādrakas were immediately to the north of the Yaudheyas extending up to the foot of the Himalayas. Madra-deśa was the plain country between Jhelum and Ravi [1], sometimes extending up to the Bias.[2] In the tract between the Bias and the Jumna lay the Vākāṭaka feudatories the Varmans of Siṁhapura and the Nāga king Nāgadatta. The other republican group of Samudra Gupta's inscription consists of the Ābhīras, Prārjunas, Sahasānīkas, Kākas and Kharparikas. None of these struck their coins before Samudra Gupta, and this for the simple reason that they had been under the Vākāṭaka governor of Western Malwā at Mandhātā (Māhishmatī) and under the Nāgas of Padmāvatī. Gaṇapati Nāga, in fact, is called the overlord of Dhārā [*Dhārādhîśa*]. We know now that the Sahasānīkas and the Kākas were nearabout Bhilsa. The modern Kākpur was their town which is within 20 miles from Bhilsa [3]; the Sāñchi hill was called the *Kākanāda*. In the time of Chandra Gupta II a Sahasānika Mahārāja, probably a republican chief of the Sahasānikas, built the Chandra Gupta Temple in the Udayagiri rocks. About the Ābhīras, we get great help from the Bhāgavata. The Bhāgavata calls the Ābhīras, '*Saurāshṭra*' and '*Āvantya*' rulers (*Saurāshṭra-Āvanty Ābhīrāḥ*), and the Vishṇu treats the Ābhīras as occupying the Surāshṭra and Avanti provinces. We know from the Vākāṭaka history that in Western Malwā there were the Pushyamitras and two other republics with their names ending in -Mitra. These were

[1] A.S.R., Vol. II, p. 14. [2] J.R.A.S., 1897, p. 30.
[3] J.B.O.R.S., XVIII, 213.

the Ābhīra republics and in their place in later Gupta history we find the Maitrakas rising as monarchs. This group beginning with the Ābhīras and ending with Kharparikas is almost in a straight line from Kathiawar and Gujarat to Damoh, below the Māḷava republic and above the Vākāṭaka kingdom. The Ābhīras in the time of the Periplus occupy Gujarat, and there is no justification in locating them in Bundelkhand as Dr. Vincent Smith did [J.R.A.S., 1897, p. 30]. He was led to do so on account of a mistaken notion that Kathiawar and Gujarat were at that time governed by the Western Satraps. Both the Purāṇas and Samudra Gupta's inscription leave no room for the Satraps in Kathiawar or Gujarat. The Western Satraps had been already dispossessed in the Nāga-Vākāṭaka period from Kathiawar. The Purāṇas here throw great light.

Purāṇic Evidence.

146. The Bhāgavata treats the Ābhīras of Surāshṭra and Avanti, the Śūras and the Mālavas of the Aravali as free republics. Their rulers are called *janâdhipāḥ*, 'national' or 'popular' [i.e. republican] 'rulers'. It does not mention the Mādrakas. It seems that the Mādrakas had already come within the Empire of Samudra Gupta as a sequence of the Āryāvarta Wars and were probably the first amongst the republics to own allegiance to the Gupta Emperor when their overlord was conquered. The Śūras of the Bhāgavata are the famous Yaudheyas. The word *Śūra* ('*hero*') is a translation of the word '*Yaudheya*', their popular title. Rudradāman, 200 years earlier, recorded that the Yaudheyas were popularly known amongst the Kshatriyas by their title '*the heroes*'.[1] The Yaudheyas, according to the Purāṇas, were good and ancient Kshatriyas. They formerly lived, like the Mālavas, in the Punjab. It is they and the Mālavas who had kept the Kushan power in check, both at its western end on the Sindh borders and the eastern end at Mathurā. They were popularly

[1] 'sarvakshatrâvishkṛita-*vīra* śabda-jātotseka-avidheyānāṁ' (E.I., VIII, 44): 'the Yaudheyas who were loath to submit, rendered proud as they were by having manifested their title of '*heroes*' among all Kshatriyas' (Kielhorn's translation).

known as '*Śūra*', '*Vīra*'. The Bhāgavata placing them next to the Ābhīras and before the Mālavas, puts them between the two, which indicates their position to the north of the Ābhīras and to the north-west of the Mālavas, i.e. the western portion of Rajputana. The Vishṇu reads:—'*Saurāshṭra-Avanti-Śūrān Arbuda-Marubhūmi-vishayāṁś cha vrātyā dvijā Ābhīra-Śūdra* [read *Śūra*]*-ādyāḥ bhokshyanti*'. Its reading *Śūdra* after *Avanti* has the variant reading *-śūra* which is confirmed by the Vishṇu Purāṇa itself in another place[1] and the *Hari-Vaṁśa*.[2] There was, however, a republic of the *Śaudrāyaṇas* whose name was derived from a proper-name *Śūdra*, not the caste-name but the personal name of the founder.[3] But the texts of the Bhāgavata and Vishṇu here evidently mean '*Śūras*' which stands for the *Yaudheyas*. The Bhāgavata and the Vishṇu do not mention at all the Prārjunas, Sahasānīkas, Kākas and Kharparikas. They had belonged to the Nāga group, being in Eastern Malwā.

146A. Then comes the Mlechchha State which is described by the Bhāgavata as the next state. This was the Kushan State. To the inscription of Samudra Gupta, the Purāṇa here acts as commentary:

Sindhos taṭam Chandrabhāgāṁ
Kauntīṁ, Kāśmīra-maṇḍalam
bhokshyanti śūdrāś ch ānty.ādyā (*or*, vrātyādyā)·
Mlechchhāś ch-âbrahmavarchasaḥ. [P.T., 55].

'*Over the banks of the Indus, and the Chandrabhāgā,* *Kauntī* (Cutch[4]) (and) *the principality of Kashmir, there will rule the Mlechchhas—the lowest of the Śūdras, who are opposed to Vedic holiness.*'

The Vishṇu reads: *Sindhutaṭa-Dārvīkorvî-Chandrabhāgā-Kāśmīra-vishayān* Vrātyā *Mlechchhā śūdrādyāḥ* [or, *Mlechchhādayaḥ śūdrāḥ*] *bhokshyanti*. The Vishṇu is anxious here to connect the Indus-Chandrabhāgā valley (the Sindh-Sāgar Doab)

[1] Wilson, V.P., Vol. II, p. 133: '*Śūra-Ābhīrāḥ*' *cf.* Harivaṁśa, 12, 837, *Śūra-Ābhīrāḥ*.

[2] See Hall's note in Wilson's Vishṇu, II, 133.

[3] See Jayaswal's *Hindu Polity*, I, p. 156.

[4] J.B.A.S., 1851, 234.

with the Dārvīkorvī (the Dārvīka valley), i.e. the Khyber Pass with its hinterland (§ 124), which shows that there was a correct appreciation of the natural frontiers of India. The Chandrabhāgā limit is confirmed by the use of the Gupta Era at Shorkoṭ in its 83rd year[1] when it is employed there without even the specification of the era, which shows that it must have been in vogue there for at least 25 years, i.e. since the reign of Samudra Gupta.

The Mlechchha rule described.

146B. The Mlechchhas are called here the lowest of the Śūdras. Here we should recall the *Mānava Code* and the other authorities which hold the Śakas in India to be Śūdras. Patañjali, *c.* 180 B.C., discussed the status of the Śakas and Yavanas who in his time had been politically turned out of India yet few of whom remained as subjects in India. The Mahā Bhārata also has discussed the status of such foreigners, Śakas and others, domiciled in India who had become Hinduised.[2] Early authorities are unanimous in giving the Śakas the status of the Śūdra who was not permitted to interdine with the twice-born Aryans. These ruling Śakas and political antagonists, on account of their political and social policy, have been lowered by the Bhāgavata as lower than the lowest Śūdras, to the position of pariahs (*antyajas*). The reason is given by the Bhāgavata itself. They not only disregarded the orthodox system ('the Vedic holiness') but they imposed a system of social tyranny. The country under them was encouraged or forced to follow their manners, ethics and religious theories: '*tannāthās te janapadās tach-chhīlâchāra-vādinaḥ.*' Politically they did persistently what the Śaka Satrap Rudradāman was made to swear not to do. He, on getting himself elected as king, took the oath that he would not exact taxes except those sanctioned by Hindu Law[3]. The

[1] E.I., XVI, 15.

[2] [I have discussed the Mahā Bhārata passage in my Baroda Lecture (1931).] *M Bh.*, *Sānti*, LXV; Manu, X, 44; Patañjali on P, II. 4. 10.

[3] E.I., VIII, pp. 33–43 [Junagarh insc., lines 9-10]: sarva-varṇairabhigamya rakshaṇārtha(ṁ) patitve vṛitena ā-praṇochchhvāsāt purushavadha-nivṛitti-kṛita-satyapratijñena antyatra saṁgrāmeshu. Then, line 12: yathāvat-prāptair-bali-śulka-bhāgaiḥ

Mlechchha kings, however, according to the description of the Bhāgavata and the Vishṇu, followed the general practice of their race—exacted illegal taxes (*prajās te bhakshayishyanti Mlechchhā rājnaya-rûpiṇaḥ*). They killed and massacred even women and children. They killed cows (which had become sacred by that time, as the Vākāṭaka and Gupta inscriptions prove). They killed Brahmins, they took away wives and wealth of others (*strī-bāla-go-dvijaghnāś cha, paradāradhanâhṛitāḥ*). They were never 'crowned', i.e., legal kings according to Hindu Law. They indulged in constant dynastic revolutions amongst themselves ["*hatvā chaiva parasparam*"; *uditoditavaṁśās tu uditâstamitās tathā*]—a condition already guessed by numismatists from their coins. There was thus a national cry, expressed by the Purāṇa text, practically inviting the Gupta emperors and the Hindus of the time to eradicate this lingering canker in the North-Western corner—an operation which Chandra Gupta II was compelled to perform and which he did perform successfully.

147. This description is the description of the 'Yauna' rule and not of the Yavanas, the Indo-Greeks.[1] The *Yauna* has been turned into *Yavana*. The Brahmāṇḍa, closing the dynasties and rulers contemporary with the Early Guptas, says in its second half of verse 199:

> '*tulyakālaṁ bhavishyanti sarve hyete mahîkshitaḥ*'

and adds by its next verse (200):

> '*alpaprasādā hyanṛitā mahā-krodhā hyadhārmikāḥ*
> *bhavishyantîha Yavanā dharmataḥ kāmato'rthataḥ.*'

'There will be the Yavanas in this country propelled by religious zeal, ambition and greed, who will be of short whims, untruthful, of great anger and unrighteous.'

With this opening verse there follows a description which is a summing-up of the Period. The Matsya, which closed with the end of the Sātavāhanas, also gives the same description, though condensed in three lines:

[1] Cf. '*The Yaunas of the Purāṇas*', J.B.O.R.S., XVIII, 201.

bhavishyantîha Yavanāḥ dharmataḥ kāmato 'rthataḥ
tair vimiśrā janapadā Āryā Mlechchhāś cha sarvaśaḥ
viparyayena vartante kshayam-eshyanti vai prajāḥ."[1]

[The Aryan population would become mixed with the Mlechchhas and the people would decay.] The **Bhāgavata** applies the same description to the Mlechchhas of Sindhu-Chandrabhāgā-Kauntî-Kāśmîra, and gives great details, as summarised above, up to the end of the chapter (Bk. XII, Chapter ii).[2] The Bhāgavata is followed by the Vishṇu in this scheme. It is thus evident that the *Yavana* of the other Purāṇas is the *Mlechchha* of the Vishṇu and the Bhāgavata. The *Yavana* here could not be the Indo-Greek *Yavana* who had passed away long before, both according to the Purāṇic treatment of chronology and dynastic details. These *Yavanas* here are the *Yaunas*, i.e. the *Yauvā* or *Yauvan* rulers who have been shown to be identical with the Kushans.[3] The Kushans bore the royal title *Yauv* or *Yauvā*, and the Kushans are placed in the Purāṇas as the Tukhāra-Muruṇḍas and Śakas. The Bhāgavata shortly after (XII, iii, 14) actually uses the form '*Yauna*'.

The Provinces of the Mlechchha State.

148. The Sindh-Afghanistan-Kashmir Mlechchhas had about four provinces, including Cutch. It is possible that some subordinate rulers under them were non-Mlechchhas, as the Bhāgavata says that the governors were predominatingly Mlechchhas (*Mlechchha-prāyāś cha bhūbhṛitaḥ*). Kauntî or Cutch was included in Sindh, as the Vishṇu does not mention it separately. Cutch-Sindh was under the Western Satraps whose coins we get for some 30 years after the Kushan submission, which we may date about 350 A.D.

[1] Ch. 272, 25-26.

[2] The next chapter is the description of the liberation of the country by Kalki from the Mlechchhas whom I had identified with Vishṇu Yaśodharman, the final destroyer of the Huns; but his description in the Mahā Bhārata and the Brahmāṇḍa agrees with the description of the Brahmin Emperor Pravarasena I the Vākāṭaka. [See also p. 46, *n.* above.]

[3] J.B.O.R.S., XVI, 287, XVII, 201.

Value of the Purāṇic information.

149. Thus we have here a trustworthy and accurate account of the Bhāraśiva-Nāga-Vākāṭaka Period and the Early Gupta Period in the Purāṇas. It is very full for the Vākāṭaka and the Samudra Gupta Periods. In fact, our literature nowhere else gives such detailed account for any other period of Hindu History before the *Rājataraṅgiṇī* takes up the history of the Karkoṭa Dynasty (7th century A.D.).

Further India.

Further India and her Recognition.

149 A. Further India was recognized as part of India in the Bhāraśiva-Vākāṭaka Period. In the Matsya Purāṇa for the first time we find that recognition.[1] Between the Himavat and the Sea, Bhāratavarsha stands, but it covers a larger area on account of Indians [*Bhāratī prajā*] living in eight more islands or sea-girt lands (dvīpas), 'which are mutually inaccessible on account of the sea intervening'. India is the ninth in that sea-girt system. This clearly means that the eight dvīpas or islands and peninsulas, inhabited by Indians, were in one direction from the Indian peninsula. The direction

[1] Matsya, ch. 113. 1–14 : [Cf. Vāyu Text, i. ch. 45, 69–86.]

यदिदं भारतं वर्षं यस्मिन् स्वायम्भुवादयः
चतुर्दशैव मनवः (1)
अथाहं वर्णयिष्यामि वर्षेऽस्मिन् भारते प्रजाः (5)
न खल्वन्यत्र मर्त्यानां भूमौ कर्म्मविधिः स्मृतः ।
उत्तरं यत्समुद्रस्य हिमवद्दक्षिणं च यत् ।
वर्षं यद्भारतं नाम यत्रेयं भारती प्रजा ॥ [Vāyu, 75].
भारतस्यास्य वर्षस्य नवभेदान्निबोधत ॥ (7)
समुद्रान्तरिता ज्ञेयास्ते त्वगम्याः परस्परम् [Vāyu, 78]
इन्द्रद्वीपः कसेरुश्च ताम्रपर्णी गभस्तिमान् ।
नागद्वीपस्तथा सौम्यो गन्धर्वस्त्वथ वारुणः ॥ (8)
अयं तु नवमस्तेषां द्वीपः सागरसंवृतः । (9)

Then follows the description of the ninth dvīpa or section of Bhārata varsha, which covers the whole of India, called here *Mānavadvīpa*.

is indicated by the situation of *Tāmra parṇî*, one of the eight Hindu dvīpas. All these dvīpas were to the east, that is, they constituted what we call to-day Further India. *Indradvīpa*, the first dvīpa in the list, has been satisfactorily identified with Burma.[1] The Malay Peninsula was well known to Indians at that time, a fact evidenced by an inscription of the fourth century A.D. inscribed on a pillar [in the present district of Wellesly] by a Hindu sea-captain (*Mahānāvika*) Budhagupta of Eastern India,[2] and it is very probable that the *Kaseru* or *Kaserumat* dvīpa which is mentioned next to Indra-dvīpa, meant the present Straits Settlements. The next class begins with Tāmraparṇî (the older name of Ceylon): Tāmraparṇa, Gabhastimān, Nāgadvīpa, Saumya, Gāndharva, and Vāruna dvīpas. Nāgadvīpa is Nicobar.[3] We know from Cambodian inscriptions that Cambodia (Indo-China) was held by the Nāgas who were superseded by the orthodox Hindu dynasty of Kauṇḍinya from India.[4] We may take 'Nāga' to be the ethnic designation of the pre-Hindu inhabitants of these colonies. Gabhastimān ['Island of the Sun'], Saumya, Gāndharva and Vāruna represent the Archipelago (Sumatra, Borneo, etc.), out of which Sumatra-Java had certainly settlements of Indians before the fourth century A.D. It is certain that the Purāṇas in the third and fourth centuries are conscious of the Hindu colonies in Further India, and treat them as parts of Bhāratavarsha.[5] Their Bhāratavarsha, which was primarily India, was at this point of time interpreted as India-cum-Greater India, which latter taking Ceylon, consisted of eight units or divisions, called *dvīpas*.

[1] S. N. Majumdar, J.B.O.R.S., 1922 (March), now reprinted in his edition of Cunningham's *Ancient Geography of India* (1924), p. 749. His identification of *Kaserumat* with the Malay Peninsula is reasonable. But the other proposals are hopeless.

[2] *Ibid.*, p. 752, citing Kern, *VG.*, III (1915), p. 255.

[3] Gerini, *Ptolemy's Geography*, pp. 379–383.

[4] *Champa* by Dr. R. C. Mazumdar, ii. 18, 23.

[5] The Vāyu shows a detailed knowledge of the Archipelago and gives in a new chapter [ch. 48] names current in Gupta times, e.g., *Aṅga* [Champā], *Malaya*, *Ya[v]a*, etc.

Samudra Gupta and Further India.

150. In line 23 in the group of Shāhānushāhi and others, i.e., the group of what we should call today the States '*under the sphere of influence*', we have '*Saiṁhalaka-ādibhiś cha sarva-dvīpa-vāsibhiḥ*', '*the king of Siṁhala and all the other islanders* (or, Oceanic rulers)', who made their submission and acknowledged Samudra Gupta as their Emperor. They paid no taxes but brought presents and expressly accepted his headship. Samudra Gupta describes this as *uniting the whole land* [Pṛithivī] *within his two arms.* His India or Pṛithivī, therefore, embraced within its bounds Further India. '*All the dvīpas*' here meant all the Indian colonies of Bhāratavarsha (§ 149 A), of the *Bhāratî prajā.* Dr. Vincent Smith thinks that the embassy of Meghavarṇa of Ceylon, come to obtain permission for erecting a monastery for the Simhalese pilgrims at Bodh-gayā, was alluded to by Samudra Gupta in his inscription as presenting tribute.[1] But the two matters seem to be quite independent. In the inscription the reference is not to the king of Ceylon only but also to the rulers of 'all the' dvīpas. That there were other Indian colonies at the time which had been in communication with the home-land is a well-known fact. We have in the third century a Sanskrit inscription in Champā [Cambodia] of a king belonging to the dynasty of Śrī Māra Kauṇḍinya[2], anticipating the favourite *Vasantatilakā* metre and the language and style of the Vākāṭaka and Gupta inscriptions. This inscription establishes that the connection of the colonies with the Bhāraśiva and Vākāṭaka India and with the revivalism of Sanskrit in the home-land had been fully maintained. All official inscriptions in India in the second century A.D., both in the South and in the North, had been in Prakrit.[3] Bhadravarman

[1] E.H.I., pp. 304-305.

[2] *Champā* by Dr. R. C. Mazumdar: Inscription No. 1. *Cf.* also J.R.A.S., 1912, 677, where Fan Ye (d. 445 A.D.) is cited as describing [Gupta] India from Kabul to Burma or Annam.

[3] With the single exception of the Junagarh inscription of Rudradāman who was particularly learned in Sanskrit and who tried to make himself an orthodox Hindu king, having come in by election.

['*Fan-Hou-ta*' of the Chinese] who defeated the Chinese forces [380–410 A.D.], was a contemporary of Chandra Gupta II. His father, a contemporary of Samudra Gupta, was fighting the Chinese Emperor at the time, and would have welcomed connection with the Indian Emperor. Bhadravarman's son, Gaṅgarāja, actually retired to India to pass his days on the Ganges and then went back to Champā and ruled.[1] The connection of the Hindu king of Funan with India since 245 A.D. is also a recorded fact. The impress of the time of Samudra Gupta on the Hindu Colonies is marked in such a degree that the Allahabad inscription is necessarily to be taken seriously—as seriously as it is taken with regard to its Indian matters. Samudra Gupta's reign coincides with a new social system on Hindu lines in Funan under Śrutavarman.[2] About the same time in the Hindu colony of Western Java we find inscriptions being written in Sanskrit in the script of 'the fourth or fifth century A.D.' And Sumatra gets so much of orthodox Hindu culture just before the arrival of Fa Hien that he found: '*various forms of error and Brahmanism flourishing while Buddhism in it is not worth speaking of*' (Fa Hien, p. 113). We have the evidence of Fa Hien that Tāmralipti, which, as we have seen, became a Guptan port by annexation in Samudra Gupta's time, was a brisk port for regular communication between India and Ceylon. To Tāmralipti the traveller had to go from Champā [Bhagalpur], which was a capital in his time—a fact fully corroborating the statement of the Purāṇas on the Gupta organisation of the Province of Champā-Tāmralipti. Fa Hien found a large merchant-ship sailing for Ceylon which he calls Siṁhala [just as in Samudra Gupta's inscription], and embarked for that island. The connection between Ceylon and India had been easy and constant enough to compel the Saiṁhalaka King to accept the imperial position of Samudra Gupta. Tāmralipti was also the chief

[1] *Champā*, pp 25–29.

[2] Coomaraswamy : *History of Indian and Indonesian Art*, p. 181 [see authorities cited therein]; Finot in *Indian Historical Quarterly*, 1925, Vol. I, p. 612.

port in Northern India for Further India. Its annexation to the Province of Champā was with a view to come in close touch with the colonies in Further India and to control the sea-trade.[1] There was here a well-considered and well-calculated policy. The inscription is not a vague record of accidental visits from Ceylon and other islands, but is a record of the results of a conscious imperial policy.

151. Evidence of Art further establishes a Guptan connection with Indian Colonies. Pieces of sculpture going back to the fourth century A.D. have been noticed as bearing the stamp of the Vākāṭaka-Gupta Art, and temples of the Gupta type have been found in Cambodia.[2] Similarly the introduction of the Gupta script and its adaptation in Burma, and the large finds of Gupta terracottas in Burma are to be noted.[3] The history of Art in subsequent centuries in Indonesia is so indissolubly knit with the Gupta art that it is to be regarded as bearing solid testimony to the introduction of Gupta influence beginning with Samudra Gupta's time. Samudra Gupta, if not politically, yet culturally, did cause the unity of Further India with the Motherland within his two arms[4].

151A. Samudra Gupta in every respect carried out the Hindu ideal of imperialism.[5] According to the Mahā-Bhārata, Siṁhala [Ceylon] and the Hindu Dvīpas or colonies were integral parts of the Indian Empire of the Hindu Samrāṭ.[6] According to that

Hindu Ideal.

1 Influx of gold was probably more from Further India, than from the South. F. India produced much gold.

2 Coomaraswamy: 157, 182, 183.

3 Coomaraswamy, *Ibid.*, p. 169. V. Smith, Early History, 4th ed., p. 297, *n.*, asserts the introduction of the Gupta Era in Burma. I learn from Mr. Umya, Superintendent, Archæological Survey, Burma, that no record in the Gupta Era has been found in Burma. But see Führer's APR., for June, 1894. On the adaptation of the Gupta script to Burmese phonetics in the Pyu inscriptions see the forms in E.I. XII. 127.

4 '*bāhu-vīryya-prasara-dharaṇi-bandhasya*'; *L.* 24, All. Insc., G.I., p. 8.

5 M.Bh., Sabhā, XIV, 9-12, XXXVII, 20.

6 *Ibid.*, XXXI, 73-74; [see also Southern Text, C. XXXIV].

ideal the whole of India including Afghanistan[1] must be comprised in that empire. But the empire must not go further west and be at the cost of the liberties of the countries beyond Afghanistan. The traditional international morality of Hindu India was noted by the Greek writers and the Arab Sulaiman.[2] The Law of Manu, which fixes the western boundary of India, was scrupulously observed by Samudra Gupta. The Sassanian king, who was troubled and weakened by the Roman emperor at the time, could have been invaded and probably easily conquered by Samudra Gupta, who in the art of war had no equal in his time. But Samudra Gupta had a law laid down to him by his dharmaśāstra—the code, '*the rule* (śāstra) *of civilisation*' (dharma). And that dharma was followed: that dharma limited a Hindu monarch's actions, both international and imperial. The history of Samudra Gupta's conquests shows that his actions were well-regulated by that law, and that he did not become a militarist.

[1] *Ibid.*, XXVII, 25, where the frontiers of Seistan peopled by 'the Parama Kambojas' and their allied tribes the 'Northern Ṛishikas' [the Ārśī people] are described. On Ṛishika and Ārśī, see *Bhāratabhūmi* by J. Vidyālaṅkāra, pp. 313-315; J.B.O.R.S., XVIII, 97.

[2] *Hindu Polity*, ii, 190-191.

PART IV

Southern India [150 A.D.—350 A.D.] and Unification of the North and the South

गायन्ति देवाः किल गीतकानि
धन्यास्तु ये भारतभूमि-भागे
स्वर्गापवर्गास्पदमार्गभूते
भवन्ति भूयः पुरुषाः सुरत्वात्' ॥

[—the INDIA-ANTHEM,
Vishṇu Purāṇa, II, 3. 24.]

सम्यक् प्रजापालनमात्राधिगतराज्यप्रयोजनस्य ।

'—[His majesty] to whom the *raison d'être of* acquiring kingship consisted in rendering good government to the people.'

[—*Inscriptions of the Gaṅga Dynasty of Southern India.*]

XV. THE SUBORDINATE MEMBERS OF THE ĀNDHRA [SĀTAVĀHANA] EMPIRE.

Purāṇic Scheme of Imperial Periods.

152. It will be convenient to have a retrospect of the Southern history to see its bearing on Northern India and the inter-connection between the South and the North before summing up the effects of the Gupta imperialism. The Purāṇas, from the time of the Āndhras onwards, give the subordinate ruling dynasties under the imperial power. They do so for three dynasties—the Andhras (=Sātavāhanas), the Vindhyakas (=Vākāṭakas) and the Guptas. It is noticeable that when the centre of imperialism shifts from Magadha, when it goes from the Kāṇvāyanas to the Sātavāhanas, the Purāṇas begin to describe the imperial dynasties with reference to their places of origin and not by their dynastic titles. The Sātavāhanas are described as *Āndhra*, i.e., arising from Andhra-deśa; similarly the Vākāṭakas are described as

Vindhyaka, arising from Vindhyadeśa. And when the Purāṇas revert to Magadha the G u p t a s are again described by their dynastic title. We shall now study the Āndhran imperial organisation as noted in the Purāṇas; the Vākāṭakan and the Guptan, we have already surveyed.

Feudatories of the Āndhras.

153. The Vāyu and the Brahmāṇḍa state that under the Āndhras there were established five contemporary families:

Vā.: *Andhrāṇāṁ saṁsthitāḥ pañcha teshāṁ vaṁśāḥ samāḥ punaḥ.*—Vāyu, 37, 352.[1]

Br.: *Andhrāṇāṁ saṁsthitāḥ pañcha teshām vaṁśyāḥ ye punaḥ.*—Br. 74, 71.[2]

On the other hand, the Matsya, the Bhāgavata and the Vishṇu do not give the number five, but describe three such dynasties. The Vāyu and the Brahmāṇḍa mention two dynasties by name, which they have in common with the Matsya and the Bhāgavata, viz., the Ā b h ī r a s and the S u b o r d i n a t e Ā n d h r a s, but they imply three, saying that under the term 'Andhras' they are giving years for two dynasties. The Vāyu and the Brahmāṇḍa in counting the five dynasties probably included in their list the M u ṇ ḍ ā n a n d a s and the M a h ā r a t h ī house (the family of Kalyāṇa Mahārathī of Mysore) who are known from their coins.[3] As these two dynasties ceased early, the other Purāṇas limit themselves to three. The Purāṇas give the years and successions of such dynasties which came down to the next Purāṇic epoch, that of the Vākāṭakas ('Vindhyakas'). The texts are:

Matsya—*Āndhrāṇāṁ saṁsthitā rājye teshāṁ bhṛityānvaye nṛipāḥ*
Saptaiv=Āndhrā bhavishyanti daś=*Ābhīras tathā nṛipāḥ.* (271, 17-18).[4]

Bh.—*Sapt=Ābhīr=Āndhrabhṛityāḥ.*

Vishṇu—*Andhrabhṛityāḥ sapt=Ābhīrāḥ*[5] (where the Vishṇu has misread the text quoted by the Bhāgavata,

1 Bibliotheca Indica Edition, Vol. II, page 453.
2 Bombay, Venkaṭeśvara Edition, p. 186.
3 Rapson, C.A.D., pp. 57, 60 (correction at p. 212).
4 J. Vidyāsāgara's ed., p. 1160.
5 J. Vidyāsāgara's ed., p. 584, Bk. IV, Ch. 24, Clause 13.

taking *Andhrabhṛityāḥ* as qualifying *sapt-Âbhīrāḥ*.)

It is thus evident that the Matsya and the Bhāgavata do not give the number of the dynasties ; they specify the Ābhīras and the 'Subordinate Āndhras' (to be distinguished from the Imperial Āndhras) as the subordinate dynasties under the Āndhras and established by the Āndhras. Mr. Pargiter has mixed up these two different sets of data as if all meaning one and the same thing, and prepared a new text which has become most confusing here. The Matsya gives one more dynasty by name, in addition to these two, the *Śrī-Pārvatîyas*, which is its independent and exclusive information. As the Matsya makes them contemporaneous with the Subordinate Āndhras, they also seem to have been established by the Sātavāhanas, but probably they were not so very important in the Āndhra times as the other two. We shall now take up the history of these three dynasties.

'Subordinate Āndhras' and Śrī-Pārvatīyas.

154. The Āndhras, corresponding to the Vishṇu's Andhrabhṛityas, i.e., the Subordinate Āndhras, who are the first to be taken up for discussion by the Matsya, the Vāyu, and the Brahmāṇḍa, completed seven successions. The Bhāgavata agrees in this except that it places the Ābhīras before the Āndhras, which is not of much consequence as these dynasties were contemporaries. The standpoint of the Bhāgavata is probably territorial, surveying from the north. The Matsya, the Vāyu and the Brahmāṇḍa give the durations. The Matsya manuscripts, by a majority, have the following reading on the two dynasties (1) the Āndhras (the Subordinate Āndhras) and (2) the Śrī-Pārvatîyas :—

Āndhrāḥ Śrīpārvatîyāś cha
te dve pañcha śataṁ samāḥ.[1]

'The Andhras and the Śrī-Pārvatīyas—the two—(have) 105 years.'

Against this, the Vāyu and the Brahmāṇḍa give their text :—

[1] Pargiter, P.T., p. 46, *n.* 32.

Andhrā bhokshyanti vasudhāṁ
śataṁ[1] *dve cha śataṁ cha vai.*

'The Andhras will rule the land, the two (dynasties) for one hundred [years] and one hundred [years] respectively.'

It is clear that under the term 'Andhras' the Vāyu and the Brahmāṇḍa include two dynasties—the Subordinate Āndhras who bore the imperial title and another, the Āndhra Śrī-Pārvatīyas. Their duration in each case is of 100 years, against the 105 years of the Matsya. Dr. Hall's copy[2] of the Brahmāṇḍa and the e- Vayu of Mr. Pargiter (which is really a Brahmāṇḍa MS.), give 100 years to the one and 100½ years to the other. Thus, in fact, all these three Purāṇas are describing three feudatory dynasties.

The expression 'the Āndhras will enjoy the land (*vasudhām*, the earth,) shows that these latter 'Āndhras' assumed imperial powers. We shall see presently that the Śrī-Pārvatīyas of the Andhra country did assume an imperial rôle, and that they were the first dynasty to do so in the South after the fall of the Sātavāhanas.

155. The Ābhīras, according to the Matsya, had ten successions and 67 years (*sapta-shashṭis tu varshāṇi daś Ābhīrās tathaiva cha; teshû tsanneshu Kālena tataḥ Kilakilā-nṛipāḥ*). The Vāyu and the Brahmāṇḍa too, give 10 successions to the Ābhīras, while the Bhāgavata gives them only 7, and the Bhāgavata does not give any duration. The Vishṇu follows the Bhāgavata.

Ābhīras.

156. To sum up: there were these three dynasties, two of which were established by the imperial Āndhras, and the other also arose at the same time and evidently under them, who, though not of much importance at the time, acquired importance on the fall of the Sātavāhanas.

Thus we have

I. The Subordinate (bhṛitya) Junior Andhras, 7 successions, 100 or 105 years.

[1] P.T., p. 46, *n.* 33; *śate* in some MSS. is changed to agree with *dve*, while *dve* refers not to the years but to the dynasties.

[2] Wilson and Hall, Vāyu, P., IV, 208. P.T., p. 46, *n.* 34.

II. The Ābhīras, 10 (or 7) successions, 67 years.
III. The Śrī-Pārvatīyas, 100 or 105 years.

IDENTIFICATION AND HISTORY OF THE SUBORDINATE ĀNDHRAS.

157. The Subordinate Āndhras are the well-known feudatory Sātavāhanas or Āndhras in whose line flourished the two Hāritīputras of the Chuṭu Dynasty, who have left their inscriptions at Kanheri (Aparānta), Kanara (Banavasi) and Mysore (Maḷavalli).[1] These inscriptions cannot be dated earlier than 200 A.D. on the evidence of their scripts.[2] Although the Banavasi record has an archaic script, the Maḷavalli inscription of the same reign has characters of 200 A.D. The latter record is in line with the Kodavali inscription of King Chaṁḍasāti—the last but one king of the Sātavāhana line (E.I., XVIII. 318), whose date, as given in the record, has been calculated by Mr. Krishna Śastri as corresponding to December, 210 A.D., which is very near the Purāṇic date for that king (228 A.D., J.B.O.R.S., 1930, 279). The genealogy of the two kings—Rājā Hāritīputra Vishṇu Skanda Chuṭukulānanda Śātakarṇi and of his daughter's son Hāritīputra Śiva Skanda-varman, 'lord of Vaijayantī,'[3] has been carefully reconstructed by Prof. Rapson on the basis of the three inscriptions of the family, together with one inscription of the first Kadamba king.[4] I cannot do better than adopt that reconstruction, having personally gone into the materials thoroughly. I, however, give a name-value to '*Viṇhu Kadda*' as Vishṇu Skanda:

[1] Rapson, C.A.D., LXXXI, XLIII, XLIX, LIII-LV, Kanheri: A.S.W.I., Vol. V, p. 86; Banavasi: I.A., XIV, 331. Maysore (Shimoga at Maḷavalli): E.C., VII, 251.

[2] Rice, *E. C.*, Vol. VII, plate facing p. 252; I.A., Vol. XIV, 1885, p. 331, plate facing p. 332. Dr. Bühler considered the Banavasi inscription to belong to the end of the first or the beginning of the second century, but Dr. Bhagwanlal Indraji considered it to be later. Prof. Rapson in C.A D., p. xxiii, would place King Hāritīputra scarcely before the beginning of the third century A.D.

[3] E.C., Vol. VII, p. 252.

[4] C.A.D., pp. liii to lv.

King Hāritīputra Vishṇu Skanda (*Viṇhu Kadda*)
Chuṭukulānanda Śātakarṇi = Mahābhoji° –
|
Mahārathī = Nāgamulanikā
|
Hāritīputra Śivaskanda varman
[*Vaijayantī-pati*].

158. There is no doubt that the dynastic name is *Chuṭu-*[*Kula*]. The term *Chuṭu* has not yet been explained. It is the same word as the Sanskrit *chuṇṭ*—'to become small'. It survives in the word '*Chuṭia* Nagpur' which means 'the minor' or 'smaller' Nagpur as compared with the bigger Nagpur in the Central Provinces. It is, very likely, a Dravidian word which was accepted by the Aryans. *Chhoṭū*=a 'younger member', is its modern Hindi equivalent which in Chuṭia Nagpur is still '*Chuṭu*,' meaning a younger brother. *Chuṭu* and *Chuṭu-kula* should be translated as 'the *Younger Branch*' i.e., the younger branch of the imperial Sātavāhanas.

'Chuṭu.'

159. According to the Purāṇas their family came to an end in the Vākāṭaka period, i.e., about 250 A.D., and that they had existed for 100 or 105 years. This will take them back to about 150 A.D. which was the most trialsome time for the Sātavāhanas owing to the rise of Rudradāman to power. Rudradāman's constitutional position has not been appreciated by Indian historians. His great strength lay in his legal status which no Śaka ruler, before or after, ever acquired in this country. His father had been fully thrown out. But he was elected king by the whole Hindu community of Kathiawar (Surāshṭra) and the neighbourhood [*sarva-varnair-abhigamya rakshanārtha* (*ṁ*) *patitve vritena*]. The Saurāshṭras who elected him king had been a republican community according to the Artha-śāstra.[1] On his election, Rudradāman took an oath by which he gave an engagement which he reiterates and proclaims in his inscription at Junagarh, promising to remain true to

Rudradāman and his effect on the Sātavāhanas.

[1] Bk. XI, [c. 125].

his *pratijñā*, i.e., to his coronation oath.[1] Rudradāman's oath and the whole tenor of his public declaration in his Junagarh inscription mean that he would behave up to his last breath like a true Hindu sovereign, and he illustrated it by saying that when his ministers opposed his decision to rebuild the Sudarśana lake on account of its heavy cost, he accepted their decision but rebuilt it from his private purse. We may take it that this elected king, behaving, as he did, like a Hindu of Hindus, must have become a very popular leader. He was learned in Sanskrit and the Śāstras, and adopted Sanskrit as his official language. He became a great menace to the Sātavāhana sovereign and he actually defeated that 'Lord of Dakshiṇāpatha' twice, but followed the Hindu law of restoring a *bhrashṭa-rāja*—a fallen enemy. His reign led to a new organisation in the Sātavāhana empire.

160. Under these conditions the Junior Dynasty—the Chuṭa Kula—along with a few other subordinate dynasties came into existence. To this period probably the 'Chuṭu-kulānanda' coins are to be assigned. The Junior Dynasty guarded the sea-coast on the west. Their capital was Vaijayantī in the Province of Vanavāsī (Kanara). We find their inscription at Kanheri in the North, and we find their coins in the South at Karwar on the sea-coast in the province of Vanavāsī. On the coins, read as of *Chuṭu-kuḍānanda* (No. G.P. 2),[2] although the letters look earlier than those of 150 A.D., the form of '*ku*' with a thickened head, and the treatment of anusvāra placed just on the top of 'na' and the form of 'sa' are later. It seems that archaic forms lingered on the coins, which amongst themselves show a period of hundred years as covered by them. It is to be noticed that the coins were not struck in the personal name of any member of the Chuṭu family but their official title—the Chuṭu Kula [*Raño Chuṭukuḍānaṁdasa* '(coin of) the Pleaser of the Chuṭu Dynasty']. And we find the same characteristics on the coins issued by the governor [of the Muṇḍa-

[1] 'satyapratijñena'; *pratijña* is a constitutional term denoting 'coronation oath'. See Jayaswal, *Hindu Polity*, ii, p 50.

[2] C.A.D., p. xxii, Plate VIII, G.P. 2, G.P. 3, 235.

rāshtra] *Muṇḍānanda*. Muṇḍarāshṭra was a province in Andhradeśa according to the Pallava inscriptions.[1]

Chuṭus and the caste of the *Sātavāhanas*—the Maḷavaḷḷi inscriptions.

161. These Chuṭu kings, the Subordinate Āndhras of the Purāṇas, being only a branch of the imperial dynasty, throw light on the caste of the Sātavāhanas. I have shown elsewhere[2] that the imperial Āndhras were Brahmins by caste. The description of the branch family confirms that view. Their gotra [stock] was 'Mānavya', essentially a Brahmin *gotra* and it was so recognised even after their time. In Mysore, Shimoga district, at Maḷavaḷḷi there was a Śiva shrine presided over by Maṭṭapaṭṭi-Deva to whom a Chuṭu king dedicated an estate and placed it as a Brahma-deya grant in the hands of a Brahmin called the Hāritīputra Koṇḍamāna of the Kauṇḍinya gotra. This gift is recorded on a six-sided pillar which was lying on the ground at Maḷavaḷḷi.[3] The name and description of the Chuṭu king are: *Vaijayantipura-rājā Mānavya-sagotto Hāritīputto Viṇhu Kadda-Chuṭu-kulānanda-Sātakaṇṇi*, who had issued his order to his Mahāvallabha Rajjuka. This gift was evidently resumed by a subsequent government. A Kadamba king subsequently renewed the grant—'with a very glad mind[4] (*parituttheṇa*)'—'for the second time' giving to a descendant of Koṇḍamāna, a maternal uncle of the king and a Kauśikīputra. The grant covered the old property and an addition of twelve new villages, all specified by name, and the gift was publicly registered on the same pillar. The gift by the previous donor is described in this as 'Śiva[Khada]vammaṇā Mānavya-sagotteṇa Hāritīputtena Vaijayanti-patinā puvva-dattitti'. Śiva Khada

[1] Coin No. 236 of the *Muṇḍananda* belongs to the same series. It was evidently connected with Muṇḍa-rashtra which occurs in the Pallava inscriptions [EI. VIII, 159]. [*Muṇḍā* in the Muṇḍārī language of Chuṭia Nagpur means a *rājā*.]

[2] J.B.O.R.S., XVI, 265-266.

[3] E.C., Vol. VII, Sk. 251-252, Nos. 263, 264.

[4] See correction by Fleet, J.R.A.S., 1905, p. 305, footnote 2. Dr. Fleet, however, has made a confusion in regarding Śiva Skandavarman as the name of the Kadamba king, while it is the name of the Chuṭu king, which has been made clear by Prof. Rapson, C.A.D., p. LIV.

v a m m a n here which is put in the instrumental (as opposed to the Kadamba king who is placed in the *prathamā*), is the former king who had made the gift (puvvadatta). He is described with the same titles as in the inscription of Vishṇu Skanda Śātakarṇi. It was a common practice in those days to add the word *Śiva* as a mere honorific before names. The king's name, according to his mother's inscription at Banavasi, was *Śiva-Khada-Nāga-Siri*, which at Kanheri, according to the same authority, is, *Khaṁda Nāga Sātaka*. The word *Śiva*, therefore, was only honorific. *Sāta* and *Sāti* stand for *Svāti* which the Purāṇas give with several names of the Andhras. *Svāti* means 'sword'. His mother was the daughter of Vishṇu-Skanda, spelt as *Viṇhu-Kada* (or, *Kada*) and *Viṇhu Kadda*, of the Chuṭu dynasty, who is also given the name *Sātakaṇṇi* in the Banavasi inscription. The former gift was actually made and recorded not by the Hāritīputra Śiva Skanda varman,[1] the lord of Vaijayantī, but by his grandfather Vishṇu Skanda (Viṇhu Kadda[2]) Sātakarṇi. And when the second inscription mentions that the Kadamba king having heard that a gift had been made by Śiva Skanda-varman, 'with a glad heart' makes the gift a second time, it means that a confusion was made between the names of the grandfather and grandson; instead of writing the grandfather's name the grandson's name was written by mistake.[3]

'Śiva' an honorific.

162. I have carefully studied the plate and I find it impossible to read *Kadambānāṁ rājā* before the word *Śiva* in line 4. I, however, find a reference to the prosperity of the Kadambas in the last line which shows that it is a Kadamba document and a Kadamba grant. The readable portion in line 4 which is the first line of the latter grant, is: *Siva-Kha[da] vamaṇā Mānavya-sa[go]ttena Hāritīputtena Vaijayaṅtī*

The Kadamba king at Maḷavaḷḷi—the Chuṭus succeeded by the Pallavas.

[1] The Kadamba king turns *Sāta* into *varman*, or adds it, which had become a style of royalty in his time, though it had not been so before.

[2] I read *Kadda*, not *Kaḍḍa*. Compare 'da' in line 2 with *da* in '*Maṭṭapaṭṭideva*', in '*nanda*' in line 1 and in '*deyya*' and in '*dinnaṁ*' in line 3.

[3] Or, that the gift had been last confirmed by Śiva Skanda, as in

paṭi[*na*] (end of the line). Before *Śiva* there were two letters (*rañā*), then a blank space. Before *Śiva*, Mr. Rice read *Siddham jayati Maṭṭapaṭṭidevo Vaijayantī-dhamma-Mahārāje patikaṭa-saujhāyichachchaparo Kadambānāṁ rājā*, out of which I can read traces of *jayati Mat.——Dha*[*m*]*mahā.jā* . . . . . . After this what Mr. Rice read as *dhirāje* is not traceable but in its place I read *ra*[*ś*]*ammā aṇpa.*[*ti*] . . . *ka* . . . . Mr. Rice's *pati kata*, etc., gives no meaning. His *dhi ra je pa ti ka ta* corresponds to my *'ra*[*śā*]*mmā aṇapa-ti*. I have no doubt that after *Dhammamahārājo* followed (*Mayū*)*raśammā āṇapa*(*ya*) *ti*. A better rubbing and facsimile would disclose the true forms of the six blurred letters after *pa* and the four letters after *ka* and before *rañā*. Mayūraśarmā was the first Kadamba king. He renewed the grant.

It is, however, not a necessary corollary that the Kadambas came immediately after the Chuṭus. The Chuṭus and the Kadambas were connected, the latter being an offshoot of the former (§ 200). Some hostile power must have intervened and that was the Pallava. No room for speculation is left in view of the Talagunda inscription wherein Mayūraśarman is recorded to have carved out his fief at the cost of the Pallava territories, and was recognized as a chief in view of his lineage, of the *Hāritīputra Mānavya*.[1] The Chuṭus thus were superseded by the Pallavas in the latter half of the third century, and the Pallava king who effected it was the king before Śiva Skanda-varman the Pallava, i.e., his father who performed an *aśvamedha*. (§ 183).

Kauṇḍinyas.

163. The Kauṇḍinyas who were on the scene as early as the second century A.D. were probably the same family who sent out a scion to Champā (Indo-China) to be the founder of the Kauṇḍinya kingdom there. They seem to have been imported from Northern India in the time of the imperial Sātavāhanas. The family was a very respected one. They are mentioned with respect in the two Maḷavaḷḷi inscriptions and were related to the royal family. We seem to

the case of the Pallava grant published in E.I., I, p. 2, where the Pallava emperor confirmed the gift made by his father (' bappa '

[1] E.I., VIII, 31-32 [insc. lines 2, 7].

have a historical corroboration here of the Champā tradition of the Kauṇḍinyas. Champā received her colony from Southern India led by the Kauṇḍinyas. Another Kauṇḍinya, in the reign of Samudra Gupta, goes to Champā and reforms the society there. He was very likely connected with this family. The Kauṇḍinyas must have been in touch with their Champā branch, which would have been certainly to their advantage. In the second, third, and fourth centuries they were thus social leaders in the South and the Colonies.

Identification and History of the Ābhīras.

164. The history of the Ābhīras is greatly explained by the Purāṇic data. Although the successions of the Ābhīras number 10 or 7, they have only 67 years to their credit. It is commonly supposed that the Ābhīras of the time of the Sātavāhanas founded a kingdom under Īśvarasena whose inscription we find at Nasik.[1] That inscription gives two important pieces of information: (*a*) that Īśvarasena who is described as king and in whose 9th year the record is dated, was not the son of a king, his father Śivadatta is described only as an Ābhīra commoner [*Śivadatt-Ābhīraputrasya*]; (*b*) the lady donor of the foundation who deposited funds with certain guilds for the pious purpose of providing medicines for sick monks of all denominations, describes herself as the mother of the *Gaṇapaka* Viśvavarman and as the wife of the *Gaṇapaka* Rebhila, which indicates that the relations had been presidents of a gaṇa republic. It seems that the Ābhīras, who rise under the imperial Sātavāhanas, had been a republic and that Īśvarasena was the first to assume monarchical title (*rājan*). He is believed to have ousted the Śaka-Satrap between the years 236 and 239 A.D. The Matsya (§ 155) marks the end of the Ābhīras expressly before the rise of Vindhyaśakti, i.e. about 248 A.D. It seems that with the rise of Īśvarasena the Purāṇas close the republican and subordinate period of the Ābhīras with him. Ten or seven successions in 67 years could

Ābhīras a republic.

[1] E.I., Vol. VIII, p. 88.

only mean republican successions, like the republican successions of the P u s h y a m i t r a s and the other °M i t r a s which the Purāṇas give and which are similarly of short durations. We do find the Ābhīras again as a republican community when Samudra Gupta comes on the scene. Īśvarasena probably went out of the Ābhīra constitution and tried to found a dynasty. In his own time the existence of G a ṇ a p a k a s is noted in the Nasik inscription. He could be even a republican 'rājan', though, more likely, he was a new monarch outside; it is, however, certain that about his time the Ābhīras as a political community ended their allegiance to the Sātavāhana house. The recognition of the Ābhīra republic by the Sātavāhanas about 67 years before Īśvarasena would be dated at about 160 A.D. They were evidently set up by the Sātavāhanas as a buffer against R u d r a d ā m a n who had been greatly harassed by the republican Y a u d h e y a s and the M ā l a v a s. The Sātavāhanas would have noticed some points of advantage in having a republic next-door to their foe, the Satrap.

Succession of the Ābhīras.

165. The confusion between the two data (10 and 7) in the Purāṇas for the successions of the Ābhīras is due to the next figure in the Purāṇas, viz., for the Gardabhilas which is 7. The Bhāgavata gives them 10 and to the Ābhīras, 7; while the other Purāṇas give the Ābhīras, 10 and to the Gardabhilas, 7. It is a case of mistake by transposition. The other Purāṇas being unanimous, the 10 successions for the Ābhīras are to be preferred.

166. In the time of the Kauṭilya, as noted above, there was the republic of the S a u r ā s h ṭ r a s in Kathiawar. The Ā b h ī r a s and the S a u r ā s h ṭ r a s seem to have been allied and akin to the Y ā d a v a s and the A n d h a k a-V ṛ i s h ṇ i s.

Identification and History of the Śrī-Pārvatīyas.

Śrī-Parvata.

167. The identity of the *Śrī-Parvata* has been recently established by Dr. Hirananda Śāstri from the newly discovered inscriptions at N ā g ā r j u n ī k o ṇ ḍ a, i.e. 'N ā g ā r j u n a's

Hill,' in the district of Guntur, on the Kṛishṇā. The inscriptions belong to the third century A.D. The hills which enclose a valley were fortified; there are remains of a brick fortification, the bricks of which are of the Mauryan type. The place was a strong military position and seems to have been a provincial capital since the Maurya times or earlier. The natural defences were strengthened artificially by brick and stone fortifications. The bricks measure 20″ × 10″ × 3″ which are the measurements of the bricks dug out at Bulandibagh.[1] It is evident that the place was a fortified capital of the empire of the Sātavāhanas, whose coins (forty-four in number) were found along with mason's tools in the remains of a monastery.

The Ikshvāku Dynasty of Śrī-Parvata, Andhra-deśa.

168. Here remains of Buddhist stūpas with carvings in the style of Amarāvatī have been exposed by Mr. Hamid Kuraishi and Mr. Longhurst. Eighteen inscriptions were found by Mr. Kuraishi, fifteen of which are incised on marble pillars which stood round the *Mahā-Chetiya* or the Great Stūpa enshrining a relic of the Buddha.[3] The inscriptions disclose the name of the place as *Śrī-Parvata*. We know the tradition that the famous Buddhist saint and scholar Nāgārjuna went to Śrī-Parvata and died there, which, curiously enough, is supported by the present name of the hill (*Nāgārjuni koṇḍa*). Yuan Chwang has recorded that Nāgārjuna was patronised by the Sātavāhana king.[4] The inscriptions are in Prakrit of the Pāli type. A number of stone structures with decorations and original buildings were erected by certain ladies under the direction of the monk-architect Reverend Ānanda. These ladies were relations of a royal house called 'the Ikshvāku [*Ikhāku*] Dynasty'. We have known this dynasty from three inscriptions discovered at Jaggayya-

[1] A.S.R., 1926-27, pp. 156 ff., 1927-28, p. 114; on epigraphy see A.S.R., 1926-27, pp. 185–189. [Since going to the Press I have received E.I., XX., i, where the inscriptions have been edited by Dr. Vogel.]

[2] A.S.R., 1927-28, p. 121.

[3] The relic itself has been now found. *Modern Review* (Calcutta), 1932, p. 88.

[4] Watters, II, 200, 207.

peṭa in the year 1882, and these inscriptions were assigned to the third century A.D. by Dr. Bühler.[1] The present inscriptions disclose the fact that several royal ladies were ardent Buddhists, while the kings were all orthodox Hindus, and their capital town (V i j a y a p u r ī) was in the valley close by.[2] Most of the inscriptions are dated in the reign of King S i r ī V ī r a-P u r i s a-d a t a, between his 6th and 18th regnal years, whose date at Jaggayyapeṭa is the year 20. One inscription is dated in the 11th regnal year of Mahārāja V ā s i ṭ h ī p u t a S i r i B ā h u-v a l a-C h ā t a m ū l a [or, Chātamūla II]. These inscriptions along with the Jaggayyapeṭa inscriptions give the following genealogy :

Chaṁtisiri=*Mahātalavara*[3] Kaṁdasiri, of the Pūkīyas | *Mahārāja* Vāsithīputa Ikhāku Siri Chātamūla [E.I. XX, 18] | Haṁmasiriṇikā

Aḍavi Chātisiri=*Mahātalavara*°[4]

Khaṁḍasāgaraṁnaka. | Daughter=Siri Virapurisadata= King Māḍharīputa | =Bhatidevā *Mahādevī* | Bapisiriṇikā, *Mahādevī* | Chhathisiri, *Mahādevī*

Kodabalisiri =Mahārāja of Vanavāsa | Mahārāja Siri Bāhuvala Chātamūla [II][5]

[1] I.A., XI, 256.

[2] A.S.R., 1927-28, 117.

[3] *Talavara* seems to be connected with what in the Law Reports figures as 'tarwāḍ', which is equivalent to an impartible rāj. Mahātalavara would mean a 'great rājā'—a big Jagirdār.

[4] Married to *Mahāḍaṇḍanāyaka* Khaṁḍa=Visākhaṁṇaka, of the Dhanakas.

[5] The names may be restored into Sanskrit thus:

Virapurisadata=Vīra Purushadatta ; Chāṁtisiri=Śanti Śrī ; Haṁmasiriṁṇikā=Harmya-Śrīkā ; Chhaṭhi=Shashṭhī (goddess Kātyāyanī); *Chāta=Śāta* [meaning,—'happy'].

Dr. Hirananda Sastri's reading 'Bāhuvala' is correct (see plate 11) where it is a clear four-cornered *b* ; *Ehu*° as read by Dr. Vogel is not borne out by the plate. In plate G the letter *b* is misformed, but the full form is in H where it occurs twice and in both cases it is clearly *b*.

Vira Purisadata married three cousins, two of whom are called *Mahādevī* in inscriptions of the same date [E.I. XX, pp. 19-20]. Bhaṭidevā was probably the eldest queen, being the mother of Chātamūla II. There were four more royal ladies who made donations but their relationship is not given. Their names are:

1. The *Mahādevī* Rudradhara-*Bhaṭṭārikā Ujanikā* ('from Ujjain'), daughter of a Mahārāja. She with Chānti Siri gave 107 pillars and a large amount of *dīnāras* for the Vihāra attached to the Mahā-Chetiya.
2. A *Mahātalavarī*, and the mother of the *Mahātalavara Mahāsenāpati* Viṇhuṣiri, and the wife of the *Mahāsenāpati Mahātalavara* Vāsiṭhīputa Mahā-Kuṁda Siri of the Prakiyas.
3. Chula Chātasirikā, *mahāsenapatnī*, wife of the *Mahāsenapati Mahātalavara* Vāsiṭhīputa Khaṁḍa-chalikireṁmaṇaka of the Hiramñakas.

There was a Mahārāja of Vanavāsa, to whom a royal lady of the Ikshvāku family [sister of Chātamūla II] was married. He was probably the last or one of the last Chuṭu kings, who from his title seems to have become subordinate to the Ikshvākus. It is clear that Chātamūla I was originally a *mahārāja*, i.e. to the Sātavāhanas; his title is generally omitted in the inscriptions, he being described merely as Siri Chātamūla of the Ikshvākus, and when the title is given [e.g. by his daughter, E.I. XX, 18 (B²)] it is always *mahārāja*, while Vīra Purisadata [except twice] is always '*King*' (*Rājan*). The son of the latter, Chātamūla II, is always '*Mahārāja*' (E.I. XX, 24). This shows that the royal position was assumed by Chātamūla I and lasted for only one generation more, having been lost in the time of Chātamūla II. That Rudradhara-Bhaṭṭārikā was the daughter of the Mahārāja of Ujjayinī proves that in the time of the Ikshvākus there was a Hindu ruler in Avanti, and not a Satrap, a fact confirmed by Purāṇic history and other sources. Rudradhara-Bhaṭṭārikā's father must have been a member of the Bhāra-Śiva Empire.

169. King Siri Chātamūla (I) had performed *Agnihotra, Agnishṭoma, Vājapeya* and *Aśvamedha*, and was a worshipper of Mahāsena, marshal of the gods. They had the Ikshvāku custom of marrying cousins. Their toleration of Buddhism is remarkable. Almost every lady of the royal family was a Buddhist but no king or any other male member has made a single donation in his own name, although they must have supplied funds to their ladies. The Ikshvākus followed the religious policy of the Sātavāhanas, their late sovereigns. Their reign was peaceful. According to one of the inscriptions of the time of Vīra Purushadata, visitors from Vaṅga, Vanavāsa, Chīna-Chilāta, Kaśmīra, Gāndhāra, etc. and Ceylonese monks frequented Nāgārjuna's Hill.

Mutual influence between the South and the North.

170. According to the script of the inscriptions of the family of Chānti Siri, she lived in the third century. Bühler placed Vīra Purisadata, who was nephew and son-in-law to Lady Chānti Siri, in the third century A.D.[1] The aśvamedha of King Chātamūla (I) seems to have been performed about 220 A.D., soon after the end of Chaṇḍasāti, the last of the Imperial Sātavāhana dynasty in Andhra.[2] The same sacrifices were performed a few decades later by the Pallava king Śiva Skandavarman (*Aggiṭhoma, Vājapeya, Aśvamedha*[3]), and with some Brahmanic additions and on a grander scale, by the Vākāṭaka Emperor Pravarasena I. The history of the North and the South here become interconnected.

171. The family was of a good Kshatriya stock from the

[1] I.A., XI, 258.

[2] His record of about 210 A.D. is found there [E.I., XVIII, 318]. With the next king, Pulomāvi (III), the Purāṇas close the dynasty J.B.O.R.S, XVI], who does not seem to have succeeded to the whole of his predecessor's kingdom.

[3] E.I., Vol. I, p. 5. The adjectives applied to Śiva Skandavarman's father are borrowed from the Ikshvāku style, denoting an immediate political succession:

(Ikshvāku) *hiraṇa-koṭi-go-satasahasa-hala-sata-sahasa dāyisu*.

(Pallava) *aneka-hiroga-koḍi-go-hala-satasahassa-ppadāyino*.

North. They married cousins like the ancient Ikshvākus. They very likely had migrated to the South in the imperial days of the Sātavāhanas when the latter reached the United Provinces and Bihar. King Chātamūla I was the first Śrī-Parvata Ikshvāku to declare his full sovereignty, probably towards the end of his reign; it is significant that his name has been mentioned in the inscriptions without a title, except in the inscription of Bhaṭidevā where he is given his feudatory title—'Mahārāja.' Vīrapurisadata alone had the title of King. Chātamūla II is only known in the inscriptions by the feudatory title of Mahārāja. He sought to revive the Southern Empire of Dakshiṇāpatha, and he inaugurated it with an *aśvamedha*. The Ikshvākus tried to be the Southern political counterpart of the Bhāraśivas of the North. Chāṭamūla (I) was evidently influenced by the example of the Bhāraśivas who had already carried out their programme with success in the North and in the Central Provinces up to the frontiers of Andhra. The intimate connection of the Ikshvākus with the North is confirmed by one of the Ikshvāku queens being an Ujjayinī lady.

172. We may take it that the Ikshvāku dynasty thought of empire-building after Chandra-Sāti Sātavāhana, about 220 A.D.[1] Taking the three generations, the family would have come to a close about 250–260 A.D., which would agree with the Purāṇas dating their fall with the rise of Vindhyaśakti. They had been brought into existence by the Sātavāhanas about the same time as the Chuṭus and the Ābhīras. The Chuṭus and the Ābhīras protected the West; similarly the Ikshvākus were posted in the East. Chātamūla II was probably the last king of the line. In the 10th year of a feudatory *Mahārāja* 'the lord father (*bappasvāmin*)' of Śiva Skandavarman Pallava, we find the Pallava government in possession of Andhradeśa,

[1] E.I., XVIII, 318. The inscription of *King Vāsiṭhiputa Sami* [*svāmin*] Chaṁḍasāti is dated in his 2nd year, in *ma* 1, *he* 2, *di* 1, which Mr. Krishna Sastri takes to be *Mārgaśīrsha bahuḷa prathamā* and calculates to correspond with December, 210 A.D. Cf. the Purāṇic date for that king (228 A.D.–231 A.D.) in J.B.O.R.S., XVI, 279. The above inscription is at Koḍavali, nine miles from Piṭhāpuram.

i.e. by about 270 A.D. (§§ 180, 187) the Ikshvākus have retired into the unknown. The time of these rules would thus approximately be :

Chātamūla I (220–230. A.D.)
Purisadata (230–250. A.D.)
Chātamūla II (250–260. A.D.)

Śrī-Parvata and Veṅgī School of Art.

§ 172 A. The A r t at Śrī-Parvata which sculptured in the round a Śaka as a door-keeper[1] is to be referred to the Sātavāhana period. Giving the honour of a door-keeper to the Śaka antagonist would fix its period, and so would do also the Sātavāhana coins found in one of the monastery remains. The freezes, and the sculptures in the round, are part and parcel of the Art of Amarāvatī which may be called the Veṅgī School of Indian Art. It goes back to pre-Christian centuries as evidenced by the Amarāvatī inscriptions (E.I., XV, 267). I think the superb animated carvings of Amarāvatī are works contemporary with the S ā t a v ā h a n a whose personal name was *Shi-yen-te-ka* or *Shan-t'e-ka* (Watters, ii 207), which seems to me to represent *Śāntakarṇa*, a name which occurs thrice in the Sātavāhana list. The tradition which Yuan Chwang heard that the king was a patron of Nāgārjuna may be apocryphal, unless Nāgārjuna flourished in B.C. The original stūpa was, according to Yuan Chwang, by A ś o k a. The Ikshvāku work was an imitation of the Sātavāhanas. Ś ā t a k a r ṇ i II alone was rich enough to decorate the Andhra tope of Aśoka; he had a very long reign (100–44 B.C., J.B.O.R.S., XVI, 278) to accomplish it, which agrees with Yuan Chwang's description of the long life of the king; and his son's reign is a recorded date at Amarāvatī (Lüders, no. 1248). The story that Nāgārjuna gave Śāntaka Sātavāhana gold out of rock to replenish his treasury depleted in building the stūpa, may have its basis in his discovering and recognising the gold ores of Mysore or Bālāghāṭ. Nāgārjuna had specialised in the knowledge of metals and chemistry among his other achievements in a long life.

[1] *Modern Review*, Calcutta, July, 1932, p. 88.

XVI. The Pallavas and Their Origin.

Position of the Pallavas in Indian History.

173. The Pallavas who superseded the Ikshvākus and the Chuṭus, the last remnants of the Sātavāhanas, have a most important position in Indian History. They are the Vākāṭakas and the Guptas of the South. They introduced Sanskrit in the South as the Vākāṭakas did it in the North. They established Śaivaism as the State religion in the South as the Vākāṭakas did the same in the North. Just as the Guptas gave a permanent stamp of Vaishṇavism on Northern India which has come down to our own time, so the Pallavas imprinted Śaivaism on Southern India which has come down to us. As the Vākāṭakas and the Guptas unified Northern India, so the Pallavas established the unity of the South which came down to the last days of Vijayanagara. The Pallavas beautified the South with sculpture and architecture, just as the Vākāṭakas and the Guptas did the North. The Pallavas introduced a system of Hinduism in the South which was common to the North and the South. That system became truly the imperial and universal social system for the whole of Bhāratavarsha, i.e. India-with-Further India. A unity which Aśoka had failed to achieve was accomplished in the India of the Vākāṭakas and the Pallavas. And that unity of civilization is a legacy enjoyed to-day. They turned Kāñchī the old capital of the Cholas, which had been outside the limit of Aryan sanctity, into another sacred Kāśī, and under them the South became as sacred a Hindu-land as the North. '*Bhāratavarsha*,' which in the time of Khāravela was probably confined to the North only,[1] was given a new definition to include the land up to Cape Comorin. '*Āryāvarta*' and '*Dakshiṇāpatha*' gave way to '*Bhāratavarsha*.'[2] And the Hindu historian in the Vishṇu Purāṇa composed a national anthem, saying,

> *Even the Gods congratulate and envy the born-Indian ; 'the Indian, born in Bhāratavarsha, is blessed', sing the Devas in heaven. 'Let us be born in that land.'*[3]

[1] E.I., XX, p. 72, Line 10.

[2] Vishṇu Purāṇa, Bk. II, Ch. 3, 1–23.

[3] *Ibid.*, 24–26 ; *See* above p. 160.

The point of view becomes Indian from that of Aryan, and the Indian [*Bhāratī santatiḥ*] includes all the children of the soil, Aryan and non-Aryan.[1]

The Pallavas arise as feudatories to the Nāgas.

174. The Pallavas who turned the South into a sacred Hindu-land were Brahmins, who, as they proudly say in their inscriptions, raised their position by their austere political deeds and became Kshatriyas. The statement is strictly true. Vīrakūrcha, the founder of the Pallava Dynasty, was invested with the insignia of full sovereignty by his marriage with the Nāga Princess, daughter of the Nāga emperor.[2] The Nāga emperor at the time, in the latter half of the third century, was the Bhāraśiva Nāga whose dominions extended through Nagpur and Bastar up to the confines of the Andhra country. Vīrakūrcha [*or*, °-korcha], an inscription of whose grandson found in Andhradeśa mentioning him as beginning the line gives him the feudatory title of '*Mahārāja*' and the description of one who though endowed with the highest Brāhmaṇa-hood (*parama-brahmaṇya*) attained the position of a Kshatriya[3], was thus a member of the Bhāraśiva empire with the position of a sub-king. In the Andhra country itself there had been no Nāga dynasty before. There were the Ikshvākus[4] and before the Ikshvākus there were the Sātavāhanas. The Nāgas who installed Vīrakūrcha Pallava must have enjoyed an imperial

[1] *Ibid.*, verse 17.

[2] यः फणीन्द्रसुतया सहाग्रहीद्राजचिह्नमखिलं यशोधनः । S.I.I., ii., 508.

[3] परमब्रह्मण्यस्य स्वबाहुबलार्ज्जितक्षात्रतपोनिधेर्विधिविहित-सर्व्वमर्य्यादस्य, E.I., i., 398 [Darśi copperplates]. Here the Mahārāja is called *Vīrakorcha-varman*. This is the oldest record mentioning his name.

[4] There was a family of the Bṛihat-phalāyanas (E.I., VI, 315) in the Kṛishṇā District who were probably feudatories to the Ikshvākus or to the early Pallavas. We do not find any trace of the family of Jayavarman Bṛihat-phalāyana before or after him. The letters of his copperplates agree with the letters on the plate of Śiva Skanda-varman, the Pallava Yuvarāja (E.I., VI, 84). Does *Bṛihat-Phala* stand for the *Bṛihat-Bāṇa*, the well-known Southern family, *phala* being the arrowhead (*bāṇa*)? The Bṛihat-Bāṇas were feudatories to the Pallavas in the time of Mayūraśarman (E.I., VIII, 32). Probably both *bāṇa* and *phala* were translations of some Tamil word.

position and must have been on the borders of the Andhra kingdom. These conditions are fulfilled only by the imperial Bhāraśiva Nāgas.

Andhra in the Nāga Empire, c. 310 A.D.

175. We get help and corroboration here from the Buddhist history. In 310 A.D., according to Siamese Buddhist history, Andhradeśa was under Nāga kings, from whom permission was taken to transfer a portion of the tooth relic to Ceylon from Dantapura in Andhradeśa.[1] The place in Andhradeśa is called *Majerika*, which I think is the name of the branch of the Godavari now called *Manjhira*.[2] The 'Nāga' king described by the Buddhists must be the Pallava king who was under the Nāga empire and was at the time (c. 300 A.D.) a descendant of the Nāga Emperor, having sprung from the Nāga princess married by Vīrakūrcha (§ 182 ff.).

Who were the Pallavas?

176. *Who were these Pallavas?* This question has been sought to be answered by various scholars since the discovery of this dynasty from their copperplates. 'Pallava' has remained a mystic, undeciphered figure. It was fashionable to regard every unexplained dynasty as being of foreign origin, and in that vogue the Pallavas became Parthians. But the conscience of the historians was not satisfied and almost instinctively they came to the conclusion that the Pallavas were natives of the country. But they regarded them as Dravidian or connected with the Dravidians of Ceylon. All these theories have ignored written records and materials which leave no room for any controversy. The Pallavas have suffered at the hands of historians a fate similar to that of the Śuṅgas. They have been deprived of their true status which is one of good, pedigreed Brahmins. The Śuṅgas had been declared to be foreigners, until the present writer was instrumental in showing that the Śuṅgas were Vedic Brahmins and the founders of a Brahmin empire, a finding which has now been universally accepted. The key of their origin was

[1] Cunningham, *Ancient Geography of India* (ed. 1924), p. 612.

[2] *Ibid.*, p. 605. Cunningham thinks that the stūpa from which the relic was removed was the same as the Amarāvatī one.

found in the orthodox literature of the country. We should employ the same method again with regard to the Pallava ethnology. The code to decipher the Pallava mystery is locked in the Purāṇas, in their Vindhyaka history. The code is this: A branch of the Imperial Vindhyakas, i.e. the Imperial Vākāṭakas, became kings of Andhradeśa which had become connected with the Vākāṭaka province of Mekalā. This Mekalā I have identified as a province of 'Sapta-Kosalā,' below the Maikal range of our maps, i.e. the British district of Raipur and the Indian State of Bastar. These Vākāṭaka sub-kings of Andhradeśa ruled in seven successions from the time of Vindhyaśakti the founder of the Vākāṭaka power, down to the time of Samudra Gupta's conquest. We have thus one index here for identification. Another index is the caste and *gotra* of the Vākāṭakas. We know from their inscriptions that the Vākāṭakas were Brahmins and that they were Bhāradvājás. The third fact is that they belonged to Āryāvarta and their language was Northern, not Dravidian. The fourth fact that we have consists in the date of Vindhyaśakti and his dynasty. And the fifth fact that we have is that when Vindhyaśakti arose, the Nāga emperors were ruling over Āryāvarta and the Central Provinces, and that Vindhyaśakti himself came to the forefront on account of them and out of them, the Kilakilā Nāgas—*tataḥ Kilakilebhyaś cha Vindhyaśaktir bhavishyati*. The sovereigns and emperors of Vindhyaśakti were the Kilakilā Nāgas, i.e. the Bhāraśiva Nāgas (§ 11 ff.). Now let us see where we can find all these five marks of identification of these Āndhra sub-kings of the Vindhyakas, in the Pallavas. The kings of the Andhra country up to *c.* 250 A.D. were certainly the Ikshvākus on the east-coast, contemporary with whom were the Chuṭu Sātavāhanas on the west-coast. The time of Vindhyaśakti is from 248 to 288 [or, 244] A.D. In this period, we find the Pallavas superseding the Ikshvākus and the Chuṭus. The Pallavas according to their own deeds and documents, executed on copperplates about 300 A.D. or a little earlier,[1] describe themselves as

[1] Cf. Krishna Śāstri, '*the Prākṛit charters of Śiva-Skandavarman and Vijaya-Skandavarman do actually belong at least to the beginning of*

Bhāradvājas, the identity of whose gotra is made further clear by the later documents of the dynasty. They were the Bhāradvājas of the family of Droṇâchārya and Aśvatthāman. They, therefore, belonged to the same Brahmin gotra to which Vindhyaśakti belonged. Their language in their copperplates is Prakrit or Sanskrit, not Dravidian. The variety of Prakrit they use in their earliest copperplates is northern. Very soon in the third generation, immediately on the close of the Nāga empire, they begin to employ Sanskrit, the style of which is Vākāṭaka. Like the imperial Vākāṭakas they are Śaiva by religion. As we have already seen, it is stated in the documents of the Pallava dynasty that the founder of the Pallava dynasty was made king by the Nāga emperor on the former's marriage with a Nāga princess. The Purāṇas give to these descendants of Vindhyaśakti, the kings of Andhradeśa up to the time of Samudra Gupta, seven successions, and the early Pallavas up to Samudra Gupta's time do number seven successions [§ 183]. Thus all the marks of identification respond to the Vākāṭaka indices. Their gotra is identical, their language and religion, their age and date, their Nāga allegiance all agree entirely. And so does the number of successions of the Pallavas up to the time of Samudra Gupta with the number of successions given by the Purāṇas to the Āndhra branch of the Vindhyaka dynasty. No room for doubt is thus left on the question of identification. The Pallavas were a branch of the Vākāṭakas. And when their inscriptions say that they were in the line of Droṇa and Aśvatthāman, they record a truthful tradition. The Vākāṭakas did belong to the line of Droṇa and Aśvatthāman, being Bhāradvājas. And I have personally found the tradition still alive at Bāgāṭ, the original home of the Vākāṭakas in Bundelkhand, that their home (Bāgāṭ) is still called the village of Droṇâchārya, the military professor of the Kauravas and the Pāṇḍavas [§§ 56-57]. The northern culture of the Pallavas in art

the 4th century A.D., *if not earlier*' [E.I., XV, 248]—a view with which I fully agree. The writing which is of the Nāga type was introduced in the South for the first time by the Pallavas; the tops of letters are headed (lined), though not box-headed.

and religion, for which they stand out as the greatest dynasty of the South, thus stands explained. The Pallavas were neither foreigners nor Dravidians, but good Brahmin aristocrats from the North, military by profession.

'Pallava.'

177. We have in the example of the 'Gaṅga Dynasty' a purely assumed dynastic title, unconnected with the gotra or personal name of the founder. Similarly the word *Pallava*, which means a '*branch*,' probably stands for the 'Junior Dynasty,' like the 'Chuṭus' of the imperial Sātavāhanas, whom they superseded. As the Chuṭus were to the imperial family of the Sātavāhanas, so the Pallavas were to the Imperial Bhāradvāja Vākāṭakas:—'branch' i.e. the Lesser Dynasty. The first Pallava king bears the name *Vīrakūrcha*; *kūrcha* means a bundle of twigs—almost the same as *Pallava*. The real name seems to be Vīra which is repeated in the name of his grandson *Vîravarman* (§ 181 ff.). The name of the other son of Vindhyaśakti was Pravīra, who was probably the younger, as he had a very long reign. As Pravīra married his son to the daughter of the Nāga Emperor and thereby succeeded to the Nāga empire, similarly Vīra had married a Nāga princess and was made king of Andhradeśa [which his father as a Nāga general had probably conquered]. The Pallava inscription correctly relates that the ancestors of Vīrakūrcha used to assist the Nāga emperors in their government, that is, they were Nāga officers; we have already seen that Vindhyaśakti was at first only an officer, probably the chief general of the Nāga emperors (§ 59). The use of the word *Bhāra* in the inscription in connection with the burden of government of the Nāga king may or may not have an echo of the *Bhāra* of the '*Bhāra* Śiva Nāga.'[1]

Pallava insignia.

178. The Pallavas naturally adopted the imperial Vākāṭaka heraldic marks, which is evident from their seal [S.I.I., ii, 521] and the subsequent history of Imperial Insignia in Southern India

[1] भू-भार-खेदालस-पन्नगेन्द्र-साहाय्य-निष्णात-भुजाग्रजानाम् ।—Velurpalaiyam Plates, verse 4, S.I.I., II, 507-508. [*Cf.* App. A, below on the place-name *Bhū-bhārā*.]

(§§ 61 and *ns.*; § 86). The Pallavas have on their seal G a ṅ g ā and Y a m u n ā, which are known Vākāṭaka insignia. They have probably also *Makara*-Standard or 'Makara-Toraṇa' in common.[1] They have the Bull of Śiva in common, facing left (proper right).[2]

'Dharma-Mahā-rājādhirāja.'

179. The Pallavas and the Vākāṭakas never come in conflict. The Early Pallavas never strike their own coin. Śiva S k a n d a-v a r m a n, the second king, introduced a new regal title. He called himself '*Dharma-Mahārājādhirāja*,' i.e. '*the rightful overlord of Mahārājas* [Emperor]' or '*the Emperor by virtue of Dharma*'. This title had not been used by the Sātavāhanas. It was an importation from the North, it was a Hindu edition or rather a Hindu counter-title of the Kushan '*Daivaputra Shāhānushāhi*. Instead of being a *Daivaputra*, the Pallava king places his claim on his adherence to the orthodox law and the orthodox civilization, which was quite in conformity with the law of Hindu constitution. He was substituting *Dharma* for the divine *Daivaputra*. It should be noted that the Ikshvākus never used this title and they were simply *Rājans* or 'kings' like their late masters the Sātavāhanas, following the old Hindu style.[3] Thus we have a full effect of the northern imperial idea in the Pallava beginnings. When the Ā r y ā v a r t a B r a n c h of V i n d h y a ś a k t i attains the imperial position just after or in the life-time of Śiva Skandavarman (I), the same idea of D h a r m a S o v e r e i g n t y on a bigger scale is found. The All-India SAMRĀṬ had a Dharma *raison d'être* as fully set out in the Mahā-Bhārata.

[1] See the open mouth of the animal in the Pallava seal in E.I., VII, 144 and on Rudrasena's coin (§§ 61, 86).

[2] See the seal in E.I., VIII, 144, and the bull on the Vākāṭaka coins reproduced in Part II of this book. The bull is made recumbent in the later Pallava documents.

[3] In one of the Ikshvāku inscriptions (E.I., XX, 23) all the three kings are called 'mahārāja'. This is one of the last records. Probably at that time the independent position had been lost. They had been originally *mahārājas*. The first Ikshvāku to adopt the title of king (rājan) was Vīra Purushadatta. His son was only *Mahārāja*.

When the main Vākāṭaka branch acquired the title of the *Samrāṭ*, the title of *Mahārājādhirāja* was naturally dropped by the Pallava family. Śiva-Skandavarman was the first and the last man in our period to have assumed the imperial style in the South.[1] That Śiva-Skandavarman was already gone before Samudra Gupta's time is evident from Samudra Gupta's inscription where the ruler of Kāñchī is Vishṇugopa. The time of Śiva-Skandavarman thus necessarily falls in the reign of the Samrāṭ Pravarasena I. From the time of Pravarasena I the Pallava king remains *Dharma-Mahārāja*, and the title allowed to the first Gaṅga king who was installed in the time of Pravarasena, was *Dharma-Adhirāja* (§ 190). The style of *Dharma-Mahārāja* becomes fixed with the Pallavas and the Kadambas in the South, and it travelled from the South before 400 A.D. to Champā (Cambodia)[2].

180. Śiva-Skandavarman, as the Crown Prince, rather as 'the junior governor' (*Yuvamahārāja Bhāradāya-sagotto Pallavānaṁ Śiva-Skaṁda-vammo*—E.I., VI., 86) issued a charter of land-grant in the Andhrā-patha from his seat at Kāñchîpura addressed to the officer at Dhānyakaṭaka, in the 10th year (of his father's reign). It shows that the Pallava dominion in the second generation had grown, at the cost of the Tamil states, to a magnitude justifying the ambition of Śiva-Skandavarman. The Dharma-mahārājādhirāj Śiva-Skandavarman describes his father[3] as *Mahārāja* Bappa-svāmin (sāmi), which shows that his father started life as a feudatory and that Śiva-Skandavarman was the first dynast to adopt the full royal title. His father had reigned for 10 years or more, the grant of the Yuvamahārāja Śiva-Skandavarman being dated in the 10th year. It seems that his father was a feudatory of the Nāgas, and succeeded to the settled and well-organized government of the Ikshvākus which is evident

[1] See Southern List of Kielhorn (E.I., Vol. VII, p. 105).

[2] There we find Bhadravarman using it. Dr. R. C. Mazumdar's '*Champā*,' Bk. III, 3.

[3] E.I., I, 6. 'Bappa' distributed *krores* of gold which should really refer to an *aśvamedha*. [*Cf.* here the description of Chātamūla I (E.I., XX, 16)]. E.I., I, 8. His son describes himself as 'of the dynasty of the *Pallavas*'. E.I., VI, 82.

from these two Prakrit copperplates of his son and the Ikshvāku records.

181. Vīravarman and his son Skandavarman II were also contemporaries of Pravarasena I. In Skandavarman II's time the official language of the Pallava Court changes from Prākrit to Sanskrit. His daughter-in-law who dates her gift in his reign (E.I., VII, 143) uses Prākrit, but Skandavarman himself (E.I., XV) and his son Vishṇugopa employ Sanskrit. And the Sanskrit style is continued by the successive generations. If the Yuvamahārāja V i s h ṇ u g o p a of Kāñchī (I.A., V, 50, 154) be the Vishṇugopa of Samudra Gupta, which seems to be certain, we have another proof of the Vākāṭaka affinity in this change of the official language of the charters. Vishṇugopa imitates the Bhāraśiva description of the Vākāṭaka documents :

Yathāvadāhṛita-aneka-
Aśvamedhānāṁ Pallavānāṁ.[1]

'*The Pallavas who had completed with full ceremonies several aśvamedhas.*'

This employment of Sanskrit dates from before Samudra Gupta's conquest.

Genealogy of the Early Pallavas.

§ 182. The genealogy of the Early Pallavas can be reconstructed from their own documents on copperplates which are copious.[2] For almost every second generation we have a copperplate. They have the system of reciting pedigree up to the fourth generation in each case. The only exception to this rule are the charters of Śiva-Skandavarman, as he had not completed four generations of kings. I note below the grants and the authorities issuing them in their chronological order.

Mayidavōlu, issued from Kāñchīpura by E.I., Vol. VI, 84, in Prākṛita.	*Yuvamahārāja* (Śiva) Skandavarman (I) in the 10th year (of his father).

[1] The Vākāṭaka historiographical style found in the inscriptions of Pṛithivīsheṇa and his successors is a stereotyped style and as such evidently goes back to the time of the Imperial Vākāṭakas.

[2] It is curious that not a single inscription on stone has been found of the Early Pallavas.

Hīrahaḍagalli, E.I., I, 2, in Prākṛita.	issued from	Kāñchīpura	by *Dharma-mahārājādhirāja* (Śiva) Skandavarman (I), in his 8th year.
Darśi, E.I., I, 307, in Sanskrit.	,,	,, 'Dasanapura, the capital' (*adhishṭhāna*)	by the great-grandson of *Mahārāja* Vīrakorchavarman.
Ōṁgōḍu, E.I., XV, 251, in Sanskrit.	,,	,, Tāmbrāpa	,, *Mahārāja* (Vijaya) Skandavarman (II) in his 33rd year.

On the basis of the genealogies given in the above title-deeds executed by these kings, the ancestry and the order of succession of the early Pallavas can be ascertained easily. We are absolutely certain that the great-grandfather of Skandavarman II and the father of Skandavarman I or *Śiva* Skandavarman was Kumāra Vishṇu the *aśvamedha-yājin*, and that Skandavarman I's son and successor was Vīravarman whose son and successor was Skandavarman II. The only question left for speculation is the position of Vīrakorcha who must come above Skandavarman I, being the founder of the dynasty. The Rāyakōṭa (E.I., V, 49) and the Velurpalaiyam (S.I.I., II, 507) plates here become helpful. Vīrakorcha or Vīrakurcha, who according to the unanimous testimony was the first Pallava king, was married to the Nāga princess according to the inscriptions, and Skanda-sishya, i.e. Skandavarman was the son of the Nāga lady according to the Rāyakōṭa plates.[1] We have

[1] In some text-books it is wrongly assumed that Skanda-śishya in the Rāyakōṭa plates is stated to be the son of Aśvatthāman from a Nāga lady. The text does not allege it. It only mentions that Skanda-śishya who was an *adhirāja* was the son of a Nāga lady. Aśvatthāman is only mentioned as one of the ancestors.

In the Velurpalaiyam plates the Skanda-śishya who is the father of Kumāra Vishṇu and the grandfather of Buddhavarman is clearly Skandavarman II, whose son, as we know from the inscription of Kumāra Vishṇu III [E.I., VIII, 233], was Kumāra Vishṇu II. In the Velurpalaiyam plates it is not stated, as has been wrongly assumed by the editor of the plates and writers of some text-books, that he (Skandaśishya) was

thus to identify Kumāra Vishṇu with Vīrakorcha-varman of the Darśi plate, who would thus be the great-grandfather of Skandavarman II. Sanskrit is found for the first time employed by the latter in the grants; the Darśi plate which is in Sanskrit seems to have been issued by him. Use of two alternative names in documents we know of from the later Vākāṭaka plates of Prabhāvatī Guptā and Pravarasena II, and earlier from the inscriptions of Aśoka. The repetition of the name Vīra as the name of the son of Skanda-varman I also proves the identity of Vīrakurcha with Kumāra-Vishṇu I, father of Skanda-varman I., grandfather's name being repeated in grandson's. The early genealogy thus will stand as follows:—

1. [Vīrakorcha-varman] Kumāra Vishṇu (ruled 10 years or more).
2. Skandavarman I, called *Śiva* (ruled for 8 years or more).
3. Vīravarman—(no record of his).
4. Skandavarman II, *Vijaya* (ruled for 33 years or more).

Skandavarman I does not give the name of his father, but refers to him only as *bappa* which stands for 'father,' as later kings refer to theirs by the same term *bappa-bhaṭṭāraka-pāda-bhaktaḥ* (E.I., XV, 254; I.A., V, 51, 155). The name is supplied by Skandavarman II's grant (E.I., XV, 251). *Vīrakūrcha*, in numerous later documents of the family, is mentioned as the real founder of the dynasty (occasionally coming after two ancestors *Kāla-bhartṛi* and *Chūta-pallava*[1], who are

the son of Vīrakorcha. In verse 7 Skanda-śishya is clearly stated to have flourished '*after*' [tataḥ] Vīrakorcha and in his line. The statement implies a break between the two [cf. *tataḥ* in I.A., XIX, 24(10), and Kielhorn's opinion thereon in E.I., V, App. No. 195, n.; E.I., III, 48]. These mistakes, and especially the latter, have led to a great confusion in fixing the identity of the Pallava kings and in re-constructing their history.

[1] Is this *Kāla-bhartṛi* the *Kāla* of the Purāṇa text '*teshûtsanneshu Kālena*' ['*when* (the Muruṇḍas etc.) *were overthrown by Kāla*']? If so, then the true name of Vindhyśakti who rises after Kāla, according to the Purāṇas, was *Chūta-pallava*; and Kāla would have been a Nāga general, and an ancestor of Vindhyaśakti.

not mentioned as kings), and as already pointed out, in one of those later copperplates it is expressly stated that he was given the status of king on account of his marriage with a princess of the Nāga emperor. The name *Vīrakūrcha* does not recur, except once, in the whole series of the Pallava plates. The character and style of the copperplate mentioning the name of Vīrakorcha is very early. As we know all the names up to the father of Skandavarman I from the record of the grandson of Skandavarman II, it is evident that Vīrakorcha is to be placed at the top, as already discussed. About Vīrakorcha being the first king there cannot be any doubt; the rest of the tradition about the still earlier names is yet unconfirmed, except the fact that the ancestors of Vīrakorcha were generals of the Nāga emperors. The latter fact is true, as they do rise in the Nāga period. They owed allegiance to no Southern king and there was no Southern Nāga king near about Andhradeśa where they first come into political existence, while the Nāga empire was next-door to Andhra, in the Central Provinces.

§ 183. The lines after Skandavarman II is similarly well-attested. Vishṇugopa, one of the sons of Vijaya Skandavarman II, has left one copperplate dated in the reign of Siṁhavarman I. Siṁhavarman I would have been proved conclusively to have been the elder brother of Vishṇugopa by the Udayendiram plates (E.I., III, 142), but unfortunately they, in my opinion, are clearly a spurious document, being written in a script of several centuries later. However, we get the same result, viz. that this Siṁhavarman was not the son of Vishṇugopa but his elder brother, from Yuvarāja Vishṇugopa's document, and the Gaṅga copperplate (E.I., XIV, 331) where Siṁhavarman (I) and his son Skandavarman (III) are stated to have installed respectively two successive Gaṅga kings [§ 190]. There are also two grants by Siṁhavarman II, son of Vishṇugopa, which recite the genealogy (E.I., VIII 159; E.I., XV, 254). Thus the later genealogy on the statements of Vishṇugopa and his son and the Gaṅga plates stands thus:

Skandavarman II.

- Siṁhavarman I
  - Skandavarman III.
- Vishṇu Gopa (Yuvarāja) issues grant, I.A., V, 154.
  - Siṁhavarman II (E.I., XV, 254; E.I., VIII, 159).

Vishṇu Gopa gives the genealogy up to Skandavarman I who is described here without 'Śiva', as also by Skandavarman II, his father.[1] Siṁhavarman II gives the genealogy up to Vīra-varman, a name which is not repeated again in the family line. These two branches really constituted one continuous line reigning one after the other; Vishṇu Gopa's plate (I.A., V, 154) is dated under the reign of his elder brother, on the extinction of whose line Vishṇu Gopa's son evidently succeeded. But there was still another junior branch from Skandavarman II. This branch is established by two copperplates (E.I., VIII, 143; E.I., VIII, 233). The first is the British Museum plate by Chārudevī, wife of *Yuvamahārāja* Buddhavarman, issued in the reign of *Vijaya* Skandavarman (II); and the second is by Buddhavarman's son Kumāra Vishṇu (III) whose grandfather's name was Kumāra Vishṇu (II) and whose great-grandfather was *Vijaya* Skandavarman. It is thus clear that Buddhavarman who is described as Yuvamahārāja by his wife in the reign of Skandavarman II was the son of Kumāra Vishṇu II, and not of Skandavarman II as generally supposed. He was Yuvamahārāja to his grandfather, and his father had evidently pre-deceased him. His relationship with Skandavarman (II) is not given in the British Museum plate. We know that *Yuvarāja*'s office was a ministerial post open to grandsons even in the life-time of their fathers.[2] Thus, the complete Pallava genealogy for our period will be as follows (those who reigned are numbered; nos. 1 to 7*a* complete our period):

[1] As we have already seen in our section on the Chuṭus (§ 161), *Śiva* was merely honorific. The repetition of the word Vishṇu in the family is probably connected with the name of Vishṇu Vṛiddha, one of the early ancestors [Bhāradvājas] whom the Vākāṭakas specifically mention. Otherwise it would be unexplained, the family being pronouncedly Śaiva.

[2] Jayaswal: *Hindu Polity*, II, 125.

1. Kumāra Vishṇu Vīrakorchavarman (E.I., XV, 251; E.I., I, 397) (*aśvamedhin*)=Nāga princess (S.I.I., II, 508; E.I., VI, 84); 10 years or more.

2. (*Śiva*) Skandavarman I (E.I., VI, 84; E.I., I, 2; I.A., V, 50.); (*aśvamedhin*) 8 years or more.

3. Vīravarman (I.A., V, 50, 154).

4. Skandavarman II (E.I., XV, 251; I.A., V, 50, 154); 33 years or more.

5. Siṁhavarman I [I.A., V, 50], reigned 11 years or more.

6. Skandavarman III (E.I., XIV, 331.)

(7) Vishṇu Gopa I (I.A., V, 50, 154); [ruled but not reigned.]

(7*a*) Siṁhavarman II (E.I., XV, 254; VIII, 159; I.A., V, 154), reigned 8 years or more.

(*Vijaya*) Vishṇu Gopa II [M.E.R., 1914, p. 82].[1]

Kumāra Vishṇu II [E.I., VIII, 233].

9. Buddhavarman [2] [E.I., VIII, 50, 143].

10. Kumāra Vishṇu III (E.I., VIII, 50; E.I., VIII, 143).

11. Nandivarman [S.I.I., II, 501; 508].

12. Siṁhavarman [S.I.I., II, 508].

I have extended the genealogy beyond our period to bring out the utility of the Velurpalaiyam plates [S.I.I., II, 501]. These plates furnish the early history of the dynasty with which we are dealing, and are important otherwise. They give the rise of the family with Vīrakūrcha and then give the genealogy from Skandavarman II. On the succession of Nandivarman I, it gives the important information that

[1] This plate is called the Narasaraopet plate. I have ascertained by correspondence with the Government of India Epigraphist that it is the same plate which is called the Guṇṭur plate or the Churā plate. The owner did not allow a facsimile to be taken. It is not dated. It was issued by 'King Vijaya Vishṇu Gopavarman, son of Siṁhavarman, grandson of Mahārāja Vishṇu Gopavarman and great-grandson of Kandavarman (i.e. Skandavarman)', from Vijaya Palotkaṭa, in favour of a Brahmin of Kundūr. It is in Saṅskrit.

[2] It seems that Buddhavarman reigned after No. 8, which is suggested by his description: भर्त्ता भुवो भूदथ बुद्धवर्म्मा in S.I.I., II, 508.

when Vishṇu Gopa (II) was dead and the other kings were all gone, Nandivarman succeeded. It means that after the extinction of the line of Vishṇu Gopa and the line of Kumāra Vishṇu III the succession opened to him. One Nandivarman, is mentioned in the Udayendiram plates [E.I., III, 142] as coming after Skandavarman III, son of Siṁhavarman I, but this plate is spurious, being in characters, as already pointed out, several centuries later; no reliance can be placed on it. Nandivarman I flourished in the line of Kumāra Vishṇu II according to the Velurpalaiyam document. On the death of Siṁhavarman I his son Skandavarman III succeeded, and on the failure of his line, Yuvarāja Vishṇu Gopa's son Siṁhavarman II succeeded. Vishṇu Gopa evidently did not accept the throne. He ruled but did not reign (§ 187). According to the Narasaraopet plates [M.E.R., 1914, p. 82] Siṁhavarman II's son Vishṇu Gopa II succeeded his father. This is confirmed by the list given in Vayalur pillar inscription.[1] After Vishṇu Gopa II the members of the third line from Skandavarman II came in—first, Buddhavarman and his son Kumāra Vishṇu III, and then his cousin Nandivarman. This is the meaning of '*sa-Vishṇugope cha Narendrabṛinde*[2] *gate tato 'jāyata Nandivarmā*'.

It became customary after Vishṇu Gopa I to call every ancestor 'Mahārāja,' whether he had succeeded to the Pallava throne or not, as in the case of Vishṇu Gopa I himself, whom his son calls only *Yuvamahārāja* but his grandson gives the title of *Mahārāja*. So the plates of Kumāra Vishṇu III call his each ancestor 'Mahārāja'. Unless we get actual grants from them we cannot be certain of their succession even in a secondary line of rulers. On the evidence of the plates only one line seems to have ruled, and till now we have no evidence of the existence of more than one ruling line of the dynasty. Vishṇu Gopa I, who alone could have been the contemporary of Samudra Gupta, was regent in Siṁhavarman II's time and was in charge of the government at Kāñchī; hence he would be called *Kāñcheyaka*. Members of the family might have been temporary

[1] E.I., XVIII, 145. This, as an original material, is useless, being an amalgam of several lists put together.

[2] Read ° *vṛide*.

local governors with titles of 'Mahārāja,' i.e. 'Governor' or 'Yuvamahārāja,' i.e. 'Lieutenant Governor'.

Early Pallava kings.

§184. Vīrakūrcha Kumāra Vishṇu performed an aśvamedha, that is, he declared himself to be the successor of the Ikshvākus. It was repeated by Śiva Skandavarman. Evidently Vīravarman lost Kāñchī[1] which had to be conquered back by Kumāra Vishṇu II.[2] The Velurpalaiyam plates do not call the latter a king. He, as a prince, seems to have conquered Kāñchī for his father. Both father and son had to fight the Cholas and probably also some other Tamil kings.[3] Skandavarman II re-established himself at Kāñchī. In his time, the Gaṅgas and also the Kadambas were set up as feudatories on the Tamil frontiers (§ 188 ff.). Their similar titles indicate that they were all Mahārājas to the Vākāṭaka Emperor. Their being Dharma-mahārājas seems to imply that they all were appointed by the *Samrāṭ*, that they belonged to a Dharma Empire established by the Vākāṭakas. There was practically a continuous fight with the Cholas until Buddhavarman broke them.[4]

Navakhaṇḍa

185. The ancestral state of the Pallavas is called Navakhaṇḍa.[5] We have a Navarāshṭra in the Mahā-Bhārata,[6] but it was in Western India. This Navakhaṇḍa should be near-about Andhra. We have Nawāgarh as one of the traditional '18 Forest Kingdoms' of Kosala.[7] Its situation is near

[1] This name is never repeated in the line; it seems to have been inauspicious and unsuccessful. His bravery, however, is noted in the inscriptions (वसुधातलैकवीरस्य).

[2] गृहीत-काञ्चीनगरस्ततोभूत् कुमारविष्णुस्समरेषु जिष्णुः (verse 8.)—E.I.I., II, 508.

[3] यन्ववाय-नभश्चन्द्रः स्कन्दशिष्यस्ततोभवत्, विजानां घटिकां राज्ञस्सत्यसेनात् जहार यः (verse 7), *Ibid.* Satyasena was probably a Chola or some other neighbouring Tamil king.

[4] भर्त्ता भुवो भूदथ बुद्धवर्म्मा यश्चोळ-सैन्यार्णव-वाडवाग्निः । (verse 8)—S.I.I., II, 508.

[5] S.I.I., II, 515 (verse 6).

[6] *Sabhā*, 31, 6.

[7] Hira Lal, E.I., VIII, 286.

Bastar, by the Nagpur division of the Bhāraśiva kingdom, from where an attack on Andhra was easy. Very likely, the father of Vīrakorchavarman was the governor or sub-king in Kosalā, and from there Andhra was acquired.

Pallava Chronology.

§ 186. Vīrakorcha Kumāra Vishṇu I must have had a fairly long career. He was an *aśvamedhin* and the conqueror of Kāñchī. Probably it was his suzerain or his father who conquered the Ikshvākus and Andhra, and he conquered the Cholas and occupied Kāñchī. His son Śiva Skanda, to be the yuvarāja and the sub-governor of Kāñchī, must have been at least 18 or 20 in the 10th year of Vīrakorcha. The capture of Kāñchī was accomplished from the Andhra throne. Vīrakorcha's marriage and his recognition as a sub-king could not be simultaneous, for in his tenth year Śiva Skanda was old enough to be the governor of Kāñchī. At his marriage, Vīrakorcha was probably only an *adhirāja* and not a *Mahārāja*, and would have got the higher title on the conquest of Kāñchī, Placing the conquest of Andhra about 250–260 A.D., we may date the conquest of Kāñchī at 265 A.D., and the tenth year of Vīrakorcha as *Mahārāja* would be about 275 A.D. when Śiva Skanda would be about 20. To verify this initial date we have a guide in the date of Vishṇu Gopa I; let us see if our proposed date stands verified by his date.

187. If Śiva Skandavarman came to the throne, say, five years later than the grant by him as *Yuvamahārāja*, i.e. in 280 A.D., and ruled for 15 years, his period [280–295 A.D.] would agree with the time assigned to him on the basis of the script of his charters as discussed above. Vīravarman, in whose time Kāñchī is lost and to whom no conquest is attributed, but who is noted for his bravery and whose name is never borne again by his descendants, seems to have died on the battlefield at the hands of his Chola enemy. The death of Śiva Skandavarman would have given a signal for an attack by the Cholas. Vīravarman could not have remained king for longer than a year or two. Vīravarman following the ancient orthodox custom had taken the name of his grandfather Vīra [Korcha]. But his name was, as already observed, never

repeated. It seems that the name Vīra which came to be associated with a political misfortune—the loss of Kāñchī and a defeat at the hands of the Cholas, was given up by the family. Skandavarman II became, for the second time, the founder of the Pallava power, and this time it became seated permanently at Kāñchī. We should remember that in his time the Vākāṭaka family was led by Pravarasena I under whom it reached its zenith, which was a point more elevated than that attained by any previous imperial dynasty. Presumably Skandavarman II received support from the Vākāṭaka emperor. He assumed the title of '*Vijaya*' deservedly. In his long reign he had sufficient time to consolidate his, and the Vākāṭaka imperial, position in the South. For over half the period of the reign of Pravarasena I he was his contemporary. We should assign him a reign of about 35 years, 33rd year being his recorded date. After him we have one record of the reign of his son Siṁhavarman I and of the governorship of his another son Vishṇu Gopa. But of his grandson Skandavarman III we have no record, and as the latter was succeeded by the son of Vishṇu Gopa I, his reign must have been a short one. Evidently, Vishṇu Gopa was defeated by Samudra Gupta before his coronation and according to the well-known custom he abdicated in favour of his son and never became legally Mahārāja, i.e. though he ruled, he did not reign. The dated chronology would stand thus:

1.	Vīrakūrcha Kumāra Vishṇu (at Kāñchī).	*c.* 265–280 A.D.
2.	[Śiva] Skandavarman I ..	*c.* 280–295 A.D.
3.	Vīravarman	*c.* 295–297 A.D.
4.	[Vijaya] Skandavarman II ..	*c.* 297–332 A.D.
5.	Siṁhavarman I	*c.* 332–344 A.D.
6.	Skandavarman III	*c.* 344–346 A.D.
7.	Vishṇu Gopa I	*c.* 346
7A.	Siṁhavarman II	*c.* 346–360 A.D.

This is fully confirmed by the date of Vishṇu Gopa which we gather from the history of Samudra Gupta.

XVII. SUBORDINATE BRAHMIN KINGDOMS OF THE SOUTH: THE GAṄGAS AND THE KADAMBAS.

The Brahmin Gaṅga Dynasty.

§ 188. Under the Pallavas there came into existence a sub-kingdom of the Brahmin Kāṇvāyanas, who after their original home adopted their dynastic name '*the Dynasty of the Gaṅgā*,' like 'the Magadha Dynasty,' of the Kaliṅga kings under the Guptas. The kings of the Gaṅga Dynasty, from the third king, were installed in each generation by the Pallavas of whom Siṁhavarman the 'Pallavendra' [' the Pallava emperor '], and also his successor Skandavarman (III) are named in their earliest genuine copperplate.[1] These Kāṇvāyanas very likely were an off-shoot of the Imperial Kāṇvāyanas of Magadha, the last king of whom (Suśarman) was taken prisoner [प्रगृह्य तं][2] and removed to the South by the Sātavāhana.[3] From the point of view of cultural history the Brahmin subordinate dynasties become important. There had been already a class of political Brahmins in the South.

A Brahmin Aristocracy in the South.

§ 189. The Kauṇḍinyas, whom we have already noticed, were introduced into the South from the North in the days of the Sātavāhana empire which once embraced both the South and the North. The tradition of certain Brahmin families coming to the South from Ahichhatra in the time of the ancestors of Mayūraśarman Mānavya,[4] who, as we shall presently see, belonged to the Chuṭu Śātakarṇi family, seems to have been based on history. The Sātavāhanas married into a few exclusive Brahmin families, e.g. of the Gautama gotra, Vasishṭha gotra, Māṭhara gotra, Hārīta gotra, etc. There was a large settlement of the Gautamas in the South [Mysore].[5] The Ikshvākus followed that tradition strictly,

[1] E.I., XIV, 333.
[2] Matsya, Pargiter, Purāṇa Text, p. 38, 3, 6.
[3] J.B.O.R.S., XVI, 294.
[4] E.C., VII, Sk. 186.
[5] E.C., VII, Introduction, p. 3.

and to some extent also the **Kadambas**. The Brahmin families occupied the position of aristocracy in the South. They remained exclusive and were intimately connected with the royal families. The Aiyars and Ayangars are still the real aristocrats of the South. The Brahmin rulers of the early centuries, now succeeded by the Vākāṭaka-Pallavas and the Gaṅgas of the revivalist period, and their matrimonial Brahmins were the makers of **Southern India**, who by introducing their culture in the South made Dakshiṇāpatha an integral part of Hindu India, and they truly extended the boundaries of **Bhāratavarsha** to include the whole of the South.

Early Gaṅga genealogy.

§190. The **Gaṅga** genealogy for our period may be reconstructed on the basis of the first undoubtedly genuine copperplate of the Gaṅgas, published by Mr. Rice in the *Epigraphia Indica*, XIV, 331, which is of the latter part of the fourth or the early part of the fifth century A.D. (*circa* 400 A.D.). I have extended the line by adding one more name from other records to fix and to verify the chronology. The genealogy will stand as follows :—

Koṅkaṇivarman, *dharmādhirāja*

|

Mādhava (I), *Mahādhirāja*

Ayyavarman (Ari[1] or Harivarman), *Gaṅga-rāja* (installed by Siṁhavarman, *Mahārāja*, of the Pallava Dynasty).

| [2]

Mādhava (II), *Mahārāja*, the *Siṁhavarman*, installed by Skandavarman III, *Mahārāja*, of the Pallavas.

|

Avinīta Koṅgaṇi, *Mahādhirāja* (married a daughter of the Kadamba king Kākusthavarman, sister of Kṛishṇavarman, *Mahādhirāja*).[3]

[1] Cf. Kielhorn's *List*, E.I., VIII Supplement, p. 4.

[2] [According to Mr. Rice, a Vishṇu Gopa was probably left out by mistake between Ayya and Mādhava II] E.I., XIV, 333; Cf. Kielhorn, p. 5.

[3] Kielhorn, p. 5. Mr. Rice, E.I., XIV, 334, thought that Mādhava II [whom he calls 'Mādhava III', counting Koṅgaṇīvarman's personal

§ 191. The marriage of Ávinīta Koṅgaṇi with a Kadamba princess is alleged by the Gaṅga documents and seems to be confirmed by the reference in the Talagunda inscription of Kākusthavarman to the political marriages brought about by Kākusthavarman. Kṛishṇavarman I whose sister Avinīta Koṅgaṇi is recorded to have married, was the son of Kākustha.[1] The time of Avinīta Koṅgaṇi is thus fixed by Kākustha's time (c. 400 A.D.). Ayyavarman, the third prince, was installed by the Pallava Siṁhavarman II whose time is about 330–344 A.D. (§ 187), and Mādhava (II) was installed by the Pallava Skandavarman III (c. 344–346 A.D.) who was the successor of Siṁhavarman. Thus these three contemporary houses fix each other's chronology, and prove that the founder of the Gaṅga Kāṇvāyana Dynasty could not have flourished earlier than 300 A.D.[2] Their time approximately would be thus (which gives them roughly an average of 16 or 17 years each) :

1.	Koṅkaṇivarman ..	.. c. 300–315 A.D.
2.	Mādhavavarman I ..	.. 315–330 A.D.
3.	Ayya or Arivarman ..	.. 330–345 A.D.[3]
4.	Mādhavavarman [II] Siṁhavarman ..	.. 345–375 A.D.
5.	Avinīta Koṅgaṇi ..	.. 375–395 A.D.

§ 192. The first prince adopted the name Koṅkaṇivarman probably for his having come recently from Koṅkaṇa. His dominion was what is known as Gaṅgavāḍī in Mysore. The Penukonda plates (E.I., XIV, 331) have been found in the Anantapur District, Madras. The Gaṅgas were the next-door

name *Mādhava* as Mādhava I] married the Kadamba princess, which is wrong on the evidence of the Gaṅga records and on the chronology for these kings discussed below (§§ 190-191).

[1] *Cf. Kadamba Kula,* the first chart.

[2] This proves that the records dated in early Śaka years (247 A.D. etc. Cf. Kielhorn's *List,* E.I., VIII, p. 4, *n.*) could not be genuine, though they recite the genealogy fairly correctly. The people alleging themselves to be descendants of old donees of lands forged a number of Gaṅga documents ; they had a fair idea of the genealogy of the Gaṅga kings.

[3] Vishṇu Gopa's existence is not certain (§ 190, *n.*).

neighbours of the Kadambas who came into existence about the same time or a generation later.

§ 193. The title *Dharmādhirāja* of the dynasty shows that the Gaṅgas, like the Kadambas, formed part of the Dharma Empire of the Pallavas.

Koṅkaṇivarman.

§ 194. The first Gaṅga king came in by right of conquest, presumably as a general of the Pallavas or the main Vākāṭakas, which is suggested by their title *Gaṅga*. He acquired a country of 'gentlemanly population' [sva-bhuja-java-jaya-janita-sujana-janapadasya], having fought terrible enemies (dāruṇa-arigaṇa°). The king was 'adorned with marks of wounds (in battle)' [labdha-vraṇa-bhūshaṇasya Kāṇvāyana-sagotrasya Śrīmat Koṇkaṇi-varma-dharma-mahādhirājasya].

Mādhava I.

§ 195. His son Mādhava, *Mahādhirāja*, was deeply learned in the sacred and polite literature of Sanskrit and was an authority on Hindu political science—'*he was skilled in expounding it and applying it in practice*: Nīti-śāstrasya vaktṛi-prayoktṛi-kuśalāsya.

Ayya (Hari) varman.

§ 196. Mādhava's son Ayyavarman '*was decorated with wounds on his body acquired on numerous battlefields*'—

aneka-yuddh=ōpalabdha-
vraṇa-vibhūshita-śarīrasya.

He had devoted his time to the study of history.

Vākāṭaka spirit.

§ 197. The Gaṅga genealogical history, summarised above, breathes the spirit of the Vākāṭaka tradition. It relates to a period before Samudra Gupta reached the South. It is in Sanskrit and had been copied from earlier documents, as it was copied in all subsequent family deeds. It was a cultured family of the type which the Vākāṭakas created.

Gaṅga civics.

§ 198. The ideal of the early Gaṅgas, both personal and civic, are remarkable. The kings decorated themselves, like Vindhyaśakti, with wounds won on battlefields. This finds an echo in Samudra Gupta inscription. The Gaṅga's civic ideal is exact and positive. The *raison d'être* of kingship was good government:

samyak-prajā-pālana-
mātr=ādhigata-rājya-prayojanasya :

'(to His Majesty Mādhava (I) Mahādhirāja) the object of kingship consisted only in rendering good government to his people.'

The Kadambas.

§ 199. The K a d a m b a s are not the direct product of the invasion of Samudra Gupta, as generally supposed, but the product of the early history of the Mānavyas. Their history has been separately discussed in a recent text-book by Mr. Maores. A few points which have not yet been noticed and which have a bearing on our period may be noticed here.

Their Descent.

§ 200. The Kadambas from their official documents, beginning with Talagunda pillar inscription, style themselves as H ā r i t ī p u t r a M ā n a v y a s.[1] Now we know that the Vanavāsī Āndhras (the C h u ṭ u s) were Hāritīputra Mānavyas (§ 157 ff.). It seems to be certain that the Kadambas were descendants of the Chuṭu Sātakarṇis. By calling themselves *Hāritīputra Mānavyas* they mark their descent from the last Chuṭu Mānavya who was a Hāritīputra. The moment the first Kadamba king acquires Vanavāsī and Kuntala, the original seat of the Chuṭus, he 'with a glad mind' restores the old grant made by the Hāritīputra Śiva Skandavarman of the Mānavya gotra and records it on the very pillar set up by the Chuṭu king for the purpose of registering the gift of the same property, which had been attached to Maṭṭapaṭṭi[2] through the same Kauṇḍinya family. The grant was made a second time,

[1] E.I., VIII, 34, footnote, by Kielhorn. Cf. E.I., XVI, p. 266, '*Mānavya-sagotrānāṁ Hāritīputrānāṁ*'.

[2] Its name survives to-day in '*Maḷavaḷḷi*'.

The interval between the ages of the scripts of the two inscriptions is sufficiently marked, and is not one of a few years, as supposed by Mr. Rice, in E.C., VII, p. 6. The language is also different. It is a new language, Mahārāshṭrī, which had never been employed before in official drafting.

implying that it had been resumed by the authority just preceding, which could not be that of any other than the Pallavas, from whom Mayūra Śarman is recorded to have acquired the territory on account of, amongst other considerations, his past 'lineage', that is, the ex-royal dynasty of the Chuṭu Mānavyas. It is dated in the 4th year of the king's reign. I regard it to be a writ of Mayūra Śarman, a fragment of his name is readable on the plate (§ 162). He was vindicating here the right of his family. He recovered his family's home-land, and revived their gift. The relationship with that ancient respectable family of the Kauṇḍinyas, who had been probably imported there by his ancestors, had continued in the meantime, as the new donee is described as the *mātula* (maternal uncle) of the donor king.

§ 201. The Pallavas as they dispossessed the Ikshvākus dispossessed also the Chuṭu Mānavyas. The Ikshvākus disappeared for ever, but the Mānavyas revived once more. At the first opportunity Mayūra Śarman Mānavya recovered his ancestral home and founded a new dynasty under the title 'Kadamba'.

§ 202. The Kadambas attempted to revive the dynastic memories. As they re-endowed the Malavalli god of the Sātavāhanas, and marked the tank and temple at Talagunda, which had associations with the Sātakarṇis, with their proud pillar and prouder inscription, so they tried to reach the northern limit of the Sātavāhana dominions in the West, for which they made repeated efforts, but they were kept back by the Vākāṭakas who strenuously retained to themselves the maritime province of Aparānta, with its Western Foreign trade.

Kaṅga and the position of the Kadambas.

§ 203. In this attempt for, what we may describe as *Sātavāhanism*, Kaṅga who flourished in the time of Samudra Gupta, is the most prominent figure. Kaṅga was the son and successor of Mayūra Śarman. He dropped the Brahmin title *śarman* and adopted the royal style *varman* with his name. He was the real founder of the Kadamba kingdom which became very powerful in his time, though only for a few years. The Pallava power, after its defeat at the hands of Samudra Gupta, was sought to be superseded by K a ṅ g a, whom the Purāṇas fully describe under the name K ā n a and K a n a k a (§§ 128-129). The Pallavas formed the southern portion of the empire of the V ā k ā ṭ a k a S a m r ā ṭ. They were '*Mahārājas*' to the Vākāṭaka Chakravartin. The Pallavas, on behalf of the Vākāṭaka emperor, seem to have exercised suzerainty over the T r a i r ā j y a, the group of three Tamil kingdoms, the leader of whom—the Cholas—they had actually conquered. K a ṅ g a v a r m a n became the ruler of three connected units—S t r ī r ā j y a, M ū s h i k a and B h o j a k a, and according to the Vishṇu Purāṇa, his rule covered also T r a i r ā j y a, i.e., he became the overlord of the South for the time being, eclipsing the Pallavas. The Pallava territory alone is excluded from his jurisdiction. It seems that Kaṅga tried to restore the Southern Empire of his ancestors after the defeat of the Pallavas and to question the right of Samudra Gupta to be the Emperor of All-India. He was, however, defeated by Pṛithivīsheṇa Vākāṭaka and had to abdicate (§ 127 ff.). After Kaṅga the Kadambas remained politically attached to the Vākāṭaka kingdom which touched the Kuntala part of the Kadamba kingdom on its own B h o j a k a ṭ a frontiers. The importance of the Kadambas lies more on the social side. They had been long in the South before the Vākāṭakas and the Guptas. Yet in the new social revival they showed new vigour and became as good agents of that revival as the Gaṅgas and the Pallavas, within their own sphere.

Making of One India.

§ 204. Thus the history of the South for the period is really a history of the Northerns in the South, both new and old, and of their efforts to introduce and establish a common civilization, *viz.* that Hinduism which proved so successful at the time in reforming and reviving society in the North. The South becomes so united with the North through these efforts that truly the old definition of B h ā r a t a v a r s h a had to be revised and extended to include the whole of the South. The northern Hindus introduce the language, the script, the worship and the culture in general, of the North into the South. They infuse new life in Further India from there, and make history. They make One-India by a common culture, the legacy of which has come down to us.

PART V.

Conclusion.

'Dharma-prāchīra-bandaḥ śaśi-kara-suchayaḥ kīrttayaḥ supratānāḥ.'

[—Allahabad Pillar.]

XVIII. Effects of Gupta Imperialism.

Samudra Gupta's Policy of Peace and Prosperity.

§ 205. The military achievements of Samudra Gupta are well known and need not be commented upon here. It should be noted that he did not over-do militarism. He was fully conscious of the value of a policy of peace. After his second campaign he never undertook any expedition, but gained his object through diplomacy and peace by bringing the Shāhānushāhi, the Hill States, the Republics, and the Colonies within the fold of his empire and the sphere of his imperial influence. His possession of an enormous quantity of gold which Northern India had not known before was the result of the inclusion of Southern India and the Colonies in his empire. The contact with the South was kept up through the Vākāṭaka House, which was soon restored, though in the Allahabad inscription the Vākāṭaka country is treated as being part of his Central Provinces and the survey of the Republics is made as if sitting at Gwalior or Eran. In line 23 of the Allahabad inscription he says that he was restoring old royal families and in line 26 he says that his officers were busy in restoring the wealth of various kings who had been conquered by the strength of his arms. Pṛithivīsheṇa I undoubtedly was one of those. Gold from the South and Further India kept on pouring-in even in the next reign. If Samudra Gupta excelled Rāma and Pṛithu in giving gold coins as he says in his Eran inscription, his son certainly excelled all figures in past history in distributing gold amongst his subjects. There is no exaggeration in this. We have the testimony of Chandra Gupta II's daughter that her father gave away several thousands of crores of [Gupta] sovereigns[1], which is again

[1] Poona Plates, E.I., Vol. XV, p. 41.

confirmed by Yuan Chwang. Amoghavarsha in his inscription admits that the Gupta king was the greatest donor of the Kali Age. This became possible on account of the beneficial foresight of Samudra Gupta. His policy of peace and reconciliation turned Prithivishena I into a faithful ally who conquered back the Kuntala or Kadamba king. The latter had seriously threatened Samudra Gupta's supremacy in the South, which probably led to his putting off the Aśvamedha or to its repetition mentioned by Prabhāvatī Guptā.[1] His colonial policy and the control of the port of Tāmralipti must have been a great source of revenue. The eastern trade with China and Indonesia was brisk at the time and was probably of greater importance than the Western trade. Both Samudra Gupta and his son Chandra Gupta emphasised their sea-frontiers, which alone they recognised on their three sides as they recognised the Himavat [Tibet] to be their northern frontier. The people were as lightly taxed as possible in both reigns, which Fa-Hien for the latter reign has particularly noticed. Samudra Gupta truly became *Dhanada* to his subjects. People could well afford to found big hospitals, and the peace of Samudra Gupta could very well enable Chandra Gupta to abolish capital punishment.

Elevated National Outlook.

§ 206. The psychology of the nation was entirely changed and the outlook became lofty and magnanimous. It was a psychology directly borrowed from the Emperor. The Hindus of his day thought of big undertakings. They contributed high, elegant and magnanimous literature. The literary people became literary Kuberas to their countrymen and literary empire-builders outside India. Kumārajīva made a literary conquest of China.[2] The Kauṇḍinya missionary established a social and cultural overlordship in

1 *anek-āśvamedha-yājī Lichchhavi-dohitraḥ* (E.I., XV, 41).

2 He, a contemporary of Samudra Gupta, left for China, where [405–412] he dictated Chinese commentaries on the Buddhist Canon. His translation of the Diamond Sūtra is a national classic in Chinese literature, from which 'Chinese poets and philosophers have drawn inspiration and instruction'. *Cf.* Giles, *Chinese Literature*, p. 114.

Cambodia. Merchants and artists made India a wonderland for the foreign eyes. There was nothing feminine in art, literature, piety or politics. The chisel produced virile gods and martial goddesses. The pen portrayed handsome and masculine men, self-conscious and proud Hindu Prussians. Scholars and Brahmins wielded sword and pen with equal facility. Aristocracy of intellect and ability was raised to a height which was hardly repeated again in this land.

§ 207. Sanskrit became the official language, and it became entirely a new language. Like the Gupta coin and Gupta sculpture, it reproduced the Emperor, it became majestic and musical, as it had never been before and as it never became after again.

The Gupta emperor made a new language, and in fact a new nation.

The seed-period of Samudra Gupta's India.

§ 208. The field, however, had been prepared by the Bhāraśivas and more so by the Vākāṭakas. Sanskrit had been employed by the Śuṅga kings in their official inscriptions. It was employed by Rudradāman, again, about 150 A.D., but the Kāvya style, as evidenced by the Champā (Cambodia) inscription which anticipates Samudra Gupta's style, is referable to the Vākāṭaka period. The Vākāṭakas had already created an All-India Empire. They had driven the Kushans to a corner. They had raised the military tradition of the people. They had brought back the Śāstras to their rightful throne. Samudra Gupta took full advantage of it and kept up the continuity of history initiated by the Bhāraśivas and fostered by the Vākāṭakas. They had paved the road through which the Shāhānushāhis and the Śaka lords could be brought to Ajodhyā or Pāṭaliputra to bend their heads before the Hindu throne. The renaissance had begun before 248 A.D. The Hindus had freed themselves already from the Kushan social tyranny and their political rule. They had already rejected Buddhism as a system unfit for their society tending to make people weak and passive. It had been, however, left for Samudra Gupta to give a constructive faith, and he gave it in the form of his *bhakti* in Vishṇu. The

Bhāraśivas had adopted Gaṅgā and Yamunā as the symbols of freed Āryāvarta, and rightly hooded Nāgas were put over the figures of the river goddesses, translating politics into the language of the chisel. The Guptas duly took over those motifs though they removed the Nāgas from their heads. The sombre Ś i v a of the Bhāraśivas and the Vākāṭakas makes room for the constructive V i s h ṇ u who stands with His hands erect upholding Hindu society, with a vigour which knows no lessening. Solid, not elegant, become the homes of Hindu gods. Square-built, rock-cut and rock-like temples are preferred to pinnacles. Self-confidence is the breeding spirit of the time. The Hindu has faith in himself : the Vākāṭaka, the Gaṅga and the Gupta speak of their manly beauty moulded by swords and arrows ; deities are compared with men and to the advantage of men. Faith in the great God Vishṇu, to whom the Gupta dedicated all his deeds and in whom he merged himself, was transmitted to the whole nation and even to Further India. This unity of man and his God was reflected in the sculptures they wrought by fashioning them after the devotees. The lofty spiritual tone reached the very zenith. Vindhyaśakti whose strength grew in great battles and whose valour could not be overcome even by gods, was yet a man exerting himself to gain spiritual merit. Mādhava I of the Gaṅga kings, whose decorations were wounds received on battlefields, declared that kingship existed only for rendering good government to the people. Śiva Skandavarman, the performer of proud sacrifices, was after all a *Dharma*-Mahārājâdhirāja. Samudra Gupta the rampart of religion, the path of the sacred hymns, worthy of study by others, was practising royalty and his duty in a way that gave him the satisfaction that he was winning his heaven and hereafter thereby. Man was made for society, and by performing his duties he was winning the kingdom of heaven. Revivalist piety thus spiritualized politics, even conquest, and left passive pietism and inert quietism of the pre-revival days to bury its past. Buddhist celibacy had lowered the position of woman. Now once more woman became the object of high honour and a political partner. In coins and inscriptions she is given equality. Wife was never so honoured as Samudra Gupta honoured Dattadevī. In the greatest moment of his triumph at Eran the Emperor of All-India proudly remembered his life-partner and the day of his marriage when her dowry consisted of only the manliness of her lord, and whose grandeur now consisted in being the ideal Hindu woman, the *kula-vadhū* and the Hindu mother surrounded by sons and grandsons.

§ 209. We are thus dazzled by this atmosphere of full manhood and glory, of conquests and culture, of activity far and wide, at home and abroad, and we forget the unknown poets and patriots and teachers of the Bhāraśiva period who sowed the seed of which the Vākāṭaka and the Gupta reaped the harvest. The hundred years of the Bhāraśivas are the seed-period of this Hindu imperialism. Literary remains of that seed-period movement we have practically none. But we recognise the tree from its fruit. That 'Dark Period' brought light and illumination to Āryāvarta and India. The spiritual movement begun in that period assumed the form of intense *bhakti* in the heroic aspect of Vaishṇavism. Who were the preachers of that cult? We know not. But we can say this much that the bible of that cult was the Bhagavad-Gītā which is repeated in the inscription of Samudra Gupta. The cult is that Vishṇu comes in the form of statesmen and heroes and readjusts society, protects Dharma and His people.

The Other Side.

§ 210. Grand and pleasing is this picture and the mind gets so captivated that it becomes most reluctant to turn away from the vision of Samudra Gupta's India. A present-day historian trained in Imperialism would naturally take delight in that picture, a picture of bold strokes, of Kirīṭa and Kuṇḍala, the picture of imperial Hinduism, of the revealed vision of the greatness of the Guptas. But does his duty end with reproducing on the fresco of the past of his race the picture of the Gupta superman? His duty does not conclude without giving the judgment of the post-Gupta Hindu who looked back on Gupta imperialism and coolly analysed it. The Hindu historian in the Vishṇu Purāṇa makes another appraisement of the matter. His concluding words[1] may be summed up thus:

'I have given this history.[2] *The existence of these kings will in future become a matter of debate and doubt as the very existence of Rāma and other Emperors has become to-day a matter of doubt and speculation. Emperors become mere legends in the current of time—the Emperors who thought and think "India is mine". Fie on Empires, fie on the Empire of the Emperor Rāghava.'*[3]

The refrain of the historian is to rail at Emperors and Conquerors. They suffer, he says from *mamatva*,—*'l'etat c'est moi'*[4].

[1] *See* V.P., Bk. IV, c. 24, verses 64–77, *cf.* also *'the Verdic of India'* (*Pṛithivī-Gītā*), verses 55–63.

[2] इत्येषः कथितः सम्यङ् मनोर्वंशो मया तव (64)
श्रुत्वैवमखिलं वंशं प्रशस्तं शशिसूर्ययोः (67).
इक्ष्वाकु-जह्नु-मान्धातृ-सगराविक्षितान् रघून् (68)

[3] यः कार्त्तवीर्य्यो बुभुजे समस्तान् द्वीपान् समाक्रम्य हतारिचक्रः;
कथाप्रसङ्गे त्वभिधीयमानः स एव सङ्कल्पविकल्पहेतुः (72)
दशाननाविक्षित-राघवाणामैश्वर्य्यमुद्भासित-दिङ्मुखानाम्
भस्मापि जातं, न कथं क्षणेन? भ्रूभङ्गपातेन धिगन्तकस्य (73)
['ऐश्वर्यं धिक्'—Commentator.]
कथाशरीरत्वमवाप यद्वै मान्धातृनामा भुवि चक्रवर्त्ती।
श्रुत्वापि तं कोऽपि करोति साधु ममत्वमात्मन्यपि मन्दचेतः। (74)
भगीरथाद्याः सगरः ककुत्स्थो दशाननो राघवलक्ष्मणौ च
युधिष्ठिराद्याश्च बभूवुरेते सत्यं न मिथ्या क्व नु ते न विद्मः। (75)

[4] Cf. *Pṛithivī-Gītā*:
पृथ्वी ममेयं सकला ममैषा ममान्वयस्यापि च शाश्वतेयम्
यो यो मृतो ह्यत्र बभूव राजा कुबुद्धिरासीदिति तस्य तस्य। (61)
विहाय मां मृत्युपथं व्रजन्तं
तस्यान्वयस्थस्य कथं ममत्वं हृद्यास्पदं मत्प्रभवं करोति। (62)
'पृथ्वी ममैषाशु परित्यजैनम्' वदन्ति ये दूतमुखैः स्वशत्रुम्
नराधिपास्तेषु ममातिहासः पुनश्च मूढेषु दयाभ्युपैति। (63)

An oversea-Empire, characteristic of the Guptan, is particularly hit at:
ततो भृत्यांश्च पौरांश्च जिगीषन्ते तथा रिपून्
क्रमेणानेन जेष्यामो वयं पृथ्वीं ससागराम्। (57)
समुद्रावरणं याति (58)
द्वीपान् समाक्रम्य हतारिचक्रः (72).

Against whom is this bitter criticism directed ? Again and again the historian uses the word Rāghava. Did not Samudra Gupta try to revive the tradition of Rāma the Rāghava, from Ayodhyā ? Did not Kālidāsa render Samudra Gupta's conquest in Raghu's Digvijaya ? The hit is palpably against the builder of the last empire chronicled in the Purāṇa—the builder of the Gupta empire whom he has left unnamed in his chronicle. He means to say that a history which is worth remembering is a history of good deeds and just services; the deeds which trample upon the rights and liberties of others are not to be canonised by the historian. If he were alive to-day, he might have said—'Remember Vikramāditya, the son of Samudra Gupta, but forget Samudra Gupta. Note only virtue, give no countenance to vice in any form or shape.' Samudra Gupta, like Alexander, killed the free spirit of his country. He destroyed the Mālavas and the Yaudheyas, who were the nursery of freedom; and many others of their class. Once those free communities were wiped out, the recruiting ground for future heroes and patriots and statesmen disappeared. The Gupta themselves, both from their mother's side and their father's side, had descended from those republican communities. They themselves were crops of those seed-communities, but they totally destroyed them.

§ 211. The social system of the republican communities was based on equality. They knew no caste. They consisted of one caste only. The orthodox system, on the other hand, was based on inequality and caste where mass patriotism could not be mobilised as it could easily be done amongst the Mālavas, the Yaudheyas, the Mādrakas, the Pushyamitras, the Ābhīras and the Lichchhavis. They were the exercise-ground for state-making, for patriotism, for individual ambitions, capabilities and leadership. But under Samudra Gupta and his descendants they all merged into an organised, officialised, orthodox caste-system and an orthodox political system which recognised and fostered monarchy and imperialism. The seed-pod for the rise of a Krishṇa, the prophet of rightful war and the prophet of the cult of duty, the seed-pod to produce a Buddha, the prophet of a universal religion and universal equality, was consumed for ever ; the seed-pod for the production of a future Bhāraśiva or a future Gupta was made extinct. And the Hindu sank. The Republics of Rajputana dissolved into the Rajputs who forgot all the traditions of their republican ancestors. And the Republics of the Punjab dissolved into the Jāṭs with all their past lost. The life-giving element was gone. The Hindus did not remember the name of Samudra Gupta with any gratitude, and when Alberūnī came to India he was told that the Guptas were a wicked people. This is another view of that picture. They were tyrants to Hindu constitutional freedom, though excellent rulers to the individual subject.

§212. The only thing which could appeal to the Hindu mind represented by the historian of the Vishṇu Purāṇa, whose political ethics never gave countenance to force and coercion, was a system like that of the Bhāraśivas, uniting in a federation of states with full individuality and individual life. The Bhāraśiva Federation was an enlargement of the *Saṅgha* organisation of the Hindu republics. It was a league of equals with a recognised leading power. If the Guptas had experimented that, they would have been better remembered by the Purāṇic historian. Following the historian of my country I would say : *Let us remember to-day only the good deeds of the Guptas and forget their imperialism.*

Durehā [Jāso] Pillar.

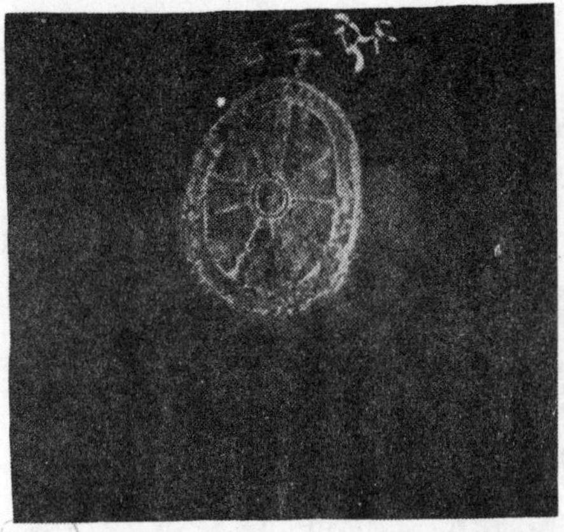

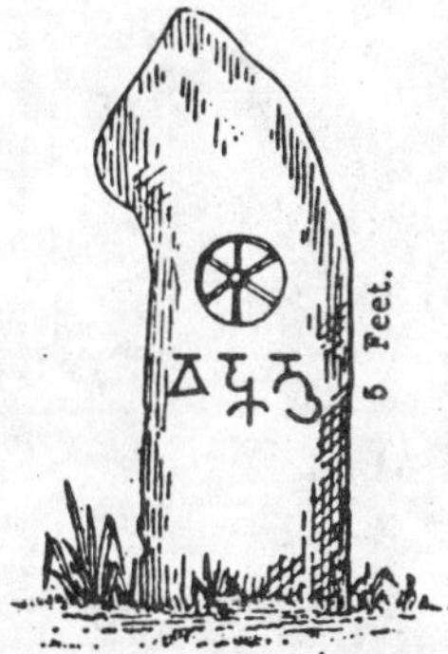

Cunningham's drawing.

Dureha [Jāso] Pillar Inscription.

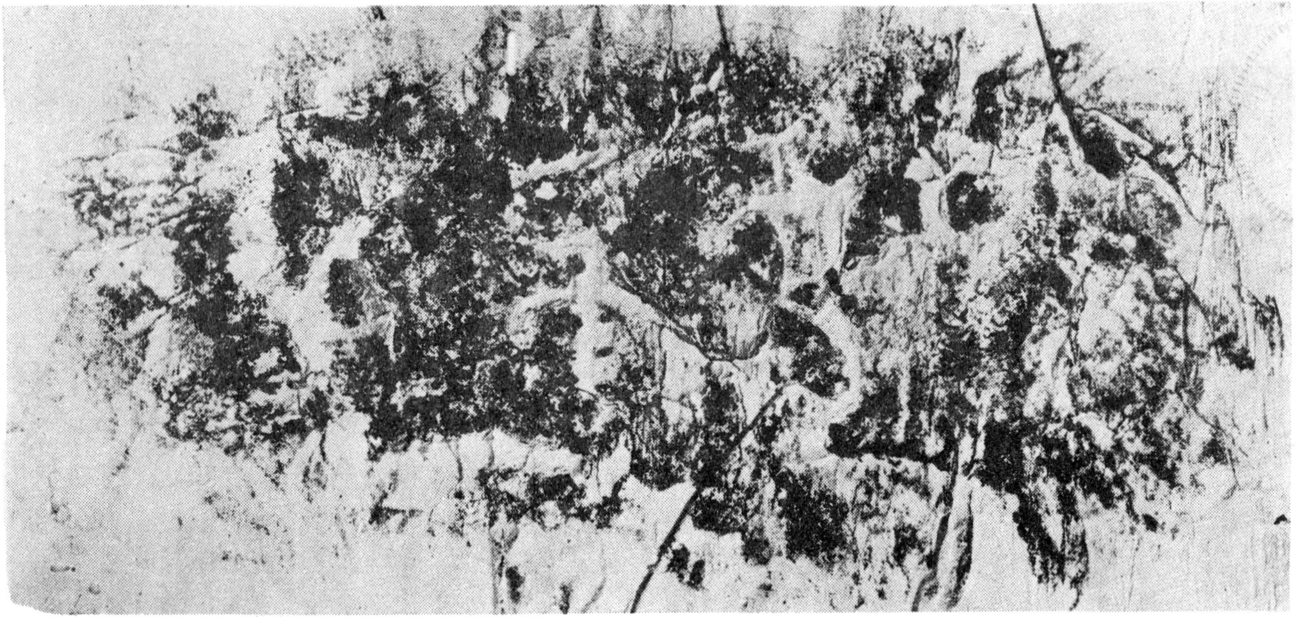

APPENDIX A.

On the Durehā Vākāṭaka Pillar, and the Nachnā and Bhūbharā (Bhūmarā) Temples.

Since completing the *History* above I took a journey (December, 1932) to verify certain facts. The result is noted below.

Durehā inscribed Pillar.

Durehā is a flourishing village at a distance of about 4 miles (S.) from the town of Jāso, the seat of the Chief of Jāso. Jāso is a small Bundela principality on the borders of Nagod (Nagaudh), Baghelkhand, Central India. Cunningham visited Durehā and noticed a stone monument which he described in his *Reports*, Vol. XXI, p. 99 (Plate 27), as 'a natural *lingam*'. He gave an eye-copy of the inscription on it and a drawing of the monument. Since his time no one else went to the place to verify Cuninngham's record. Suspecting the inscription to be of importance, in my last tour in Bundelkhand I made enquiries about the place *Dareda* as Cunningham had spelt it. I came to know from my friend Mr. Śaradā Prasad of Satna that the correct name of the village is *Durehā* and I motored with him to the place. The monument is by the side of the unmetalled road in the village, standing on an artificial elevation. It is not a lingam at all, but a pillar; the side facing the south is made smooth by chisel, while its back is rough as it was hewn out of the quarry. Unfortunately when I returned from Nachnā and took an impression of the inscription it had become dark and the operations had to be done in artificial light. Below the inscription which consists of one line there is a wheel with 8 spokes, just as on Rudrasena's coin and Prithivīshena's inscriptions of Ganj and Nachnā. Cunningham gives this inscription below, not above, the wheel in his eye-copy. It seems that the drawing given by him was done from memory, not on the spot, as the order of the inscription and the wheel is transposed and the shape of the stone is also not truly drawn. The stone is not round.[1]

A flashlight photograph was taken after filling the lettering with French chalk, but as I could not fully follow the forms of the letters in darkness, the third letter was not fully filled in and its left-hand loop incision (which has come out in the impression[2]) was missed. There is a flaw in the stone to the right of the third letter which gives a false impression of there being a letter. It is produced by a higher level of the surface. The last two letters were completely missed by me on the stone in the darkness; but they have come out in the impression. I give a photograph of the whole stone to show its shape. The stone is painted white by the villagers and a few letters in white paint are written above the inscribed portion. It is now called *Maṅgalanātha* (*Śiva*).

The inscription reads *Vākāṭakānā*[*m*] which evidently refers to the royal *insigne* the wheel, *chakra*, below. The whole would read '*the* chakra *of the Vākāṭakas*'. It was obviously set up in the Vākāṭaka territory.

Its letters belong to the early Vākāṭaka time. The first letter *Va* is earlier in form than the same letter in Pṛithivīsheṇa's inscriptions. Its second letter *kā* agrees with the form of the same letter with the same value in the impression of Pṛithivīsheṇa's inscription reproduced by General Cunningham in his plate (A.S.R., Vol. 21, plate XXVII, second inscription). The third letter *ṭa* has a wedge on the top and the box is not developed. The fourth letter *ka* has no box on its top; nor does the last letter *na* has the form of the time of Pṛithivīsheṇa, it belongs to an earlier type. *M* is also of an early form. Hence the majority of the letters appear to indicate a date earlier than that of the known inscriptions of the time of Pṛithivīsheṇa.

Distances of Sites. I may note here the distances between important ancient sites in the area.

Durehā is about 5 miles to the north-west from Nachnā. Bhūbharā (Bhūmarā) to Khoh is 5 miles (to the south) across the hill. Ganj to Bhūbharā the distance is 13 miles. Khoh is on the southern side below a high range (about 1,500 ft.), and Nachnā below its northern slopes. Khoh is in the Nagod State

[1] See Plate IV. [2] See Plate V.

Gond Type at Bhūmarā.

Bhūbharā [Bhūmarā] Voussoir Bricks.

while Nachnā is in Ajaygarh. Durehā is in Jāso. There were two large towns in the early centuries—one on the site of Gaṇj-Nachnā and the other at Khoh. These were twins, united and separated by the chain of the mountain on the top of which was situated the Temple of the so-called 'Bhūmarā', more common and correct pronunciation being *Bhūbharā*. The temple is near the village Majhgawāṅ ('the middle village'), at a distance of 1½ miles from the village Bhūbharā [which everyone I met at the locality and at Nagod called by this name].

Bharahut features and their origin.

Bhūbharā is a village of the Goṇḍs, who have features as in Bharahut sculptures.[1] Bharahut and Bhūbharā are within Nagod territory and within about twenty miles from each other as the crow flies. In the middle lies Uch-harā, the residential fort of the Rajas of Nagod.

Bhūbharā inscribed bricks.

There was a brick-wall round the temple of Bhūbharā. Thousands of bricks still lie in a square round the temple remains. Most of these bricks where I examined the heap (East Gate) disclosed Brāhmī letters of *c.* 200 A.D. I have brought to the Patna Museum two such bricks. They are important as affording some reliable data on the date of the temple. The letters on the rough bottom-side read *darva-ārā*[*la*] on one and *darva* (l. 1) -*ārālā* (l. 2) on the other.[2] *Darva* is 'hood' and *ārāla* or *ārālā* is 'arch', from *ārā*, 'segment of a circle', 'a spoke'; cf. Sanskrit *arāla*. These marked bricks are, as a matter of fact, voussoir bricks. *Ārā* seems to mean a voussoir, and in *ārālā* we seem to discover the technical architectural Hindu term for the horse-shoe arch. The name *darva-ārālā*, 'hood-arch', may refer to the shape of the arch, or to the purpose of accommodating hoods of Nāga images. It is evident that the outer wall of the temple had niches with round arches for reception of images. The smooth face of one brick has a clear *bhū* inside a bigger letter which is a large *bhā*. This large letter is followed by a large *rā* and a *ya* with an anusvāra.

[1] See Plate VI. Female types have a still greater resemblance.

[2] See Plates VII and VIII. The surface of the bricks has been made lighter to bring out the lettering in the photograph.

The whole inscription reads *Bhūbhārāyaṁ*, 'at Bhūbhārā.' The other brick on the top-side has *ā* at the left corner and *rā* at the right. They have arrow-marks to show the correct direction to the mason. The bricks are voussoir bricks in shape. The measurements of the bricks are: (1) 7″ × 8″ × 9″ (one side broken, at present 6″, originally probably 8″ like the opposite side); the thickness is 2½″, and the fabric very strong; (2) 8″ × (7″, broken) 9″. It seems that bricks were made below the hill and were marked for *Bhūbhārā* which was evidently the name of the hill where the temple was built. Probably bricks were made together for several buildings and were thus allocated.

There being no inscription on the stone remains of the 'Bhūmarā' temple, the brick inscriptions are very useful in fixing the age of the temple. The temple cannot be later than 200 A.D., it should be, as the letter-forms certainly indicate, of about 150–200 A.D.

'Bhākul dev.'

The name of the mukhalingam, now lying flat in the temple, is *Bhākul dev*, according to the tradition current at Majhgawāṅ and the neighbourhood. This seems to stand for *Bhāra-kula-deva*, '*the Deity of the Bhāra kula (dynasty)*'. The date of the bricks would warrant the inference that probably this was the Śiva-lingaṁ founded by the Bhāra-Śiva king mentioned in the Vākāṭaka inscriptions. In any case its period is the Bhāraśiva period.

Place-names having Bhara or Bhāra.

There are place-names in the neighbourhood, e.g. *Bharahaṭā* and *Bharaulī*. Near Satna there is *Bharjunā* where ancient sculptures are found. Pre-eminently in the same group of nomenclature and area stands the well-known *Bharahut*.

Area to be explored.

Bhūbharā [village] marked the boundary between the Gupta empire and the Vākāṭaka kingdom during the Gupta period, according to the boundary pillar inscription of Bhūbharā (*thāṛī pāṭhar*) which is traceable at present in the jungles. Bhūbharā and Majhgawāṅ are in the thick of the jungle. We found fresh foot-prints of a pair of huge tigers who had walked back by the time of our return over our shoe-marks. Reports of similar temples on the hill still existing have reached me. The hill should be explored.

[Reverse Side]

[Obverse Side]

J. B. O. R. S., 1933

Nachnā Temples.

Bhairava-Siva (Chaturmukha) Temple (Pinnacle over Āmalaka restored recently and Portico added.

A window in Pārvati Temple showing Date-Palm Design.

Vandalism.

The Bhūbharā temple has been subjected to modern vandalism. The glorious door with its jambs and sculptures has been removed; that is, the temple has been practically demolished; and the parts have been taken to the Indian Museum at Calcutta and to Fort Uch-harā, where numerous parts have been fortunately saved and preserved by Lal Saheb M.-Kumāra Bhārgavendra Singh, President of the Council of Nagod. But they are lying scattered. The exquisite face-lingam is lying uncared for in the jungle within a shrine which has been rendered tottering by the removal of the massive door and the sculptures which faced and lined the sides.[1] This link between Bharahut and the revived Hindu plastic art has been subjected to a fate worse than Bharahut.

Nachnā.

The Nachnā temple has been the subject of a worse treatment. The famous Pārvatī temple has been, within the last few years, deprived of its outer walls completely.[2] With its pieces one side of the tower of the Śiva temple has been repaired by a local Brahmin,[3] who is said to have discovered gold coins buried in jars at Nachnā. The walls of the Pārvatī temple imitating rocks and caves have thus wholly disappeared, and their animal sculptures which are amongst the most beautiful specimens of Hindu plastic art are either lying scattered on the ground or taken away. A few of them have been rescued by a friend of mine.

Pārvatī and Śiva temples.

The Pārvatī temple and the Śiva temple are works of the same artists and are contemporary ones. Mr. Codrington is wrong in saying that the Śikhara of the temple of Śiva is a later construction and 'superimposed' (*Ancient India*, p. 61). I have examined the temples and had the advantage of the expert opinion of an engineer whom I had taken with myself. The

[1] Lal Saheb whose attention was drawn to the present condition of the temple has kindly promised to take steps to preserve what still remains.

[2] See the *Modern Review* (Calcutta), April, 1933, for its illustration.

[3] See Plate IX. The room in front of the Śikhara temple is a recent addition. The side photographed shows the original śikhara, except for the pinnacle which is modern.

Śikhara temple is the earliest in India existing in its original form. The carvings and the technique are the precurser of the Gupta and the later art. The Śiva-faces on the lingaṁ are superb.[1] One of them with a Bhairava expression has its palate wonderfully well done, which one realizes by feeling it. I hope, some artist will make a thorough study of the temple and sculptures on the spot, and some official attempt would be made to rescue the buildings and the remains.

Age of Nachnā Temples.

A good datum on the age of the Nachnā buildings is the cult-figure of Śiva. The face to the south is Bhairava. Śiva was worshipped in his auspicious (*Śiva*) form by the Bhāraśivas; the forms at Bhūbharā, and Nakṭī(Khoh) and the one discovered by me (see below) are all of that aspect.[2] The Vākāṭaka Rudrasena I, on the other hand, worshipped that god in the *Mahā-Bhairava* form (G.I., p. 236). It was interdicted to make Bhairava in the main shrine (*na mūlâyatane kāryo Bhairavas tu*...Matsya 258. 14). Hence we have his fierce face (*tīkshṇa-nāsâgra-daśanaḥ karālavadano mahān;* 258. 13) combined with other faces.[3] Two more Bhairava-Śivas in the same style are found at Jāso, one on a platform in the village, fashioned in the same red stone as the Bhūbhārā sculptures, and another in black stone in the Jāso temple (brought there and deposited from some neighbouring site). The Nachnā temples will go back to the time of Rudrasena I, for Pṛithivīsheṇa worshipped the god in the *Maheśvara* form (G.I., p. 237). The Pārvatī temple has the date-palm trunk design in one of its windows.[4] This design is prominent at Bhūbharā. R. D. Banerji has pointed out the intimate structural and material affinity between the Pārvatī and Bhumara temples (*Memoir*, No. 16, p. 3). Nachnā is nearer Guptan Art and serves as a link between that and Bhūbharā.

New discoveries.

Near the village of Bhūbharā close to a well under a tree I found a mukhalingam belonging to the same period as the Bhūbharā-Majhgawāṅ

[1] See Plate X. [2] See Plate XI.

[3] See the two faces reproduced in Plate X. The sanctum is dark but for the windows. With difficulty this photograph was taken.

[4] See Plate IX.

Vākāṭaka Siva:

Two faces of
Bhairava-Siva 〈Chaturmukha Lingam〉
at Nachna.

Bhāra=Siva Sivas.

Bhūbharā [Bhūmarā] Siva

Eka=mukha-Lingam—Nakti=ki-talai.

Bhūbharā Eka=mukha Lingam Śiva

Bhākul dev.[1] Between Ganj and Nachnā I found a square stone temple with a few sculptures on a *bāwalī* (stepped well) which have exactly the same technique as the Nachnā sculptures. The temple contains a plain lingam. The spot is called Chaupaṛā.

Local Tradition of Past Dynasties.

From Lal Saheb of Nagod and other persons I came to learn local traditions about the past dynasties which ruled over Uch-harā, Nachnā, and Nagaudh. The 'Bhars' are said to have been the former rulers of Nagaudh and Nachnā and the Sanyāsins, of Uch-harā. These Sanyāsins are the historical 'Parivrājaka Mahārājas' of the inscriptions, and 'the Bhars' might probably be the Bhāra-Śivas. There is no room in history from the Chandel times or rather from the Gupta times to the present day for a Bhar dynasty. It is possible that Mahārāja Jayanātha and his family who were neighbours of the Parivrājakas were a branch of the Bhāra-Śivas.

Tẹhere is no Bhar village at Bhūbharā. But I was told by Lal Saheb, who is the adopted son of the late Chief of Nagaudh and knows every inch of the ground, that the Bhars in the State wear sacred thread and have the status of inferior Kshatriyas. They may or may not be connected with the Bhāra-Śivas. I am inclined to regard them as unconnected.

At Bhārahut I heard the tradition that there had been a Telî dynasty there. This probably refers to Tailapa, as in the proverb of 'Gāṅgū and Telî' (Gāṅgeyadeva and Tailapa).

[1] See Plate XI. Curiously enough, I found a similar, though later, sculpture at Koch, near Tikari, Gaya, indicating the Bhāraśiva influence in Magadha. [The Koch image will be illustrated in a subsequent issue of J.B.O.R.S.]

APPENDIX B.

On Chandravalli Inscription of Mayūraśarman.

The Archæological Survey of Mysore Annual Report, 1929, published in 1931, came to my hands after I had completed the above *History*. In the Report (p. 50 ff.) Dr. M. H. Krishna has published a new inscription of Mayūraśarman where Mayūra śarman's name clearly appears. This inscription may be compared with the Kadamba inscription of Maḷavalli in which I have read Mayūraśarman's name (§ 161). In both records he is '*Mayūraśamman*'. In the new record, which is engraved on the embankment of a lake at Chandravalli by the fort of Chitaldrug in three short lines, Dr. Krishna has read certain geographical names as '*Pāriyātrika, Sakasthā[ṇa], Sayindaka, Puṇāṭa, Mokari*'. He has given a photograph of the rock which at places is very indistinct, and he has given a drawing (eye-copy) of the letters. From the photograph I have checked the reading which needs modification.

Dr. Krishna's reading of the first line I fully accept: it is:

(1) *Kadaṁbāṇaṁ Mayūraśammaṇā [viṇimmi]aṁ*

The second and third lines he reads as

(2) *taṭākaṁ, dūbha Trekūṭa Abhīra Pallava Pāri-*

(3) *yātrika Sakasthā[ṇa] Sayindaka Punāṭa Mokariṇā.*

And he has translated them as

'(Mayūraśarman) who defeated Trekūṭa, Abhira, Paḷlava, Pāriyātrika, Sakasthāna, Sayindaka, Puṇāṭa, and Mokari'.

But *Mokariṇā* will mean 'by Mokari', i.e. by Mayūraśarmman a Mokari, *Mokariṇā* qualifying the above *Mayūraśarmmaṇā*. Nor can *dūbha* be taken for '*defeated*'. The reading is obviously not correct. Following the photograph I read the two lines thus:

[Symbols: between lines 1 and 2 there are symbols of the sun and moon, denoting perpetuity]

(2) *taṭī*[.] Kāñchī-Trekūṭa-Ābhīra-Pallava-[pu]rī-
(3) [yāti]keṇa Ṣāṭahanīstha-Sendraka-puri-damana-kāri[ṇā].

The three lines will mean:

'Mayūraśarmman, of the Kadambas, who marched against Kāñchī and Trekūṭa (Trikūṭa)—the Ābhīra and the Pallava capitals—and who subdued the Sendraka capital at [1]Sātahanī, built the embankment'.

The first two capitals were of the Pallavas and the Ābhīras respectively; the order is wrong in the inscription; having mentioned *Trekūṭa* the writer put down Ābhīra. The Sendraka seat seems to have been at *Sātahanī* which name as the name of a province we already know. As the names of capitals are sought to be given, I am more inclined to take this Sātahanī as the name of a town.

In *taṭī* the long *ī* was seen by Dr. Krishna (p. 54), but he refused to read it, to connect with it the next *ka*. Dr. Krishna has drawn in his tracing the form *pu* after *Pallava* but has read it as *pa*, with the result that he obtains *Pāriyātrika*. The next letter *ṇa* he has missed. The supposed *ka* of his *sakasthāṇa* is clearly *ta*; *ha* and *nī* (the next letters) he has completely missed. Evidently a part of the ligature in *Sendraka* is taken by him as a part of a *y* which does not exist. There is an *i*- or *ī*-mātrā on *r* (read by Dr. Krishna as ṇā of his *Puṇāṭa*); the suggestion of a straight line to the right at the tail-bend of the letter is no part of the letter which can be clearly seen under a magnifying glass.

It will be seen that Mayūraśarman has not yet assumed any royal title.

The date of the inscription on palæography would be *cir.* 300 A.D. The late Chalukyan form of *r* is to be noticed in *Sendraka*. Dr. Krishna's date (250 A.D.) is influenced by his wrong reading.

We are thankful to Dr. Krishna for bringing the record to light and for deciphering most of the letters, which must have entailed great labour.

[1] Or. '*in Sātahanī*'.

APPENDIX C.

On Chandrasena, and Nāga Marriage.

Chandra-sena (pp. 113, 117): On Chandrasena as a ruler in the district of Gaya see Cunningham, *Reports*, XVI, 41-42 General Cunningham heard the tradition at Dharāwat [a village near Kauwāḍol] that the king of the place was Chandrasena whose lake *Chandra Pokhar* measuring 2,000 ft. × 800 ft. is still existing. He is said to have married a fairy. His time was before Guṇamati, the Buddhist scholar (p. 46). Seals in Gupta characters were dug out by Cunningham at Dharāwat.

Nāga marriage and Kalyāṇavarman's marriage (pp. 113, 118): The marriage of Kalyāṇavarman was peculiar in that the young king did not go to Mathurā for his marriage; on the other hand the bride was brought to Pāṭaliputra. This custom of bringing the girl by her parent's party to the bridegroom's house for marriage was a Nāga custom, which has been brought out by Mr. Hira Lal Jain in his edition of the Jaina text the *Nāya* [=*Nāga*]-*Kumāra-chariu* of Pushpadanta, Karanjā Series, 1933 (p. xxvii).

N.B.—*Ajantā*: I have ascertained now that the correct pronunciation is *Ajantā*, not *Ajaṇṭā* which I adopted above from Vincent Smith [*E.H.I.*, 442].

APPENDIX D.

Bhiṭā Excavations on the Hindu War on the Kushans and On Vākāṭaka Seals and Inscriptions.

I.

Kushans at Bhiṭā.

Two attacks on the city.

B h i ṭ ā as exposed by the spade[1] offers itself as an epitomé of Indian history for at least sixteen centuries, if not more. The site had been occupied from about the Tenth Century B.C. to the Tenth Century A.D. In these two millennia, we are here concerned with the remains of the K u s h a n-t o-G u p t a P e r i o d. Sir John Marshall found that the site discloses **two military attacks** on it, both of which fall within our period. To quote his words: (regarding the fourth stratum)

(*a*) 'That the house was hurriedly deserted, owing to some 'catastrophe, in the Kushaṇa period, and afterwards suffered to fall 'to ruin, seems manifest from the coins and other articles left lying 'on the floors, and by the subsequent accumulation of débris in the 'rooms and court, but how long the edifice had been standing when 'this happened, it is impossible to determine with any degree of 'certainty.'

(*b*) [Regarding the fifth stratum] 'This second evacuation, which 'took place in the early Gupta epoch, seems to have been as pre-'cipitate as the first and to have resulted from some hostile attack on 'the city; for many missiles, such as catapult and sling balls, were 'found in the houses and lanes and most of the houses themselves 'were burnt, while in the house which I am describing, even the 'sacred images of the gods were abandoned to their fate.'[2]

1 '*Excavations at Bhīṭā*' by Sir John Marshall, A.S.R, 1911-12, pp. 29 ff.

2 *Ibid.*, p. 34. *Cf.*, p. 37, 'Like the houses of Nāgadeva and Jayavasuda, this one must also have been deserted hastily in the Kushaṇa times, as indicated by the minor objects found on the floors' [*re*-Building No. 23].

Attack in the Bhāraśiva Period.

The exact period of the first attack is indicated by the finds on the original floor of the house of the fourth stratum which is to be distinguished from the débris above reaching the fifth stratum. Seventeen copper coins of Kanishka and Huvishka were found on the floor of the fourth stratum and three clay sealings [Nos. 19, 20, and 73], the characters of which are in the early Kushan script. The débris were three feet deep when a new building thereon was constructed. Sir John has given the date of this construction as the end of the Third Century A.D. We can be certain that this new construction was done a short time after the date of the seal of Nāgadeva (No. 5), which Sir John Marshall has described as having late Kushan script. This was found two feet above the floor of the fourth stratum (p. 48). The débris, according to Sir John, had accumulated in the natural course (p. 34). A further and still more positive datum is afforded by the fact that in the excavations although no Kushan coins later than those of Huvishka were found, a mould (No. 35, p. 65) for minting gold coin of **Vāsudeva** was discovered. This shows that the sack must refer to the early years of Vāsudeva, not a single coin of whose reign has been found there. We might note here that seventeen coins of his predecessor, Huvishka, seven coins of Kanishka, and three coins of Kadphises II were found in different parts of the excavations. In the period after the sack, we have such names as Nāgadeva [about 200 A.D.] and Amātya Nāgadāma [No. 40, *cir.* 200 A.D.]. A large number of 'anonymous Kosam' coins were recovered but they have not been published. They may include coins of the Bhāraśivas. The seal of *Amātya Nāgadāma* closely agrees in script with that of the Bhāraśiva coins. The title *Amātya*, which is on several seals of the period, denotes a reversion [by the Bhāraśivas] to the old Hindu system of government. It seems that in the Bhāraśiva period the town was under their *Amātyas*.

The second military operation against the city in the early Gupta epoch must refer to the first Āryāvarta War of Samudra Gupta in the first few years of

R u d r a s e n a who has got one coin only (No. 100) to his credit in the excavations.[1]

Position of Bhīṭā.

Bhīṭā is 10 miles S.S.W. from Allahabad.[2] It is on the southern bank of the Jumna. The City stood at the gate of the C h e d i country. We find it fortified before the Maurya time, according to the excavations. The name of the place was S a h a j ā t i, which is found in a terracotta seal matrix in the house called by Sir John Marshall the '*House of Guild*'. It is seal No. 1 which is the oldest record found at Bhīṭā. It is in Māgadhī and reads *Śahajātiye nigamaśa*. Every letter of the seal is at least a century older (if not earlier still) than Aśoka's letters. Sir John's reading (*Śahijitiye*) is incorrect. The town of Sahajāti is mentioned in the Vinaya Piṭaka (Chullavagga, Chap. XII) where at the time of the Second Council (about 100 years after the Buddha's death) the Venerable Revata is approached by the brethren of Vaiśālī who reach it by a boat.[3] Sahajāti was in the Chedi country and it was so in the time of the Buddha's disciple Chuṇḍa.[4] Numerous seals, found in the house of the President of the City Corporation, from Government Civil Officials and Military Officers and a Vākāṭaka prince [see below] prove that it was probably a military station in the Bhāraśiva and the Vākāṭaka period, as it evidently had been before. The seals would have been attached to government orders and also probably to orders for drawing money from the President who acted also as the State bank. The seals cover several generations. The city had grown as a commercial station, being situated almost at the terminus of the Jumna,

[1] His son Pṛithivīsheṇa has also only one (No. 73).

[2] Cunningham, Vol. III, p. 46.

[3] Rāhula Sāṅkṛityāyana, *Buddhacharyā*, pp. 559 and 561, where the identification has been suggested.

There is no warrant for Sir John's supposition that the old name of Bhīṭā was *Vichīgrāma* of which a sealing (not seal-matrix) was discovered in the excavations. A matrix (No. 11) with the personal (man's) name *Vichī* found in another place proves only this that a man of the name of *Vṛischi* lived there.

[4] Aṅguttara Nikāya, VI, 5, 4, 5; X, 1, 3, 4; X, 2, 4, 5.

and serving as the internal port for transport between the Doab and Central India via the ancient Deccan Road.[1]

II.

Vākāṭaka Seals at Bhīṭā.

Importance of Sahajāti grows.

The period of peace after the overthrow of the Kushan power is a gradation from 150/200 A.D. [the period of the Amātya administration] to the next century which is marked by a different class of officers under the Vākāṭakas to whom the Empire passed from the Bhāraśivas. Documents from princes of the blood, governors, generals, and the emperor come into evidence, showing that Sahajāti had risen into importance and that it was then in close touch with the then imperial capital of the Vākāṭakas.

Mahārājâdhirāja's Seal.

In a script of about 250 A.D., '*in northern characters of the 2nd or 3rd Century A.D.*'—(Marshall, p. 52), we have a most important seal. The letters of this seal, No. 29, are not Kushan and are distinctly pre-Guptan. They are a class by themselves. They read: '..*ṭaka mahārājâdhirāja*'.[2] The '*ja*' is just like the Kushan letter, and '*ra*' with a small seriph is still straight, while '*ka*' has a straight cross-bar. The '*ha*' assumes a form approaching that at Jaggayapetta and it is yet distant from the Allahabad pillar form. It is thus, on the whole, a writing of the latter half of the Third Century A.D., marking a period of transition. A distinct character, however, is given to it by the first letter *ṭa* which curiously enough, has

[1] Bhadanta Sāṅkṛityāyana has drawn my attention to the other two towns in the Chedi country occurring in the Pāli Canon, namely, *Bhadda-vatikā* and *Sahañ-chanikā*. Bhaddavatikā is Ptolemy's *Badraotis* which falls in Chedi. Is *Sahañ-chanikā* the same as *Chanakā* of the Purāṇas ?

[2] Sir John Marshall's reading '..*raka Mahārājâdhirāja*' is inaccurate with regard to the first letter, which can never be '*ra*' in any period of Indian palæography. The vertical which he took to be a '*ra*' turns with a loop towards the cross-bar of the next letter '*ka*' which it almost touches [below the left end of the bar], and there is a box-head like a '*ta*' attached the top of the letter.

a box-head. It is the earliest specimen of the box-headed Vākāṭaka writing. The beginning of the legend is broken. Considering the shape of the seal, there seem to have been two more letters as Sir John Marshall has assumed. The first two missing letters, in my opinion, were *Vākā* (and not *Bhaṭṭa*- as suggested by Sir John Marshall). The whole legend gave '*[Vākā]ṭaka-Mahārājâdhirāja*'. '*Mahārājâdhirāja*'—a new title—appears here for the first time. It was a Hindu rendering and adaptation of the '*Shāhānushāhi*' title of the Kushans which denoted their imperial position. Pravarasena I alone could be the Vākāṭaka sovereign to assume this title, which after his four aśvamedhas expanded into that of *Samrāṭ*. The seal, like the coins of Pravarasena, is dated. It bears numerals of a type which must have become archaic in his time: 30, 7 (=37). Like the other records of this king we have to take it to be in the era counted from the foundation of the family, i.e. his father's coronation, 248 A.D. We have already seen (*ante* p. 79) that the reign of Vindhyaśakti covers 36 years, and the seal being dated in the 37th year, it must refer to the second year of Pravarasena's reign. The second face of the sealing bears the bull figure which becomes the chief emblem of the dynasty and is stamped on all the seals of high State-officials and generals of the period [see below] and on the Pallava documents. It becomes the crest of the Vākāṭaka Government. This seal was found 18" (eighteen inches) above the Kushan level and eleven feet below from the top, which works out to be the level of the Third Century A.D.

Seal of Gautamiputra.

The next important document is the seal of Gautamiputra (No. 25) which was discovered in the débris below the floor built in the Fourth Century A.D. The seal of Gautamīputra is artistically the best seal of Hindu India and Sir John Marshall rightly observes: '*In respect of execution the seal excels any object of this class which has yet been discovered in India*' (p. 51). On account of the title Gautamiputra, Sir John Marshall thought that the ruler in the seal was an Āndhra king. But it is not correct. The system of being described by the mother's name was prominent in Brahmin and Kshatriya families (more prominent in the former), e.g. in the inscriptions of the Śuṅga time (at Ayodhyā, Pabhosā, etc.). The Āndhra Sātavāhanas who were Brahmins similarly followed the custom. The Vākāṭakas, who were Brahmins originally and assumed their Kshatriya rôle under the imperial influence of the Nāgas and on account of marriages into their family, would naturally observe that custom. That Gautamīputra Vākāṭaka assumed it as his official name is a fact attested by the Vākāṭaka inscriptions. His name stands out with the implicit claim that he was from a Brahmin mother. There are several facts which establish the identity of the Gautamiputra of the seal with the Gautamīputra of the Vākāṭaka inscriptions. The Āndhras never employ Sanskrit while all the known Vākāṭaka inscriptions, like the seal, are in Sanskrit. The Āndhras were not *vṛishadvaja* (*'having in their banner Śiva's bull'*). The dynasty of the Gautamiputra of the seal is different from that of the Sātavāhanas. He is called here 'The Increaser of Śrī Vindhya [*Śrī-Vindhya-bardhana-Mahārājasya*[1] 'the *Mahārāja who is the increaser* (of the family) *of Śrī Vindhya*, which may be compared with *Cheti-rājā-Va(ṁ)sa=vadhanasa* of the Hathigumphā inscription]. It means that he belonged to the family of **Śrī Vindhya**, i.e. of King Vindhyaśakti, the founder of the Vākāṭaka family and grandfather of Gautamīputra. On the coins of Rudrasena and Pṛithivīsheṇa the same hill symbol appears which is to be found in the middle of this seal and which from the later seals of the Śivalinga of Kālañjara (No. 15) is to be identified as the **Vindhya Hill.** The Vākāṭaka coins have got the Vṛisha of Śiva on which Śiva is seated in Rudrasena's coin. That corresponds with the '*Vṛishadvaja*' of this seal. The Vākāṭakas, according to the inscriptions, were Śaiva, and in the seal the prince claims that his royalty had been dedicated to Maheśvara (i.e. Lord Śiva) and his son Mahāsena. Probably the original *Ishṭadevatā* of

[1] The whole text of the seal (running round the margin) is: *Śrī Vindhyabardhana-Mahārājasya Maheśvara-Mahāsenâtiśrishṭa-rājyasya vṛishadvajasya Gautamiputrasya*. It is slightly misread by Sir John Marshall as *Śrī Vindhyabedhana°*. There is neither any horizontal *e* mark, nor any room between the ligature *ndhya* and *ba* for such a mark.

Vindhyaśakti was the famous Śiva *Kālañjara*[1] who is apparently the same as *Kāleśvara* appearing in a later seal (No. 14). The Āndhras never had Śiva as their Ishṭadevatā, nor had they the title of *Mahārāja* which the owner of this seal bears.

According to the Vākāṭaka inscriptions, Gautamīputra was the son of Pravarasena I and father of Rudrasena I, and in the Vākāṭaka plates he bears the same appellation Gautamīputra (without any personal name) as here. He seems to have been a Mahārāja (governor) under his father who was Mahārājâdhirāja. The letters are consciously moulded with the aim of perfect symmetry, and the forms adopted are all square which makes the scribe adopt some archaic forms (e.g. of *ha* and *ma*). They are slightly later than the letters of the seal No. 29 in their general tendency in spite of the older forms.[2]

In this seal (No. 25) we find not only a document of Gautamīputra but also the name of the first king of the family [Śrī Vindhya].

Seal of Bhīmasena.

Seal No. 27 gives the name of **Bhīmasena.** It was found among the débris accumulated above the Kushan floor (pp. 32 and 51) and Sir John Marshall rightly assigns it to the Second or Third Century A.D. This Śrī Bhīmasena is identical with the Śrī Bhīmasena of the Ginja inscription discussed above (*ante* p. 108), of the year 52 of the Vākāṭaka era, from which his date is fixed (300 A.D.). It has a standing Nandi-bull and the figure of Gaṅgā (compare it with the more distinct figure in seal No. 26, discussed below)[3] The writing closely resembles the writing at Ginja (E.I., Vol. III, pl., p. 305). The bow-and-arrow mark which is on the seal is not an exclusive Southern Indian

[1] The god Kālañjara has two later seals, discovered at Bhīṭā (viz. 15, 16). Both *Kālañjara* and *Kāleśvara* probably signify the same deity.

[2] See the *i*-mātrā on *m* in *Gautami°*.

[3] Where on Vākāṭaka seals or coins, e.g. on Rudrasena's coin or Bhīmasena's seal, the Vṛisha or Gaṅgā or both face or point towards the standard, it means that the standard is Vṛishadhvaja and that it bears these symbols on it. The device is obvious, for it would be too cumbersome to depict these figures inside a banner on such small objects as seals and coins.

device. It is also found in seal No. 73 which bears Kushan characters. Bhīmasena was the actual governor of the area in the year 300 A.D. which is conclusively proved by the neighbouring Ginja record. In the seal his mother's name is also given, he being called *Vāsishṭhīputtra*, not *Vasasuputtra* as read by Sir John Marshall. The whole legend reads: *Rājño*[1] *Vāsishṭhī-puttrasya Śrī-Bhīmasena[sya]*. He is called *mahārāja* at Ginja. It seems that he also was a son of Pravarasena I, from another wife who belonged to the Vāsishṭha gotra.

Seal of Śivamāgha.

Seal No. 26 belongs to another Vākāṭaka governor and was recovered from the same stratum as the seal numbered 27. The legend is in similar characters but slightly later in date: '*Mahārāja Gautamiputrasya Śrī Śiva-māghasya*'. It has the same crest of the Nandi bull and the Ganges as on the seal of Bhīmasena, and the title *Mahārāja*. The figure of the Ganges standing on a *makara* is clear here. Her left hand is on the hip in both the figures and the right hand points to a standard. Mahārāja Śivamāgha[2] is known from a stone inscription at Kosam inscribed during his rule (E.I., Vol. XVIII, p. 159, pl. No. ii). He was actually the Governor of Kauśāmbī in the beginning of the Fourth Century A.D. He seems to have been dead or transferred by the Vākāṭaka year 86[3] (334 A.D. which falls within the reign of Pravarasena I) when another governor Mahārāja *Śrī Bhadrama* ..was ruling at Kauśāmbī.

Thus we have these further records of the time of Pravarasena I:—

Vākāṭaka-Mahārājâdhirāja (Seal No. 29) [Year 37=285 A.D.]

Mahārāja Gautamiputra (Seal No. 25).

[1] It was read by Sir John Marshall as '*Rājña*'.

[2] Sir John Marshall was doubtful about the vowel-force to *ma* and he has read doubtfully *m[e]gha*. But *mā* is clear both here and in the Kosam inscription. I take this opportunity to correct the statement, *ante* page 87, § 76, where I assumed the reading of Rai Bahadur Daya Ram Sahani (*Śiva-m[e]gha*) and his view, that they were Gupta governors, to be correct.

[3] E.I., XVIII, 160, pl. No. 3. Rai Bahadur Daya Ram Sahani read the date as 88.

Rājā Bhīmasena (Seal No. 27) [at Ginja, 'Mahārāja', year 52=300 A.D.].

Mahārāja Śivamāgha (Seal No. 26).

Mahārāja Bhadrama..(Year 86=334 A.D.).

Queen Rudramatī's Seal.

Seal No. 30, of *Mahādevī* Rudramatī, with Nandi bull (couchant), is the latest royal document of the Vākāṭakas. We do not yet know whose queen she was. We have nothing later here than the time of Pṛithivīsheṇa. It has letters of the Fourth Century A.D. and was found in the prę-Guptan level.

These seals and other Vākāṭaka seals of officials (to be discussed presently) prove the universal employment of Sanskrit in the Vākāṭaka Court from the very beginning, and the existence of a high stage of art and culture which is in no way inferior to that evidenced by the Gupta coins.

We have quite a number of sealings of officials belonging to the period. They are clearly distinguishable on account of the distinctive royal Vākāṭaka emblems on them.

Officers' Seals.

Seal No. 33 is of *Jayanta*, a cavalry officer (*aśva-pati*). It has the Vākāṭaka wheel-mark. Seal No. 36 belongs to *Amātya Īśvarachandra*. This also has the Vākāṭaka wheel-mark. Seals Nos. 37 and 38 of *Amātya Dharmadeva* may or may not belong to the class as the Vākāṭaka royal marks are absent thereon. Seal No. 44 is distinctly Vākāṭakan in script and symbols. It has the Nandi bull and a wheel. The owner was a general—*Daṇḍanāyaka Śrī Śaṅkaradatta*. Similarly seal No. 45 has a (couchant) bull and also probably a wheel and is from *Daṇḍanāyaka Grāmabala*. Seal No. 46 is similar to seal No. 45 and is from *Daṇḍanāyaka La*... Seal No. 48 (not reproduced) appears to be similar to the above seals and is from *Daṇḍanāyaka Yajña-vī*.... Seal No. 49 has a couchant bull; '*Daṇḍanā* [*yaka*] *Umasya*'. No. 51 is exactly similar to No. 44 : a standing bull with a mark of the sun between the horns, similar to the figure on No. 44: *Daṇḍanāyaka Va*. No. 52 of *Pratihāra*.. *Viśākha Rudradāma*. It has the couchant bull as in No. 45 but more artistically done. No. 54 is similar where the name is *Gaṅgadeva*. No. 57 has a powerful representation of the bull facing the figure of Gaṅgā which stands between the bull and the standard of Śiva's trident-and-battleaxe (*cf.* seal No. 14 of Kālañjara). No. 78 has a couchant bull with *Rudrasiṁha* in characters of the fourth century (a little later than those described above).

The bull-figures may be compared with those on the Vākāṭaka coins and the Pallava seals. Majority of the bull figures on the seals exhibit great art and so does their lettering.

APPENDIX E.

Paikuli Sassanian Inscription (293/4 A.D.) and its bearing on the Vākāṭaka Period of Indian History.

The (Kurdistan) Paikuli Inscription, edited by Prof. ERNST HERZFELD in Forschungen Zur Islamischen Kunst (Series No. III) under the title PAIKULI MONUMENT AND INSCRIPTION OF THE EARLY HISTORY OF THE SASSANIAN EMPIRE (in two volumes), Berlin, 1924, has a bearing on the period of Indian History discussed above. It refers to the Ābhīras, the lord of Avanti, 'Satraps', and the Kúshán king.

The inscription was discovered by Sir Henry Rawlinson who made an eye-copy of it in 1836. It was edited by Thomas in his '*Early Sassanian Inscriptions, Seals and Coins*' (JRAS., 1868). Prof. Herzfeld undertook several journeys to Paikuli and recognized that it was a bilingual record. His work could only be published by the generosity of Sir Dorabji Tata and through the kind interest of Prof. Browne of Cambridge. Out of gratitude to them the German scholar has published his work in English.

The inscription was engraved by the order of King Narseh, and the subject is the war between him and Varhrán III.

Pápak, son or descendant of Sásán, flourished as a vassal chief near Shíráz whose son Ardashír became the founder of an empire and assumed the title of *Sháhánsháh i Érán* (emperor of Erán) on April 28th, 224 A.D., on the defeat of the Arsacidan suzerain Ardaván. On the eastern side of his empire he included therein Khorásán, with the result that the *Kúshán Sháh*, the next neighbour, amongst others, sent his envoy to declare his allegiance. This account is taken from Tabarí, which stands confirmed by the coins of Pápak and his son Sháhpuhr, elder brother of Ardashír I, and of Ardashír I (originally published by Thomas and Cunningham; *Paikuli*, i, 36). Ardashír's son, Sháhpuhr I, ruled in 241–272, who called himself '*Emperor* (*King of kings*) *of Érán and non-Érán* (*anérán*)'. The next sovereigns Hormizd I (272-273) and Varhrán I (273–276) were short-lived. Varhrán II (276–293) was greatly harassed (283 A.D.) by the Roman Emperor (M. Aur. Carus) and by the rebellion of his own brother Hormizd in the east (289 A.D.). On the death of Varhrán II a dynastic war broke out (293 A.D.) between Varhrán III (son of Varhrán II) and his grand-uncle, Narseh. Narseh proved successful and reigned from 293 to 302 A.D. in which year he was succeeded by his son Hormizd II (302–309 A.D.).[1] The Paikuli Inscription relates to this dynastic struggle of 293 A.D.

In this civil war the 'lord of Avantī' [*Avandikán xvatávya*] took the side of Varhrán III. And according to the inscription, 'all kinds of Satraps' (*Sátrap gónak gónak*) congratulated the new king (Narseh) on his victory. So also congratulated him 'the king of the Ābhīras' [*Ábírán Śáh*].

It is noteworthy that these princes are 'all enumerated as independent princes' (Herzfeld, p. 43). Prof. Herzfeld's surmise that they had been subject to the Sassanian throne up to the war is not supported by the inscription. Had they been subject, they would not have been treated as independent by the victorious emperor. They had aided as mere allies their neighbour Varhrán III who had been governor and ruler of Sīstān. The German scholar has been influenced by the unproved theory of Dr. Vincent Smith of a supposed 'unrecorded' Sassanian invasion of India [Sindh, the Punjub, etc.].

I cite below the passages having bearing on India from the Paikuli Inscription. The text is bilingual—Pársík and Pahlavík; where the original text is given the language is indicated by (*Pr.*) or (*Ph.*) In line 24 we read:

'straight to the country of Asúristán they do not 'come......with that army come together......own......

[1] After him the succession is:
Sháhpuhr II (309–379);
Andhar Narseh (309);
Ardashír II (379–383);
Sháhpuhr III (383–388);
Varhrán IV (388–399).

'Sakánsháh (i.e. the rival of Narseh), and Vahunám 'until....TANDY, and by (?) them (25) the lord of 'Avanti [Avandik(á)n vat(á)vya, (*Ph.*)[1] the Sakánsháh, and Vahunám......TRAN I arrive*d* (pp. 105, '107).

It is thus clear that the lord of the Avandikán was a chief ally of Varhrán (III) the Sakánsháh. Line 29 says that Vahunám was captured and bound and was brought on a donkey (after being paraded) to the royal Porte.

Lines 44 to 47 enumerate the kings and rulers who recognized the new king (pp. 117, 119) after the victory—an event which may be dated in or about 294 A.D., the year following the battle. The text is as follows:

'And the king of the Kúshán [*Kuš(á)n ŠĀH-(Ph.)*] ....., 'and to us the Caesar [*Késare-(Pr.)*], and the Roman [*hróme-(Pr.)*][2]...

'(45)......(42) and the king of Khwárizm, and Zámásp the...pat of the Kúshdán, and Dígpambak(?) [the..., and Sayyidí, the Shaikh of the Arabs [Harváník (*Pr.*), Arváník (*Pl.*)], and Pak, the eunuch, and Béruván, son of (?) Spandorát, and the king of the Páradán, and Varáčgurt the king, and the king of Zand-Afrík, and the king of Makúrán, and X. the king of....., and Tírdát the king, and 'Amru, the descendant of the Abgars,......and the king of Ábhíra [*Ābírán ŠĀH -(Pr.)*], and Síká-......

'(46)......(43')......—ṾRYN YPPṬ that their BYTAK......—satraps of all kind, (Vará)zgirde, the lord [*Xvatáy* (Pr.) *xvatávya* (Pl.)] of the Sakhúričán, and Khvarasmán, the lord of the Mókán, and Bagdát, the lord of the Zúrádián, and MitrȦLasén, the [lord of the] Bóraspičín, and Bátí, the lord of the Zúradatčín, and X. the lord of the [Ap]réšumičán, and Márwak [the lord of] the Ishtakvín, and......the lord of the Térakhčín,...

'(47)......the lord [of the...], and the other princes ......our instruction they become, and the whole Empire

[1] The Pársík text has decayed here.

[2] Read 'the Roman Caesar's': '*and*' in the text is wrong.

anew (?) I wish (?) (or: they congratulated me) and some came personally to our Porte, others envoys...... PAKR ......, and by(?) him the Empire, and the place......, and to our service they come......he holds, on him [they] say...... End.'

The Kúshán Sháh who is put on par with the Roman Kesar (Cæsar) was the Kushan king. The word KÚSHÁN in the inscription has been treated as a territorial unit; evidently the dynastic name (after the name of the first king *Kushaṇa*) gave the territorial designation of *Kúshán* to the Balkh-Badakshan region. The Kúshán Sháh here must be the Kushan emperor, to be mentioned even before the Roman emperor. The group of kings headed by these two emperors (lines 44-45 of the Pársík text, and lines 41-42 of the Pahlavík text) are undoubtedly independent kings.

It is noteworthy that the *Abírán Śáh* or the king of the Ābhīra country is in that list of kings. We know that the first Ābhīra king—Īśvarasena—founded the Ābhīra kingdom about 240 A.D. (§164 above). The Ābhīras before him were republican (§164). They appear again as republican in 350 A.D. in Samudra Gupta's time. The Ābhīra king in 293-294 A.D. was thus one of the descendants of Īśvarasena whose records are dated in his own royal years and not in the Śaka era. The Ābhīra king up to 294 A.D. was an independent sovereign ruling over a part of Aparānta (insc. at Nāsik) and the neighbourhood. He must have sent his envoy to Narseh like other kings (line 48). In the reign of Pravarsena I (284–344 A.D.) who is followed by Samudra Gupta, the Ābhīra kingdom must have been suppressed, evidently soon after 294 A.D.

The king of the Páradán is the king of the Pāradas of Sanskrit or Pāladas of Aśoka. I have shown elsewhere[1] that these Pāradas were a northern nation, in north Afghanistan, and their modern representatives are the Bārad-zái. The existence of a king of the Pāradas in 293-294 A.D. proves that the community ceased to be republican which they had been in the days of Aśoka, and that the Pārada king was independent

[1] IA, 1933, p. 121, ('*Places and Peoples in Aśoka's Inscriptions*').

and not under the Kúshán Sháh, who thus does not seem to have had the whole of Afghanistan under him.

The second group of 'all sorts of Satraps' is taken by Prof. Herzfeld to be an Indian group. He identifies them ('twelve') as Indo-Scythians. He is mostly influenced by V. Smith's view that Kathiawāḍ and the territories upwards were under the Śakas up to the reign of Chandra Gupta II. He also identifies the lord of Avanti as a Śaka Satrap. When Prof. Herzfeld counts 12 Śaka Satraps, he evidently includes in them the lord of Avanti and the king of the Ābhīras, for the 'Satraps of all kind' text has only 10 rulers. The view that the group of the Satraps is all Indian is not accurate; nor can the Ābhīra king come under the Indo-Scythian class. But a few of them are certainly Indian.

The lord of Zúrádián is certainly the lord of the Surāshṭras, as pointed out by Prof. Hertzfeld (p. 43). The Surāshṭras had been republican in the time of Kauṭilya. Soon they came under the imperial rule of Chandra Gupta Maurya and Aśoka. Then they came under Rudradāman who was elected by them their king about 150 A.D. In 293-94 A.D. they are under a ruler (xvatavya, not necessarily a 'Satrap') whose name BAGDĀT may be identified as BHAGADATTA or BHAGADĀTA. Now we know all the Kshatrapa names from 150 A.D. to 332 A.D.—in practically an unbroken succession (Rapson, C. A. D., cliv–clvii), and no name having the slightest approach to Bhagadatta is found in that list. Prof. Rapson has pointed out in connection with the name ĪŚVARADATTA, that the DATTA-ending is foreign to the Kshatrapa family (p. cxxxiii). Surāshṭra had been the seat of the Western Satraps. The appearance of Bhagadatta in Surāshṭra in 294 A.D. confirms the conclusion already advanced in our History (§§81, 164) that Surāshṭra had been won back from the Western Satraps before the Gupta time. Bhagadatta seems to belong to the confederacy of the Ābhīras, cf. the name 'Ābhīra *Śivadatta*'. The Saurāshṭras are described as a republican community at the rise of Samudra Gupta by the Bhāgavata Purāṇa, that is, they had been so in the time of the VĀKĀṬAKAS also (§82). It is likely that this Bhagadatta was a republican chief, which is evidently suggested by the Paikuli term '*all sorts of Satraps*'. If they had been only of the class of 'Śaka' Satraps such a description was not needed. The description is constitutional; several constitutional classes of independent, though small, rulers are intended.

Prof. Herzfeld identifies Mókán as the district around Quetta. Its lord was Khvarasmán. The learned scholar thinks that MitrALasén (the lord of Bóraspičín) was a Śaka Satrap. But the Śaka Satrap at the time was *Mahākshatrapa* Bhartṛidāman (289–295 A.D.) with his *Kshatrapa* Viśvasena (294–304) and his predecessor was Viśva Siṁha (Rapson, p. clvi). We have a total absence of the Mahākshatrapa's family in the Paikuli list. It is thus evident that they were not free to have diplomatic dealings and they must have been represented by the Kúshán Sháh. The independent Indian sovereigns mentioned in the list were Hindu rulers, who at the time existed, according to the Purāṇic data, in Avanti, Ābhīra, and Surāshṭra (§§73A, 74, 81 145 ff.), probably forming a confederacy. MitrALasén may be a leader of 'the Three Mitra' Republics (Pushymitra, Paṭumitra, and Padmamitra), and Bóraspičín is probably from *Vāravatī*, capital of the *Vāravatya* Yādavas who were near Valabhī, and whose rulers bore the title of *Pushpa*.., according to the Mañju-Śrī-Mūlakalpa (ch. 53, p. 625).[1] It is not possible to identify any of the other names as Indian, except perhaps MÁRWAK as MĀLAVAKA, which is discounted by the unknown *Ishtakvín*.

The data of Paikuli admirably confirm the Purāṇic data for 293-294 A.D. The date falls within the first ten years of the Vākāṭaka imperial time under Pravarasena I. We have noted above (p. 87) that the province of Malwā, where these free communities of the Āvantyas and the Mitras had been ruling, seems to have been acquired about 300–310 A.D. by the

[1] Pushpa-nāmo tato proktā Vāravatyāṁ purodbhavaḥ |
Valabhyāṁ * * * * *
anantā nṛipatayo proktā Yādavānāṁ kulodbhavāḥ |
Cf. ĀMMK., p. 604 were *Vāray(v)atyāḥ* are *Yā(d)avāḥ*.

Vākāṭakas as their over-lord. Just before that they appear to be absolutely independent. It must have been they and the Saurāshṭras who drove the Śaka Satrap out of that part of the country. The Purāṇic history of the Ābhīra kingdom (rise about 248 A.D., § 164, p. 170 above) stands confirmed by Paikuli which records the Ābīrán Šáh as an important sovereign in 293-294. Their appearance in the time of Samudra Gupta (350 A.D.) as a republic shows that under Pravarasena I the Ābhīra monarchy came to an end, about 300–310 A.D., when the Province of Malwa came under the Vākāṭaka House. Their individuality was preserved in the form of their republican government. This history leaves no room for a Śaka Satrap in Koṅkaṇa, Kathiawīḍ, Gujarat, and Malwā in 293–300 A.D. The Śaka had been pushed out to Cutch-Sindh before 293 A.D.

THE KUSHANS AND THE SASSANIAN EMPIRE.

Certain Sassanian coin-legends, and titles, noted by Muhammadan historians, throw light on the condition of the Kushan emperors in the Bhāraśiva-Vākāṭaka period. The former were already available from Cunningham and other numismatists, and the latter have been collected from literary sources by Prof. Herzfeld, who has prepared the following chart exhibiting the titles (I have inserted *K.* before the names of kings):

[*From the* Paikuli Inscription, *p. 51.*]

Pāpak Shāh, about 200–220.

- *K*. Sháhpuhr, Shāh, † previous to 224.
  - Sháhpuhr, harkapati † after 294.
- *K*. Ardashír, Sháhánsháh, 224–241.
  - *K*. Sháhpuhr I, Sháhánsháh, 241–272.
    - *K*. Hormizd I, Vazurk Kúshánsháh and Sháhánsháh, 272-273.
    - *K*. Varhrán I, Vazurk Kúshánsháh and Shahánsháh, 273–276.
      - *K*. Varhán II, Vazurk Kúshánsháh and Shāhánsháh, 276–293.
        - *K*. Varhrán III, Sakánsháh, and Sháhánsháh, 293.
      - Hormizd, Ormies.
    - *K*. Narseh, Sháhánsháh, 293–302.
      - *K*. Hormizd II, Sháhánsháh, married daughter of Kúshánsháh, 302–309.
        - Adharnarseh;
        - Hormisdas;
        - Sháhpuhr Sakánsháh;
        - *K*. Sháhpuhr II, Sháhánsháh; 309–379.
          - *K*. Sháhpuhr III, Sháhánsháh, 383–388.
          - *K*. Varhrán IV, Kirmánsháh, and Sháhánsháh, 388–399.
        - *K*. Ardashír II, Budh-Ardashíránsháh, and Sháhánsháh, 379–383.
    - Pápak Mihrán, bítákhsh of Georgia, 265–342.
  - Ardashír, Kirmánsháh.
  - Narseh, Vispuhr i Sásánakán, † after 294.
  - Péróz, Vazurk Kúshánsháh, Vispuhr i Sásánakán, † after 294.

The rise of Ardashīr, the first Sassanian king (224–241), falls in the Bhāraśiva period. Before his rise the Bhāraśivas had already driven the Kushans from the Gaṅgā-Yamunā Doab, that is, Ardashīr found the Kushan emperor weakened and he took advantage of it. According to Tabarī, Ardashīr took away Khorásán but according to the Armenian historian whom Nöldeke prefers, his empire did not include Balkh. In any case, he did reach the borders of the Kushan home-province and exercised some sort of superiority over it. He seems to have threatened to invade the Indian dominions of Junāh who opened negotiations from Sirhind (§38, p. 50). But it is not until the time of Hormizd I (272–275) that the Sassanian king calls himself GREAT (*Vazurk*) KÚSHÁNSHÁH in addition to SHÁHÁNSHÁH, which is repeated by Varhrán I (273–276) and Varhrán II (276–293). This title is given up by Narseh (293–302), though temporarily revived by Péróz some time after 294 A.D. The title denoted over-lordship on the Kushans. In 302–309 A.D., Hormizd II married the daughter of the Kushan king (Kábul Sháh) and the Kushan position improved.

Thus from 272 up to 292, for 20 years, the Kushans got the protection of the Sassanian king and assumed the position of a vassal king. In that period the Bhāraśivas and after them Pravarasena I would have operated against the Kushans in India. After 293 A.D. they must have been more pressed by Pravarasena, who may be regarded to have broken their power in India, whereon the Kúshánsháh shifted himself into Kabul. The Sassanians were hard-pressed by the Romans and could not be of assistance to the Kushans. The final suppression of the Kushans, who revived in 302–309, is to the credit of Samudra Gupta and Chandra Gupta II. There does not seem to be any room in history for a conquest of the Sassanians over North-West or Western India. That the Sassanian rule extended over Sīstān is proved by their title SAKÁNSHÁH and is confirmed by Kālidāsa who places the Pārasikas next to Sindh in the invasion of Raghu: *sthala-vartmnā*, through the Bolān Pass, as opposed to the sea-route from Aparānta to East Persia.

APPENDIX F.

Vākāṭaka Emperor and Gupta Family.

Prabhāvatī Guptā on the constitutional status of Early Guptas.

Prabhāvatī Guptā on constitutional status of Gupta Kings.

A Vākāṭaka document—the Riddhapur plates now in the possession of the Mahant of Rithpur, Amraoti, Berar, and published by Mr. Gupte in J.A.S.B., 1924, 53 [1]—gives a piece of information which contradicts the statement of the Gupta inscriptions regarding the beginning of the Gupta family. Mahādevī Prabhāvati-Guptā, the authoress of the record and mother of Mahārāja Damodarasena-Pravarasena, who issued the grant from Rāmagiri (Ramṭek, near Nagpur) in the 19th year of Mahārāja Pravarasena II, was at the time probably the oldest living member of the Gupta family.[2] She says that Mahārāja G h a ṭ o t k a c h a was the **first king** of the Gupta dynasty (*Guptānāmādirājo Mahārāja-Śrī-Ghaṭotkachaḥ*).[3] This statement contradicts that of her grandfather Samudra Gupta on the Allahabad pillar that Śrī Gupta was [the first] *Mahārāja*. This claim is not accepted by the Vākāṭaka family. It seems that the first prince

[1] Plates reproduced are unfortunately in the negative. They have to be read with the help of a mirror.

[2] The translation and reading of line 11 [J.A.S.B., XX, 58, 60] need correction: in '*sāgra-varshaśatadivaputra-potrā*', one anusvāra on *di°* is missed; *dimva=dinva*. *Sāgra-varshaśata* has no reference to the Queen who has been taken to have been 100 years old by the editor of the plate; it refers to the 'son and grandson' [or sons and grandsons]—'*whose son and grandson are men (endowed) with fully centennial happiness*'. Such a wish was appropriate especially when she had already lost her eldest son prematurely.

[3] The same import is to be found in the other grant of this queen (E.I., XV, 42) in '*Guptādirājo*' qualifying [*Mahārāja*]=*Ghaṭotkachaḥ*, where its bearing could not be clear owing to the uncertain reading before *Ghaṭotkachaḥ*. [My footnote [4] at p. 113 *ante* has to be modified according to the Riddhapur plate.]

recognized by them was Ghaṭotkacha, who must have been a contemporary of Pravarasena I. In this contradiction between the statements of the grandfather and granddaughter there is a contradiction between the two dynasties, which discloses historical hostility.

Historical hostility and constitutional claims. The titles of her paternal ancestors are given by her thus:

1. *Mahārāja* Śrī Ghaṭotkacha (E.I., XV, 41; J.A.S.B., 1924, p. 58).
2. *Mahārāja* Śrī Chandra Gupta (I) (both plates).
3. *Mahārājâdhirāja* Śrī Samudra Gupta (E.I., XV; in J.A.S.B., 1924, '*Mahārāja*').
4. *Mahārājâdhirāja* Śrī Chandra Gupta II (both plates).

Against this we have Samudra Gupta giving the following titles to his forefathers and himself:

Mahārāja Śrī Gupta.
Mahārāja Śrī Ghaṭotkacha.
Mahārājâdhirāja Śrī Chandra Gupta.
Mahārājâdhirāja Śrī Samudra Gupta.

In the 13th year of her first son Divākarasena she gave her grandfather the title of *Mahārājâdhirāja*, but about 40 years later, when her father was gone, she called Samudra Gupta only '*Mahārāja*' and recognized her father only as the *Mahārājâdhirāja*. All this connotes the historical constitutional position of each Gupta ruler in the eyes of the Vākāṭaka House. The latter (1) did not recognize Gupta to have been a ruler at all, (2) and did not recognize Samudra Gupta as a rightful *Mahārājâdhirāja*, as he had begun life as a Vākāṭaka subordinate and as a *Mahārāja*, and it was only as a rebel that he killed Rudrasena I, while Chandra Gupta II was the first recognized *Mahārājâdhirāja* over the Mahārājas of the Vākāṭaka House. The Vākāṭaka House (3) never recognized Chandra Gupta I as a *Mahārājâdhirāja*; in the time of Pravarasena I such a claim was unthinkable, and Chandra Gupta's assumption of such dignity would have been then and always considered by the Vākāṭakas as an act of sedition.

APPENDIX G.

On Further India and Insulindia, 150 A.D.–350 A.D.

The subject of Further India and Indian Archipelago has been touched upon in pp. 154–158, *ante*. Here it is proposed to discuss the colonial history mainly with reference to the home-land for the period 150 A.D.–350 A.D.

The State of Champā (Annam), according to Chinese authorities, was founded in 137 A.D.[1] Champā seems to have been mentioned under the name *Aṅgadvīpa* by the Vāyu Purāṇa [ch. 48]. The name *Champā* was adopted by sanskritizing the ethnic name of the local population *Cham*. The Kauṇḍinyas who founded the State were, as pointed out above, the Kauṇḍinyas brought from Northern India to the South by the Sātavāhanas. The Sātavāhanas were a naval power: they marked their coins with the figure of a ship, they were always anxious to keep the maritime provinces of the West-Coast and the East-Coast under them. The Kauṇḍinyas were intimately connected with the Chuṭu Sātakarṇis by ties of relationship. It may be assumed that their migration to Annam and foundation of a kingdom, which defied the Chinese empire and established its independence, must have been politically connected with the Sātavāhanas. *Kin-lien*, which seems to be the Chinese rendering of *Kauṇḍinya*, successfully attacked the southernmost districts of the Chinese empire, and in 138 A.D. the Emperor contracted peace with him under which Chinese territory was evacuated by him. The Sanskrit inscription of Vō-chaṇh (now in the Hanoi Museum) lends confirmation to the Chinese data. It is in Sanskrit and resembles the script of Rudradāman. One of the descendants of Śrīmāra (whose name is lost in the inscription) records that in the Assembly he publicly declared that whatever moveables

1 Chavannes, *Les religieus éminents*, p. 203; Vogel, *Yūpa Inscriptions of Mūlavarman*, p. 188; Majumdar, *Champā*, pp. 1[illegible], 21.

and immoveables he had given (*visṛishṭa*) to his brothers and sons, etc., were to be respected as their personal properties after his death. The script of the inscription is of the Second or Third Century A.D. It seems that this king was not very far removed from Māra, the founder. The original Brahmin caste (*Brahma-Kshatriya*) and the family name *Kauṇḍinya* are given in two later inscriptions of the dynasty in which dates in the Śaka era are given: *chaturshu varshaśateshu Śakānāṁ vyatīteshu*[1] and 579 respectively.[2] The employment of Sanskrit points to a contemporary revival of Sanskrit in the Mother-Country of the Kauṇḍinyas.

The Kauṇḍinyas kept up a continuous war of aggression against the Chinese empire from 248 A.D. They seem to gather strength about that year. In 248 A.D. they made a naval attack, defeated the Chinese fleet which had been sent against them, and took the capital of Hanoi, whereupon a treaty was concluded by the Han emperor who ceded the whole of Cheo-ling. The name of the Hindu king ended in *Varmā* (Chinese *Fan*). The next king spelt by the Chinese as *Hiong* (270–280 A.D.) extended his kingdom of Champā to the north at the cost of the Chinese emperor who concluded a treaty with him in 280 A.D. His successor Yi was again a powerful king; he died in 331 or 336 A.D. He sent an embassy to the imperial court of China (284 A.D.). The next king maintained the vigour, but about 359 A.D. there was a reverse and a period of depression up to 377 A.D. Bhadravarman revived the offensive in 380–413 A.D. He and evidently his family had borne the Pallava title *Dharma-Mahārāja*.[3]

It will be seen that the history of the colony of Champā follows the curves of the history of the Mother-Country. The Purāṇas mark a victorious point of time with 248 A.D. which

[1] Mi's'on stele. Finot, B.E.F.E.O., III (1903), 206–211; IV (1911), 264; Majumdar, *Champā*, No. 7.

[2] Finot, B.E.F.E.O., IV, 918, Majumdar, No. 12.

[3] The Kauṇḍinyas established also a kingdom in Poli. Groeneveldt, *Notes on the Malay Archipelago and Malacca, compiled from Chinese sources*, Verh. v.h. Bat. Gen., xxxix, 1880, p. 81, cited by Dr. Vogel in his *Yūpa inscriptions of King Mūlavarman*, p. 194, *n*.

is the beginning of the offensive and successes of Champā against China. The Vākāṭaka-Pallava dynasty had a set-back about 350 A.D. And then there is another imperial age in India about 370 A.D. under the consolidated power of the Guptas when we find that the colonies attorn to the Gupta House. It is impossible not to perceive the effects of the changing history of the Mother-Country on Champā during the period we are concerned with.

The script of Bhadravarman's inscriptions is Pallava and his title is also Pallava. It seems that after 248 A.D. when the kings of Champā adopt the Pallava dynastic name ending in *varman* they come under the system of the Pallavas in accordance with the march of history in the main-land.

From the Sanskrit Inscriptions of King Mūlavarman, found on four Yūpa (sacrificial) posts of stone at Koetei in East Borneo, edited by Dr. Vogel,[1] we find that before 400 A.D. a dynasty was founded in Borneo, the third king of which performed the Vedic Yajña *bahusuvarṇaka*,[2] and gifted lands, kine, a *kalpa-vṛiksha* (gold-tree) and money to Brāhmaṇas in the island. His father's name was Aśvavarman and grandfather's name was Kuṇḍuṅga. Aśvavarman was the founder (*vaṅśakartā*) of the dynasty in Borneo. The verses are in *anushtubh* and *āryā* metres. The *Yajña* was performed at Vaprakeśvara, evidently a Śaiva sacred place in Borneo. The script of Mūlavarman is closely the Pallava script. The name *Kuṇḍuṅga* is a Southern Indian name, *cf*. *Kuṇḍu-kūra* in the Pikira grant. We have instances of Aryans in the South adopting Dravidian names. It is almost impossible to hold the theory advanced on the strength of this name by the Dutch Indologists that the family was probably native of Borneo and was Hinduized. To suppose that in the second generation

[1] Brids. Kon. Inst., 1918, pp. 167–232 (with plates). *Cf*. IA., IV, 355; Dvivedī Commemoration Volume [Hindi, Benares, 1933], p. 220 (with good plates).

[2] Śrī Mūlavarmma-rājendro
yashṭavā bahusuvarṇakam
tasya yajñasya yūpoyam
dvijendrais samprakalpitaḥ (p. 213)

they could be so much and so rapidly Hinduized as to perform Vedic sacrifices and make such intimate Hindu gifts is a hard demand on probability. Kuṇḍuṅga does not seem to have flourished in Borneo as the founder was Aśvavarman.

The script at Koetei, after a very able and exhaustive treatment, has been dated by Dr. Vogel in the middle of the fourth century, 'a somewhat earlier date than that proposed by M. Finot who has assigned them to approximately 400 A.D.' Now a generation before 350 A.D. will bring us about 325 A.D. which is the time of the Pallava King Skandavarman II, the Conqueror ('*Vijaya*'), whose date we have ascertained to be C. 297–332 A.D. (p. 195 above). The script agrees with the script of the time of this Pallava king and his successor Siṁhavarman I.[1] We know that in the time of Vijaya Skandavarman Sanskrit became the language of the Pallava inscriptions. It seems that the kingdom in Borneo was founded in or about the time of Vijaya Skandavarman, who firmly got established at Kāñchī and had a long and prosperous reign. The sacrifices of the orthodox Pallava type, and no performance of an aśvamedha, and the name-ending in imitation of the Pallava designation, would lead us to infer not a peaceful local venture of an individual, but an undertaking directed by the Pallava emperor or under his ægis.

Similar is the case of the Hindu kingdom of J a v a . The earliest inscriptions in the island are of P ū r ṇ a v a r m a n , and they are in Sanskrit. They have been edited by Dr. Vogel in *Oudheidkundigen Deienst in Nederlandsch-Indië*, Deel I, 1925, pp. 15–35 (with plates) under the title "The Earliest Sanskrit Inscriptions of Java". They are four in number and are all in the western part of Java, in the province of Batavia, inscribed on rocks. The Chi-Arutön (spelt also Tiaroeten or °teun) inscription is a dedication of two foot-marks (*padadvaya*) evidently as a memorial to the dead king. The capital of the king is called Tārūma-Nagara. It reads:

(1) vikkrāntasyâvanipateḥ,

[1] The script should be compared with the inscriptions of Mayūraśarman on stone discussed above (pp. 167, 221).

(2) Śrīmataḥ Pūrṇṇavarmaṇaḥ,
(3) Tārūmanagarendrasya,
(4) Vishṇoriva padadvayam.

A similar record in Śragdharā with foot-prints is at Jambu, in the middle of a stream near a confluence, which is rightly explained by Dr. Vogel as the cremation place of the king. There the inscription mentions the king as having flourished before (*purā*) at Tārumā. The Chi-Arutön Inscription is in my opinion a similar funeral memorial, probably at the place of his Śrāddha. The Jambu foot-prints are called *padavimba-dvayaṃ*, which reminds us of the custom still living amongst the Bengal Hindus of taking actual foot-prints of a dead elder before cremation. The third inscription is (at Kĕbon Kopi) to commemorate a favourite elephant of the king which bore the name *Jayaviśāla*. Evidently on its death the memorial was given by the king, like the memorials to noted or favourite horses in the Mughal times. The fourth record is at Tugu (Bĕkasih). It is in five stanzas of anushṭubh. It registers the excavation or deepening of two streams, one (nadi) called Chandrabhāgā which had been 'dug' first by the *Guru*, father of king Pūrṇavarman. This ancestor is called r ā j ā d h i r ā j a :

(1) purā rājādhirājena Guruṇā pīna-bāhunā, khātā khyātām purīm prāpya
(2) Chandrabhāgârṇṇavam yayau ||

The *Rājādhirāja* had excavated the stream and brought it to the capital and thence it (the Chandrabhāgā) reached the ocean. The other stream was cut by King Pūrṇavarman in the 22nd year of his reign. Its name was Gomatī. To a length of 6,126 bows (*dhanus*), i.e. either 7 or 12 miles (Vogel, p. 33) it was cut or deepened (khātā) in 21 days (*dinais siddhaikaviṅśakaiḥ*)—from the 8th Krishṇa Phālguna to the 13th Śukla Chaitra (i.e. in *amānta* system). This stream had destroyed the camping-ground (*śibirâvanim*) of the king's grandfather, a *rājarshi* (royal sage). The king made a gift of one thousand kine to Brāhmaṇas on the completion of the work. The inscription bears the mark of a *triśūla* on its top.

The script is of the three inscriptions is exactly Pallava,

while that of Chi-Arutön is Vākāṭakan. The inscriptions have been executed with great skill, showing a practised hand in writing and a practised chisel familiar with Sanskrit lettering. In other words, they are the workmanship of Hindus. This remark equally applies to the Koetei Inscriptions and the Champā Inscriptions. Intimate affinity is noticed in the scripts of Bhadravarman (Champā), Mūlavarman (Borneo), and Pūrnavarman (Java). They are all within a century or so amongst themselves. The system of amānta year-reckoning is South-Indian.

The title of Pūrṇavarmana's father, *rājādhirāja*, is comparable with the identical Gupta title and the Gaṅga title of *Mahādhirāja*. It is certain that the family of Java was Śaiva and had come into existence in the Pallava time, and that it knew the influence of the Guptas which is indicated by the title of the king's father and the Vākāṭaka script at Chi-Arutön which is accompanied with a shell writing—an essentially northern writing—between the big toes of the foot prints. Taking the date of the inscription *c.* 450 A.D. as suggested by Dr. Vogel, the time of the grandfather of Pūrṇavarman will be about 375 A.D., and the time of the foundation of the family about the same as that of the Borneo dynasty of Aśvavarman. The names of northern rivers (Chandrabhāgā, Gomatī) should not be a matter of surprise, as the Pallavas themselves were northerners and their whole court and subordinate rulers were northerners.

Hindu Colonial States in the Archipelago and Further India were thus established facts in the Vākāṭaka-Pallava period, and they seem to have been connected politically with the Mother-Country. With the advent of Samudra Gupta as the Indian Emperor having stepped into the shoes of the Vākāṭaka Emperor, those colonies in Insulindia and Further India—as an already organized system—transfer and render their allegiance to the Gupta Emperor, who notes the easy fact.

The evidence of the Guptan influence has been already noticed. The reference to Vishṇu (Vikrānta) at Chi-Arutön is probably another index of the new influence of the Guptas. We know the description of Sumatra from FaHien who found it almost a completely orthodox Hindu land like Guptan India.

Insulindia was thus fully connected with the political and cultural changes in the mainland.

Chạmpā was probably the earliest colony, it being a key to the Chinese trade and the point from which the islands of Java and Borneo were easily accessible. The great naval activity and attainment in navigation by the Hindus in the Far Eastern Seas are attested by the Champā history in Chinese, by FaHien, and Champā inscriptions which mention her naval wars. The trade of the Far East seems to have been in the possession and control of Andhra, Kaliṅga, and Bengal (from where the *Mahānāvika*, the great sea-captain, Buddhagupta [from *Raktaṁ-ṛittikā*, Rakta-māṭi in Bengal] marked an inscription in Malay before 400 A.D.)[1]

The Vāyu Purāṇa gives a full description of Siṁhapura, a capital in Further India, evidently in Malaya. It notes the fact of islets of very small dimensions and mentions their groups (*anudvīpas*) as attached to bigger islands. Its detailed knowledge of the islands proves the intimate connexion of the Insulindia with Samudra Gupta's India. which is borne out by his own inscription and the inscriptions noted above.

1 Vogel, *Yūpa Inscriptions of K. Mūlavarman*, p. 185.

INDEX

(*References are to pages.*)

INDEX OF AUTHORITIES CITED.